MADE IN PARADISE

Previous page

Off-screen husband and wife, Warren Beatty and Annette
Bening, play on-screen lovers as they stroll on location at
Moorea in 1994's *Love Affair*. The South Seas scenes were
filmed in French Polynesia, and the famous passenger-freighter
Aranui was used for the exteriors of the film's cruise ship. This
is at least the third version of the romantic fairy tale, including
1932's *Love Affair* (starring Humphrey Bogart) and 1957's *An
Affair to Remember* (starring Cary Grant and Deborah Kerr).
The Beatty version is the only one shot, in part, in the South
Pacific; Moorea is about 12 miles from Tahiti and renowned as
one of the most beautiful islands on Earth. Fiji actor Manu
Tupou appears in a cameo opposite Katharine Hepburn, who
plays Beatty's aunt.

This page

The first moving pictures to show Hawai'i's surf was shot in
1906 by a Thomas Edison crew. But the surfing movie, as a sort
of sub-genre of South Seas cinema, really got underway in the
1940s with Bud Browne's *The Big Surf* (1943) and *Hawaiian
Memories* (1945), shown here, with surfers and outrigger
paddlers streaking past Diamond Head, off Waikiki.

MADE IN PARADISE

HOLLYWOOD'S FILMS OF HAWAI'I AND THE SOUTH SEAS

BY LUIS I. REYES

With Contributions By Ed Rampell

MUTUAL PUBLISHING

Cover photos, clockwise:
The two dukes—John Wayne and Duke Kahanamoku in *Wake of the Red Witch*.

Elvis Presley and Joan Blackman in *Blue Hawaii*.

Dorothy Lamour and Jon Hall in *The Hurricane*.

Mary Ann Ventura and Jeff Chandler in *Bird of Paradise*.

Ricardo Montalban and Herve Villechaize in *Fantasy Island*.

Keanu Reeves and Patrick Swayze in *Point Break*.

Elvis Presley in *Paradise, Hawaiian Style*.

Tarita and Marlon Brando in *Mutiny on the Bounty*.

MADE IN PARADISE
HOLLYWOOD'S FILMS OF HAWAI'I AND THE SOUTH SEAS

BY LUIS I. REYES

With Contributions by Ed Rampell

Cover Design by Wizard of Art, Ltd.
Interior Design by Jane Hopkins

Special Thanks to the South seas Cinema Society

Library of Congress Catalog
Card Number: 9578397

Cover design by The Wizard of Art, Ltd.
Interior design by Jane Hopkins
Endsheet photo © 1995 by Martin Charlot
Lyrics from *Down On Ami Ami Oni Oni Isle* reprinted with permission from Royal Music Publisher

First Printing October 1995
1 2 3 4 5 6 7 8 9
Casebound: ISBN 1-56647-089-7
Softcover: ISBN 1-56647-108-7

Mutual Publishing
1127 11th Avenue, Mezz. B
Honolulu, Hawaii 96816
Telephone (808) 732-1709
Fax (808) 734-4094

Printed in Korea

All photos courtesy of the Luis Reyes collection unless otherwise noted.

My Blue Heaven stars Dan Dailey and Betty Grable as radio stars in a musical comedy that includes a Pacific tie-in. This movie typifies Hollywood's trend of including Hawaiian song and dance in musicals which otherwise have nothing to do with South Seas cinema. Una Merkel, Jane Wyatt, and Mitzi Gaynor—who went on to play in the genre movies *Down Among the Sheltering Palms* and *South Pacific*—co-star in *My Blue Heaven*. This 1950 picture is not to be confused with the 1990 Steve Martin comedy with the same name about a criminal in the witness relocation program who insists on tipping FBI agents like Rick Moranis.

Table of Contents

Film Titles Table of Contents

Above

Lee Marvin, Elizabeth Allen, Mike Mazurky and John Wayne in *Donovan's Reef*.

▼ ▼

DEDICATION

This book is dedicated to Auntie Momie and Uncle Howell (Betty and Howell Kaleohano); the Kaohi *ohana*; Jolynn Kaohi Chew and all the Boringuis; Pat Hurley Cafferty; Dr. Paul K. Yee; Joseph Prokop and family; John "Duke" Wayne; my son Luis Ignacio Keonimana Reyes; and my wife, Ronda Jean Reyes, whom I married on Kauai, Hawai'i.

SPECIAL DEDICATION

To Jack Lord, the man most responsible for the development of the modern Hawai'i film industry, and to all the members of the Hawai'i film and television production community.

ACKNOWLEDGMENTS

Mike Hawks, Peter Bateman, Critt Davis, Doug Hart, Leith Addams, The Staff Of The Academy of Motion Pictures Arts and Sciences Library and Center for Motion Picture Studies; The Television Academy Library; producer Charles Floyd Johnson; Ricardo Tremillos, University of Hawaii; producer Howard W. Koch; producer Brian Frankish; Georgette T. Deemer, Manager, Hawaii Film Office; Judy Drosd, Film Commissioner, Office of Economic Development, County of Kauai; Georja Skinner, Maui Film Commission and Molokai and Lanai Islands; Diane Quitiquit, Big Island Film Office; Walea L. Constantinau, Oahu Film Office; Randy Spangler; Rita D. Ractliffe; DeSoto Brown; Jeff Baskin; Warner Bros. Archives; Eddie Brandt's Saturday Matinee; Larry Edmunds Book Store; the South Seas Cinema Society and most of all to Bennett Hymer who shared the vision and Jane Hopkins who designed it with *Aloha Nui* in her heart.

THE SOUTH SEAS CINEMA SOCIETY

The South Seas Cinema Society is devoted to establishing South Seas cinema as a full-fledged film genre and to the study, preservation, and dissemination of knowledge of the moving images of the Pacific Islands through publications, archiving, documentaries, film festivals, oral histories, etc. The

Elvis Presley serenades Joan Blackman with an ukulele in a studio publicity picture with a Diamond Head backdrop for the 1961 musical *Blue Hawaii*.

Society collects films, videotapes, posters, stills, lobby cards, sheet music, and other movie memorabilia relating to South Seas cinema. Its founders include: ▼ Robert C. Schmitt, whose father accompanied silent films on an organ in a Cincinnati theater. Mr. Schmitt came to Hawai'i in 1947. He served as State statistician for many years and wrote the groundbreaking work, *Hawaii in the Movies, 1898-1959.* ▼ Part-Hawaiian DeSoto Brown is a Bishop Museum archivist, collector extraordinaire of twentieth-century Hawaiiana, and author of several books in the same field. He was a consultant for the 1992 documentary *Hawaii on Screen.* ▼ Part-Hawaiian Matthew Locey has worked on numerous movie and TV productions as an assistant director, including *Aloha Summer, The Karate Kid II, Magnum P.I.,* and *Jake and the Fatman.* Mr. Locey has his own production company, PAU, and is one of the few Polynesian members of the Directors Guild of America. ▼ Ed Rampell majored in cinema at Hunter College on his native island of Manhattan. Mr. Rampell is a full-time freelance writer who has visited more than 100 Pacific Islands since 1976. He reports for numerous news outlets, including Radio Australia, and is the North and Western Pacific bureau chief of *Pacific Islands Monthly* magazine. ▼ For more information write: South Seas Cinema Society, c/o Locey, 174-2 Noke Street, Kailua, Hawai'i 96734, USA.

ENDSHEETS

Painter/filmmaker Martin Charlot is the creator of the 1986 mural "Stars in Paradise," that is displayed at the Kahala Mall Consolidated Theater Complex on Oahu. He is the son of painter Jean Charlot, who taught Diego Rivera and other Mexican muralists the art of the fresco mural. Martin's parents were introduced to each other by Sergei Eisenstein while he was shooting *Que Viva Mexico!* Martin's 1964 black-and-white documentary *Kalapana,* about a traditional Hawaiian village on the Big Island of Hawai'i, unfolds an aesthetic sensibility and sensitivity to island culture. In the same year, he directed *Apocalypse 3:16* in Hawai'i, a chilling horror story with biblical undertones. Renowned in Hawai'i as a muralist, he has also written screenplays. To pursue a film career, Martin recently moved to Los Angeles, where he has studied acting with Fiji actor Manu Tupou.

In what may be the most famous love scene in movie history, Deborah Kerr and Burt Lancaster embrace at Halona Cove, Oahu, which locals nicknamed "From Here to Eternity Beach" after the movie based on the James Jones novel. This scene is very much in the tradition of the South Seas genre, which has long linked lovemaking to water with languid lagoons, flowing waterfalls, and swirling seas.

Preface

Being an island boy by way of Puerto Rico and Manhattan, I have always been powerfully drawn to the South Sea islands of the movies and television. When I was a child, these productions offered me the rare opportunity to see attractive people of color portrayed in their own cultures with a semblance of strength and dignity.

Films like *From Here to Eternity* and *Donovan's Reef* and TV shows such as *Hawaii Five-O* filled my imagination. I would find myself daydreaming of sparkling white sand coco palm-lined beaches peopled by gentle and beautiful island maidens. It was easy to daydream when I was enduring harsh snowbound winters in an overcrowded New York City tenement apartment. The island settings gave me a sense of freedom from the restraints of a conventional world, an escape to a timeless Eden, where I could leave everything behind and begin again.

In 1982, when I went to Hawai'i for the first time, the Islands were everything I imagined they would be and more. My college friends from Hawai'i and their families overwhelmed me with their *aloha* spirit, kindness, generosity and warmth, and the Islands' history unexpectedly gave me a new appreciation of my own background.

I visited the Bishop Museum in Honolulu and discovered with awe a small display area acknowledging the Puerto Rican contri-

Below
Bing Crosby on location in Hawai'i for *Waikiki Wedding*.

butions to Hawai'i. I had been unaware that at the turn of the century many Puerto Ricans left their Spanish-speaking island in the Caribbean to work on Hawai'i's sugar plantations. Geographically, Hawai'i was not that much different from Puerto Rico and, like Hawai'i, was home to a mixture of races. With some adjustments, the new immigrants easily made their home in these Pacific Islands.

In contrast, never in all my time in New York had I seen any official government or cultural display that acknowledged Puerto Ricans as part of the New York immigrant experience. I came away from the Bishop Museum with a greater appreciation of not only my own cultural heritage, but Hawai'i's as well, where out

of an influx of immigrant labor and clash of cultures came an ethnic and cultural fusion. Hawai'i's fascinating intercultural blend grounded in Polynesian traditions is what makes it a very special place for me.

▾ ▾ ▾

Being a movie buff, during my island stays I would try to visit as many of the spectacular movie locations of films shot on Kauai and Oahu. But, for all of Hawai'i's colorful movie-making past, what little information existed about these locations was found only in travel brochures and government information packets. I could not find any source that discussed in depth the Hollywood films that had been made in whole or in part on the islands. (It was only in 1988 that Robert C. Schmitt published his *Hawaii in the Movies: 1898-1959*.)

This book explores almost all the Hollywood films shot in or about Hawai'i, as well as other South Sea locales, including behind-the-scenes stories of making movies in the Islands and the development of Hawai'i's present-day film and TV industry.

The book focuses on the more notable Hollywood-based theatrical feature films (mostly post-sound era) and network television programs, although some of the non-Hollywood-made films, particularly the emerging New Zealand cinema, are also briefly discussed in chapter four.

Omitted are many films distributed by smaller distribution and production companies such as Monogram, PRC and Allied Artists. During the thirties and forties, these companies released many low-budget, island-theme movies using standing jungle or tropical island sets, stock footage and costumes. These studio-based island sets were still being used well into the 1950s but enhanced with Technicolor stock footage as in such films as *The Girls of Pleasure Island* (1952, Paramount) *Down Among the Sheltering Palms* (1953, Twentieth Century Fox) and *The Lieutenant Wore Skirts* (1956, Twentieth Century Fox). Only those World War II films with a major story line based in Hawai'i or actually filmed in the South Seas are included.

In compiling the movies, it became apparent that many of these films had striking similarities and, in our opinion, constituted a genre. This book may represent the first effort ever to treat South Seas cinema as a distinct

Above
Glorai DeHaven co-stars with Billy Gilbert, Mitzi Gaynor, and Jack Paar in 1953's run-of-the-mill, WWII-in-the-isles *Down Among the Sheltering Palms*. Five years later, Mitzi Gaynor returned to paradise in another wartime island epic, *South Pacific*.

Left
Nat King Cole in ***The Blue Gardenia***, a Warner Bros. picture which also starred Anne Baxter, Richard Conte, and Ann Sothern.

I also try to separate fact from fiction concerning contact between Western and Polynesian cultures as expressed in these films. For the most part, the movies have created a romantic native paradise to serve as the setting for adventures enjoyed by white Americans or Europeans (usually males). The clash of Western and Polynesian cultures, as well as the exploitation and devastation of natural surroundings and native cultures through disease, commerce and Western religion, has been largely simplified or distorted by Hollywood movies.

The book is based on numerous interviews I conducted with actors, producers, crew members and locals, as well as on magazine and newspaper articles. Information was also obtained from publicity material at the Academy of Motion Pictures Arts and Sciences Library and the Center for Motion Picture Study in Los Angeles and the Academy of Television Arts and Sciences Library in North Hollywood, California. In the course of writing this book I revisited the many films and TV shows I had already seen and viewed many others that were new to me.

Members of Honolulu's South Seas Cinema Society helped review the manuscript, adding to its accuracy. Special thanks are due to Ed Rampell, who gave generously of his time and knowledge, and to DeSoto Brown and to Robert C. Schmitt, whose book *Hawaii in the Movies: 1898-1959* was an invaluable source of information.

I hope these pages will bring back memories of good times at the movies and in front of the television, watching colorful, larger-than-life celluloid images of tropical adventure, romance, song and dance in the films of Hawai'i and the South Seas, and for the more serious film buff perhaps a greater appreciation and awareness of the South Seas film genre.

Aloha Nui Loa,
Luis I. Reyes

Foreword

Looking back, Robert Louis Stevenson's *Swiss Family Robinson* was my first association with a classic adventure story and a tropical island. In my schoolboy days, it was one of the books students had to read.

My first island film experience was in the Walt Disney version of the tale, shot in Tobago. Then a young actor, I had a wonderful time swinging on vines, falling off waterfalls, playing with wild animals, fighting pirates and romancing a young girl on a sandy palm-lined beach. Later I would find out that the Caribbean is very different from Hawai'i in feeling, style and mood.

In 1968, I arrived in Hawai'i for the first time on a military air command flight going from San Francisco to Saigon as part of a USO Vietnam Tour. We stopped at the Honolulu airport at 11:00 p.m. to refuel. It was then an old funky airport with Quonset huts. I remember very vividly the headline in the January 22 newspaper—"Duke Kahanamoku Dies." I spent an hour on the ground reading about the former Olympic swimming champion and the man who best personified Hawai'i.

Several months later back in Los Angeles, writer/producer Leonard Freeman, with whom I had worked before, called and said "I'm doing a TV series in Hawai'i called *Hawaii Five-O*. Would you like to be in it?" A pilot (test) two-hour movie episode had been filmed and for some reason they wanted to replace one of the actors. Hawai'i, fast moving cop show—it sounded like fun and something good for me to do. After seeing the pilot I said yes.

There I was again disembarking at Honolulu's old funny, funky airport. Honolulu was much more of a city than I ever thought it would be. While there weren't many tall buildings then, there was a cosmopolitan feeling to the place created by the many ethnic groups that lived in the islands. I certainly wasn't disappointed. I had a wonderful introduction to Hawai'i from the locals who worked on the show and quickly introduced me to the nuances of island life. The show and its crew got a lot of acceptance in the community and we tried to do as much as we could for civic and charitable groups. We met a lot of people while we were filming on location, as tourists and locals were always happy to see us.

In my mind, the best thing about Hawai'i in the late sixties and early seventies was that people went there to have a good time and to be happy. An atmosphere where people are happy is exciting to live in. You might call this part of the Aloha Spirit.

I didn't meet Jack Lord until a few days after I arrived, and I was impressed by his stature and cordial manner. We went right to work and it was long hours, six days a week.

A Quonset hut near Pearl City housed the permanent sets, including McGarrett's office. We dubbed this makeshift studio "Mongoose Manor." *Hawaii Five-O* broke ground in Hawai'i for an ongoing television series, especially the kind of show we were doing, involving multiple island locations.

The first year we shot 25 shows over a ten and a half month period. Sometimes it would take us eight, nine or even ten days to shoot a one-hour show. There were technical difficulties, since we had to truck all the things we needed to multiple locations. By the time we were up and running for a couple of years, our filming season was down to seven and a half months. A key factor was the move in the second year from "Mongoose Manor" to centrally located studios behind Diamond Head. Also, everything became more efficient due to the firsthand experience and knowledge gained by our crew and cast. We developed that first largely local crew which remained a crack unit over the twelve seasons. When the *Magnum P.I.* TV series started shooting, it used essentially the same crew for eight years.

When I first embarked on this show, I hoped to get thirteen weeks, or a season of work. Little did I know then that I would be in Hawai'i eleven years later, still doing the series.

Hula dancers sway to the song "Lani" in *Hell's Half Acre* (1954).

Hawaii Five-O creator and executive producer Leonard Freeman, was first and foremost a writer. Jack was the star. Everything else fell into place after these two. The characters were strong and the quality of the story lines was very good, which explains why the show has held up in reruns and syndication around the world through the years. Last time I checked, about a year ago, the show still had a weekly audience of 105 million people.

Hawaii Five-O was a morality play set in an exotic setting where the good guys triumphed over the bad guys. There was little if any character psychology or inner personal turmoil in the script. We just caught the crooks. Our team was representative of the melting pot of Hawai'i, but also symbolic of an America where different ethnic groups could work together side by side. In Hawai'i, groups retain their identity but subordinate their ethnicity to the idea that the whole is greater than the parts. The series demonstrated that through McGarrett, myself as Dano, Chin Ho Kelly and Kono.

I was thrilled to see Hawaiian history and culture used as a backdrop for many of the show's story lines. Hawai'i is a place that is constantly changing and evolving but still deeply rooted in tradition.

I would like to think that Hawaiian tourism jumped dramatically from the constant exposure Hawai'i received on a weekly basis from the series. I participated in a Hawaii Visitors Bureau tour of seven mainland cities, as well as a promotional film. There was terrific cooperation from the people of Hawai'i and the armed forces. I loved going to work every day, and each show was different and fun. *Hawaii Five-O* introduced me to a magnificent place in the South Pacific called Hawai'i, where I lived and made my home for twenty years. I stayed on after my involvement in the series came to an end. It's an accomplishment to have done 270 hours of television in Hawai'i. My Hawai'i years will always remain for me one of the shaping influences of my life, and for that I consider myself very lucky.

James MacArthur, "Dano"
Palm Desert, California
May 1995

"The Academy Award Baby" is what Hollywood called this entrancing little miss, whose lullaby, *Sweet Leilani*, won a Motion Picture Academy Award as the best song of 1937. Here is Leilani and her daddy, Harry Owens, the music-writing maestro. They were brought to Hollywood by Paramount especially for the big musical show *Coconut Grove*, for which Owens wrote several new numbers and in which he appears as an actor and as leader of his own Royal Hawaiian Orchestra.

Introduction
South Seas Cinema—Is It a Film Genre?

by Ed Rampell

"Oh, you never heard of jello,
Or of Abbott and Costello...
You never heard of Mr. Gable,
And you never heard of Ginger Rogers, auwe!...
We're a lot of happy creatures,
'Cause there are no double features,
It's no wonder that we always wear a smile.
We wouldn't know Mickey Mouse
From Mickey Rooney,
On Ami Ami Oni Oni Island,
Ami Ami Oni Oni Isle."
— Betty Grable singing Mack Gordon and Harry Owens'
"Down On Ami Ami Oni Oni Isle"
in 1942's *Song of the Islands*.

Above

Sons of the Desert (1933) is considered to be Laurel and Hardy's finest feature. In it, the boys deceive their wives into believing tha they are off to Hawai'i in order to cure Ollie's bad cold. But instead of being Honolulu-bound, the duo sneaks off to Chicago. Laurel and Hardy returned to paradise in their very last film, *Utopia* (1950). Stan inherits a South Seas atoll where the boys move to avoid high taxes. They establish a libertarian government after uranium is discovered. However, the anarchistic society draws unwanted emigres from around the world to "Robinson Cruisoeland," and President Ollie is overthrown in a coup. *Utopia* literally epitomizes the genre's process of "anti-Utopian subersion": once Westerners encounter paradise, Eden must be undermined and debased.

South Seas cinema is an enduring and endearing film genre that has delighted audiences for years. Since the birth of the Kinetoscope, it has involved many of the motion picture industry's top talents. From the 1890s to the 1990s, from the nickelodeon to the movie palace to the cineplex to the CD-ROM, filmmakers and fans have enjoyed the imagery of Hawai'i and other Pacific Islands on the silver screen.

The first known "Paci-flicks" were shot in the then-Republic of Hawai'i on May 10, 1898. They were travelogues by an Edison camera crew, en route by ocean liner from Asia to the East Coast. The oldest surviving New Zealand footage chronicles the 1901 visit of a member of British royalty to the antipodes. Anthropology as a serious social science and moving pictures emerged during the same historical era. Ethnologists swiftly seized upon the medium as a means for recording vanishing cultures in Oceania and elsewhere. From the infancy of the cinema, with 1913's *The Shark God* and *Hawaiian Love* shot on location on Oahu, Hollywood came to play the dominant role in South Sea filmmaking.

An endless list of filmdom's greatest geniuses and most popular performers have worked in this island idiom. Thomas Edison, D.W. Griffith, John Ford, Josef von Sternberg, Robert Flaherty, F.W. Murnau, Raoul Walsh, Mervyn LeRoy, Cecil B. DeMille, King Vidor, John Huston, Steven Spielberg, and many others have produced and directed Pacific pictures. Illustrious actors such as Marlon Brando, Sir Laurence Olivier, John Wayne, Montgomery Clift, Henry Fonda, Gary Cooper, Burt Lancaster, Kirk Douglas, Clark Gable, Charles Laughton, Errol Flynn, Humphrey Bogart, Ronald Reagan, Bing Crosby, Bob Hope, Anthony Quinn, Lee Marvin, Jon Hall, Harry Houdini, Harold Lloyd, Charlie Chaplin, Douglas Fairbanks, Sr., Abbott and Costello, Elvis Presley, Mel Gibson, Kevin Costner, Jason Scott Lee, Keanu Reeves, and Tom Hanks have co-starred in South Seas cinema, along with actresses Dorothy Lamour, Gloria Swanson, Joan Crawford, Rita Hayworth, Deborah Kerr, Sophia Loren, Jane Russell, Frances Farmer, Betty Grable, Esther Williams, Ava Gardner, Marlene Dietrich, Mia Farrow, Brooke Shields, Jessica Lange, Meg Ryan, et al. Some

Two beautiful reasons why Clark Gable and his mutineers find island life idyllic.

M-G-M Presents "MUTINY ON THE BOUNTY"

Copyright © 1935 Loew's Incorporated   COUNTRY OF ORIGIN U.S.A.   3   Property of National Screen Service Corp. Licensed for display only in connection with the exhibition of this picture at your theatre. Must be returned immediately thereafter.   R57-54

Photo courtesy of the Ed Rampell Collection.

Above

Topless girls and nubile, pneumatic, naked nymphs in native nirvanas have long been a staple of South Seas cinema, where more flesh was glimpsed than in any other Hollywood genre up until the late 1960s. Even in 1935's *Mutiny on the Bounty*, the Tahitian *vahine* (Mamo Clark and Movita Castenada) are barebreasted (although modestly covered by leis and tresses), indicating why the mutineers tossed Bligh and the breadfruit overboard and returned to paradise.

of Tinseltown's most beloved characters are linked to Paci-flicks—Charlie Chan, Moby Dick, King Kong, Gulliver, Robinson Crusoe, Gidget, and the dinosaurs of *Jurassic Park*. South Sea screenplays have often been based on books by literary lions like Herman Melville, Daniel DeFoe, Robert Louis Stevenson, Jack London, Somerset Maugham, James Michener, Charles Nordhoff, James Norman Hall, Zane Grey, James Jones, and Norman Mailer.

While South Seas cinema goes back almost to the birth of the movies and has involved many of filmdom's glitterati, film historians, critics and academics have not recognized the island movie as a motion picture genre with its own distinguishing attributes. Reviewers and the like have ignored South Seas cinema's special qualities, including it with the adventure movie and costume drama genres.

It was as if the Pacific picture did not have the qualifications that rated classification and categorization as a distinct genre—like film noir, the musical, or the western—although some South Sea films can sometimes fit into other genres, for example, the romance or the musical. Perhaps the lack of recognition was racial, since South Sea films often involved nonwhite roles and its plot or story line sometimes dealt with interracial relationships.

Some of Hollywood's Hawai'i and South Sea flicks have been lightweight entertainment, but this has been true for other genres, as well. South Sea films run the entire gamut of artistry, from "good fun," put-your-brain-into-neutral escapist B pictures, to the highest realms of cinematic art. Two Pacific films have won Academy Awards for Best Picture (1935's *Mutiny on the Bounty* and 1953's *From Here to Eternity*), and other films in the genre have received Oscars and accolades.

What is the essence of, and traditions that determine, South Seas cinema? How and why do we look at these movies, and what do we make of them? First of all, it is important to define South Seas cinema and how the term is used here. The South Seas is a generic term that refers to most of the Pacific Islands of Polynesia, Micronesia, and Melanesia, which make up Oceania. The South Seas also refers to a state of mind, to a prevailing fantasy of a tropical wonderland in the Pacific. North of the equator, Hawai'i is no longer geographically categorized as being in the South Seas. On the other hand, more films have been shot in the Hawaiian archipelago than on any other Pacific Island and, with the possible exception of Tahiti, no other place has been so projected onto the popular imagination as an earthly paradise.

South Seas cinema proper is a genre encompassing movies set in the Pacific Islands, but it is important to note that there are qualifications to this thumbnail definition*. In particular, there are numerous crossovers in terms of classification. For example, 1943's *Guadalcanal Diary* is set in the Solomon Islands, but it more properly falls in the war movie genre (for this and other reasons, many WWII pictures are not included in the text). *From Here to Eternity* (1953) is a war movie and adult drama. However, since it is clearly (and authentically) set on an Oahu military base and milieu and culminates with a pivotal event in Hawai'i history (Imperial Japan's surprise attack at Pearl Harbor), *Eternity* belongs in the genre.

Jurassic Park was partially filmed on Kauai, but the story is supposed to take place on a fictional isle off the coast of Central America. On the other hand,

Hollywood films shot and set in the continental U.S. such as 1942's *Ship Ahoy*, which have no other tie to the South Seas genre than a musical number with a Pacific theme, are at least in part related to South Seas cinema. The cross-pollinating and bleeding of genres into one another leads to broad parameters in defining South Seas cinema as relating to Pacific Islanders, their islands and cultures.

Loosely defining South Seas cinema as films made in and/or about Hawai'i and other islands of Polynesia, Micronesia, and Melanesia (three geographical areas sometimes referred to as Oceania), its most distinguishing feature is that, more than any other Hollywood genre, it deals with the theme of PARADISE. This utopian quality, often portraying the isles as earthly Edens, sets South Seas cinema apart from other film genres. It is only natural that Hollywood, which specializes in the manufacturing of dreams, would be drawn early on, and throughout the years, to a part of the world that, more than any other place on the globe, has come to symbolize paradise in the imagination of Western man.

Another Hollywood genre that deals with a utopian theme is science fiction. But sci-fi pics like H.G. Wells' *The Shape of Things to Come* (1936) and *War of the Worlds* (1953), *Invasion of the Body Snatchers* (1956 and 1978), *2001: A Space Odyssey* (1968), the *Star Wars* series, and even the *Star Trek* movies, are more projections of dire prophecies and anxieties into the future than assertions of millennial epiphany.

Before the invention of the motion picture, captain's logs, novels, and paintings portrayed Pacific Islands as heavens on earth. This ready-made archetypal image was inherited by Hollywood. One of the key ingredients of paradise, according to Hollywood, is cooperative mutual aid, as opposed to competitive survival

---

*Only those movies in this book dealing with the South Seas or island themes fit into this genre; some using Hawai'i only as a setting or locale incidental to the plot, obviously don't.

of the fittest. In the films the isles are often represented as sanctuaries far from the madding crowd of the industrial nightmare—Oceanic oases of tropical abundance. In 1932's *Bird of Paradise*, Joel McCrea as Johnny Baker has no trouble "going native" ("native" being Hollywood's generic term for Pacific Islanders) and living off the bounty of the land on the mythic isle of Lani ("heaven" in Hawaiian) with his Polynesian beauty Luana, played by Dolores Del Rio. They slice open a coconut, and milk pours out, even though in real life (as opposed to reel life) the process of opening coconuts and making coco-milk is more complicated.

In the early days of the cinema, colorfully titled anthropological tomes, like Malinowski's *Sex Lives of Savages* (in the 1995 Irish comedy *Circle of Friends* this book is frequently mentioned by a professor to his students as a contrast to repressive church doctrine) and Mead's *Coming of Age in Samoa*, reinforced Oceania's image as an instinctually liberated haven of free love, previously celebrated by ship captains like Bougainville (who dubbed Tahiti "Nouvelle Cythera," after the Peloponnesian island where Aphrodite, goddess of love, first emerged from the sea), novelists like Melville, and artists like Gauguin.

In Hollywood's interpretation, the South Pacific became a paradise because nature, in this winter-free environment, is benign and luxuriantly lavish. Freed from the confines of nine-to-five drudgery, people inhabit an uninhibited leisure society. Naturally, this island euphoria leads to a perennial happiness in settings of eternal summer—what Melville admired as "perpetual hilarity" in 1846's *Typee*, the first great novel set in Polynesia.

As Oceanic El Dorados, the isles are often portrayed as being better than civilization. South Seas cinema has much implied and explicit criticism of Western society. In 1932's *Rain*, based on the Somerset Maugham story, the Pago Pago-based white hotelier Horn, portrayed by Guy Kibbee, tells a traveler: "You behold here the last remnant of a paradise. That's my quarrel with reformers, all dried and shrivelled up... Now take these islanders; they're naturally the happiest, most contented people on Earth. They ask nothing of life except to eat, dance, and sleep. Thinking gives them a headache. Trees and the sea give them all they need to eat, so they don't have to fight. They're satisfied with their gods, with their winds and waves..."

In the 1935 *Mutiny on the Bounty*, Franchot Tone plays Midshipman Roger Byam, the ship's interpreter. He learns that the Tahitian word for money is "monee," a corruption of the English word which the Polynesians learned from the British. Prior to the coming of the white man, Tahitians did not have money and, therefore, no word for this means of exchange. In a barter subsistence society, the relationships between people are more natural.

In many South Sea films, the Islanders are innocent, noble natives who live in sublime simplicity and

are morally superior to Westerners. Jon Hall is a case in point, often playing an untainted, Rousseauian *bonne sauvage* who lives in harmony with nature. In 1940's *South of Pago Pago*, the sarong boy is preferred by Frances Farmer over her former partner, the coarse, crude, exploitive Victor McLaglen. Hall's Polynesian Chief Kihane is clearly the ethical, physical, cultural, and even intellectual better of McLaglen's white character, who attempts to enslave the people of Manoa to gain possession of their pearls. And Hall teaches Farmer's saloon girl character the true meaning of love.

Islanders' *joie de vivre* is aptly expressed in the song "Happy Talk" in 1958's *South Pacific*, which Bloody Mary (Juanita Hall) sings to Lt. Cable (John Kerr) as his charming Liat (France Nuyen) pantomimes the words that evoke a life of ease and pleasure on the mythic Bali Ha'i isle. Likewise, in 1942's *Song of the Islands*, Betty Grable—who's quite becoming gamboling about in a grass skirt and leis—sings of tropical bliss:

"...Mr. Cupid really goes to town
Down on Ami Ami Oni Oni Isle.
Everybody feels terrific
And romantically prolific
And you never see a face without a smile
It's against the law to wear a frown
Down on Ami Ami Oni Oni Isle.
...When you're underneath a banyan
With a beautiful companion,
Close your eyes and dream it up a little while,
Open them and if you're in heaven
It's Ami Ami Oni Oni Island..."

The happy-go-lucky settings—and sets—for these equatorial raptures are often languid lagoons where beautiful brown-skinned girls inhabit a natural native nirvana. Underwater shots, as well as scantily clad *vahine* (women) and *tane* (men) in sarongs, loin cloths, and grass skirts are a staple of these scenes, which often include partial nudity, in and out of the water. "Happy Talk"

was shot at a lovely Kauai waterfall. *Song of the Islands* opens with Islanders romping at a studio cascade that feeds a pool.

Amorous, aquatic images started with the languorous lagoon and waterfall revealed by F.W. Murnau and Robert Flaherty in 1931's *Tabu*, shot on Bora Bora. This scene filmed on location at a limpid pool of water in French Polynesia is probably the grandfather of the watery sex scenes that suffuse South Seas cinema and reached their Oceanic apotheosis in three *Blue Lagoon* movies made in Fiji.

Toplessness—suggested or explicit—is another staunch standard of South Seas cinema. Whether in documentaries, like 1925's *Moana of the South Seas*, or features like Hollywood's three *Bounty* epics and more recently in 1994's *Rapa Nui*, filmed on Easter Island, barebreastedness was one of the genre's points of interest well before the relaxing of motion picture censorship in the 1960s. In the name of anthropological realism, Pacific women have been glimpsed *au naturel* before their white sisters. Even Dorothy Lamour's sarongs were revealing by 1930s and 1940s standards.

The imaging of the isles as having uninhibited inhabitants in various states of dress and undress led to the breaking of another long-time motion picture taboo— interracial sex. Women free of Freudian hang-ups make themselves readily available to white men, and vice versa. Their love inspires Western men to mutiny and Pacific women to forsake ancestral homelands and sail away with their white boyfriends to uncharted isles, like Pitcairn. As Robert C. Schmitt, author of *Hawaii in the Movies, 1898-1959*, notes with amusement: "...above all, interracial romances turn up with stupefying frequency in these movies."

White/nonwhite sex is still a forbidden love and touchy subject—to wit the notoriety of Spike Lee's *Jungle Fever*, released in the last decade of the supposedly enlightened late twentieth century. But sixty years earlier,

Clark Gable as English mutineer Fletcher Christian was able to make love with the Hawaiian actress Mamo Clark as the Tahitian Maimiti in 1935's *Mutiny on the Bounty*. During the same era, Ray Milland carries on with sarong girl Dorothy Lamour in *The Jungle Princess* and *Her Jungle Love*, Joel McCrea honeymoons with Dolores Del Rio in *Bird of Paradise*, and so on.

In all these cases the males are white and the women, brown. But in *South of Pago Pago*, sarong boy Jon Hall (who was, according to studio publicity, part-Tahitian) plays a *kanaka* (indigenous Pacific Islander) who has a torrid love affair with Frances Farmer. Another example of this trend is 1979's *Hurricane*, with Hawaiian actor Dayton Ka'ne romancing blonde, blue-eyed Mia Farrow.

A possible explanation for the popularity of Western lovers could be that whites brought the art of kissing to Oceania, where the *hongi*, or rubbing of noses, was common. In 1938's *Her Jungle Love*, Ray Milland has the enviable task of teaching voluptuous *vahine* Dorothy Lamour to smooch. Likewise, in 1962's *Mutiny on the Bounty*, Marlon Brando teaches his on-screen and off-screen love, Tarita, to kiss.

Photo courtesy of the DeSoto Brown Collection.

Cross-culturalism, in the form of learning one another's language, is also a recurring genre theme. In the 1935 *Mutiny on the Bounty*, linguist Franchot Tone's Polynesian paramour shares a humorous English-speaking scene with him. Tone, as Midshipman Byam, is impressed by Tehani's (Movita Casteneda) knowledge of the king's English, until he realizes that the only word the Tahitian knows in Shakespeare's tongue is "yes." In *Song of the Islands*, Victor Mature and Jack Oakie falsely believe that Betty Grable (as a white local girl) can't speak English, and, with much merriment, the only word they all apparently know is "aloha." There is a similar gag in *Pagan Love Song*, as Howard Keel underestimates Tahiti resident Esther Williams' ability to speak English. In 1958's *Enchanted Island*, Dana Andrews as Melville's alter ego makes a stab at speaking Marquesan, with disastrous consequences: he unwittingly praises the mortal enemies of Oceania's fiercest cannibals in front of the wrong tribe.

In addition to showing more skin and being sexier over the years than most other Hollywood genres, there are other distinguishing hallmarks to the South Seas genre. No South Sea movie is worth its salt without a flotilla of native outrigger canoes rushing off to meet and greet the arrival of the white man's ship. Often, the sails of the tall ships are glanced from on high—perhaps by a lookout in a palm or by hunter/gatherers on a mountain; a cry, conch shell, and/or sharkskin drum are heard; Islanders drop what they're doing, dash out to their ca-

Above

Brian Donlevy aims his machine gun in *Wake Island* was rushed to the screen in 1942, not long after the actual WWII battle west of Hawai'i. Director John Farrow's stirring action pic typifies Hollywood's wartime agitprop morale boosters, aimed at the home front. To a great extent, the island-hopping campaign in the Pacific Theater debunked the South Sea celluloid stereotype of paradise. The apocalyptic Second World War became the genre's ultimate anti-utopian subversion. From Pearl Harbor to Guadalcanal to Iwo Jima, and so on, WWII turned Oceania into an inferno, with indigenous peoples caught in the Axis-Allied power rivalry. The islanders generally play minimal—if any—roles in Hollywood's WWII movies, as imperial Japan and the Western colonial powers fight in Pacific peoples' home isles.

noes, and paddle or swim out to the Western vessel, laughing along the way.

This scenario is repeated in many Pacific pictures, including all of Hollywood's *Bounty* sagas and 1990's *Joe Vs. the Volcano*. In 1955's *Mister Roberts,* Islanders—including former Hawaiian Olympic and surfing champion Duke Kahanamoku—paddle out to welcome the Naval supply ship the USS *Reluctant*. In 1966's *Hawaii*, a double-hulled Polynesian canoe bearing an *ali'i* (high chiefess) leads a fleet of outriggers to greet the New England missionaries' sailing ship.

Another classic *kanaka* cliche is the bizarre native ritual. These primitive rites, full of wild dancing, costumes, customs, and even cannibalism, often culminate in an orgiastic frenzy. In the 1933 and 1976 versions of *King Kong*, pseudo-Melanesian ceremonies result in the betrothal of the great ape to Fay Wray and Jessica Lange. In the 1950 remake of *Bird of Paradise*, there is firewalking, and Debra Paget sacrifices herself in a volcano. The 1955 *Pearl of the South Pacific* has a religious pageant notable for its gigantic reproductions of precontact Pacific tiki gods. In 1979's *Hurricane*, there is a strange ceremonial deflowering of a young Polynesian virgin. Even the weddings that close both 1961's *Blue Hawaii*, starring Elvis Presley, and 1963's *Donovan's Reef*, starring John Wayne, have undertones of the exotic ritual trend.

Closely related to these spectacles is the native feast: an elaborate luau of *kanaka* cuisine, complete with pigs roasted in earthen ovens, tropical fruits, kava (the Oceanic elixir), and coconut drinks, as seen in 1932's *Bird of Paradise*, 1937's *Waikiki Wedding*, 1942's *Song of the Islands*, 1958's *Enchanted Island* (based on Melville's first novel, *Typee*), 1962's *Mutiny on the Bounty*, and so on.

Another genre cliche is goofy geography. Stories often take place on isles that do not exist. Skull Island—the home of King Kong—is completely fictitious, although it seems to be a Melanesian outlier on the periphery of Indonesia. In *Song of the Islands*, Ami Ami Oni Oni Isle is a nonexistent island supposedly located in the Hawaiian archipelago. On the other hand, real isles have made up the names of several movies, such as 1942's *Wake Island*, 1943's *Guadalcanal Diary*, and 1976's *Midway*. In 1941's *South of Tahiti*, the indigenous people are portrayed as having a Southeast Asian culture, while in reality the Austral, Gambier, and Tuamotu isles and atolls south of the real Tahiti are—like Tahiti itself—part of French Polynesia, and inhabited by Pacific Islanders.

For some reason, geographical locations are popular in the titles of this genre. Among the first is 1922's *South of Suva* (the capital of Fiji). The fictional isle of Manoa is located *South of Pago Pago*, the harbor at American Samoa. Most of *South Pacific* is set in the then-New Hebrides, now called Vanuatu. *Moana of the South Seas* takes place in Savaii, in what is now Western Samoa. About a dozen other films have been made with the words "South Sea" in the title, including 1941's *Aloma of the South Seas*, 1950's *South Sea Sinner,* and 1953's *South Sea Woman*. South may be the location of choice, but it is not the only direction found in movie titles: there's also 1953's *East of Sumatra* and 1969's *Krakatoa, East of Java* about the volcanic eruption that took place in Indonesia (actually west of Java), and so on. Then, of course, there are the titles that are "Beyond the" somewhere, such as the "Blue Horizon" or "Reef," or "Thunder Over" someplace, like "Tahiti," etc.

Goofy geography is not the end of it. Flora and fauna often appear on islands where no such plants or animals can be found. There's a parade of tigers, cobras, and chimps in the Dorothy Lamour sarong sagas, although there are definitely no indigenous monkeys, et al, in all of Polynesia, where the most dangerous land beasts are wild hogs. Bengal tigers, a leopard, and monkeys were imported to the Big Island of Hawai'i for location shooting of the 1963 safari drama *Rampage*, starring big game hunter Robert Mitchum and Sabu, supposedly set in Malaysia. A Universal backlot was turned into a tropical set, with 20,000 plants arranged to resemble an ersatz Pacific Island for the 1942 Abbott and Costello comedy *Pardon My Sarong*. In the 1979 *From Here to Eternity* TV mini-series, the Pearl Harbor surprise attack was shot near Long Beach, California, and the Canary Island date palms shown are not found on Oahu.

Although remakes and sequels are not unique to this genre, South Seas cinema is full of them. Hollywood spawned three *Bounty* sagas—in 1935, 1962, and 1984—starring Clark Gable, Marlon Brando, and Mel Gibson as the born-again Mr. Christian. (Tasmanian Errol Flynn, a descendant of

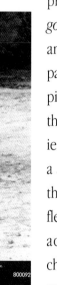

the real mutineers, starred in a 1932 Australian version, *In the Wake of the Bounty*.) The first version of *The Blue Lagoon* was lensed in 1949; the Brooke Shields remake was shot in 1980; while a sequel to the remake, 1991's *Return to the Blue Lagoon* was, like its predecessors, lensed in Fiji.

Improvements in motion picture technology, as well as in transportation and communications links, account, in part, for some of the cinema reincarnations. The 1933 *King Kong* was studio-based, while the 1976 version was partially made on Kauai's remote Na Pali coast. While the predominantly studio-made Gable *Mutiny on the Bounty* had stock footage and Tahiti background shots, the latter two adaptations were largely shot

Above

Brooke Shields and Christopher Atkins in *The Blue Lagoon*.

on location in French Polynesia. John Ford's original *The Hurricane* was shot in black and white on a sound stage with Samoa second unit footage; the 1979 remake was shot in color, on location on Bora Bora.

While partial nudity and sensuality have always been a part of South Seas cinema—especially for indigenous extras and cast members—Hollywood's increase in explicitness and candor in sexuality over the years can be clearly seen by comparing the three versions of the prepubescent *Blue Lagoon* saga to each other and, likewise, by comparing the trio of *Bounty* pics. The same is true of the two *Hurricane* movies. In all cases, there is a successive increase in the amount of exposed flesh and on-screen sex acts, reflecting the changing times and mores.

Natural disasters, too, are a recurring theme in South Seas cinema. As Schmitt notes in his seminal study, *Hawaii in the Movies, 1898-1959*: "At least eleven of the pictures made in or about Hawai'i featured volcanoes, either real (usually Kilauea) or fictional. Most of these volcanoes were filmed in fiery eruption, often in studio simulation, threatening either to claim the heroine, overrun a village, or even blow up an entire island." The wrath of Madame Pele (sometimes erroneously referred to as a male god) or a similar fiery deity is a recurring theme, as recently as 1990's *Joe Vs. the Volcano*.

A volcanic eruption takes place in the 1941 Jon Hall-Dorothy Lamour Technicolor vehicle, *Aloma of the South Seas*. In 1937's *The Hurricane*, the sarong boy and girl survive a cyclone (which won a special effects Oscar), while in the 1940 knock-off *Typhoon*, Lamour plays opposite Robert Preston and the big blow. In 1943's *White Savage,* Hall, Maria Montez, Sabu, and Sidney Toler experience an earthquake. In 1953's 3-D *Drums of Tahiti,* Tinseltown Tahitians seeking independence from France are hit by both a volcano and a hurricane! The gigantic IMAX documentary *Ring of Fire* brought the disaster dimension into the 1990s, with the world's largest screen images of Hawai'i volcanic activity.

Danger lurks in the deep, too, as Polynesia's most dangerous creatures are found underwater. In 1931's *Tabu* and fifty years later in *Beyond the Reef* (also called *Shark Boy of Bora Bora*), Polynesians deal with killer sharks in the waters of Bora Bora (where shark feeding is now a favorite tourist pastime). In 1948's *Wake of the Red Witch*, which stars the two Dukes—Kahanamoku and John Wayne—the latter does battle with a giant octopus. And, of course, in the 1930 and 1956 versions of *Moby Dick*, Captain Ahab (played by John Barrymore and Gregory Peck) hunt the great white whale with dire consequences. (It's interesting to note that the Great American Novel takes place in the South Pacific—not in America).

The genre's natural disaster and sea beast trends fit into the concept of "anti-Utopian subversion" propounded by University of Hawai'i English Professor Glenn Man in his paper "Hollywood Images of the Pacific," presented at the 1989 Moving Images of the Pacific Islands Conference. The Paradise propounded and shown by these films must be subverted, because they are, initially, presented as being superior to Western civilization. The American Way cannot be portrayed as inferior to the Fa'a Samoa (Samoan Way) or any other island way of life. South Seas cinema is full of implicit and explicit criticism of the West, and a Euro-centric civilization can't allow itself to be criticized—for long.

This is further complicated by the fact that the islands are generally presented as being better off before contact with the West than they are after. Historians refer to this initial contact as the "fatal impact," the "first taint," and "before the holocaust." The year 1995 marks the 400th anniversary of the first known contact between Polynesians and Europeans. When Spanish Captain Mendana arrived at Fatu Hiva in the Marquesas in 1595, his fleet slaughtered hundreds of Marquesans.

On the other hand, in the early days of Hollywood's other genre which highlights indigenous people, the western, Native Americans (before Arthur Penn's 1970 *Little Big Man*) are generally stereotyped as barbaric tribes which must be conquered. In the western, the West is seen as a place that must be settled and civilized by Westerners in order to be improved. But this is usually not the case within the philosophical framework of South Seas cinema. It is a replay from the collective unconscious of the biblical mythos, of the expulsion of Adam and Eve from Eden after they taste the fruit of the tree of knowledge. Ignorance, after all, is bliss.

Thus, the empire must strike back: in the metaphorical form of natural catastrophes and terrifying underwater creatures, but also in the form of the intrusion of Christian values and its various proponents into South Sea life. The omnipresent, omnipotent white man comes in a variety of forms and guises, and often reaps a whirlwind of destruction in the islands.

In Robert Flaherty and W.S. Van Dyke's 1928 *White Shadows in the South Seas*, the intruder takes the shape of a white trader. (In Flaherty and Murnau's 1931 *Tabu*, the merchant that the Tahitian is indebted to is Chinese.) In 1940's *South of Pago Pago*, 1941's *South of Tahiti*, and 1957's *Pearl of the South Pacific*, pearl traders interject skullduggery into the isles. In 1983's *Nate and Hayes*, Tommy Lee Jones plays the Pacific's Bluebeard, Bully Hayes, as pirates invade Pohnpei and Fiji.

Not all of the troubles in paradise are caused by adventurers or entrepreneurs. In 1966's *Hawaii* and Hollywood's three adaptations of Somerset Maugham's *Rain*, missionaries disrupt the natural order with their harsh, Calvinistic creed at odds with the happy-go-lucky isle ethos. With characters like the Charles Laughton/Trevor Howard/Anthony Hopkins Captain Bligh, and Raymond Massey's uncompromising colonial governor in the French Polynesia-set *The Hurricane*, the interloper becomes the militarist and the colonizer.

Chaos comes to Polynesia via the *Bounty* mutineers, who not only generate tension in the international relations between Tahiti and England, but also carry Tahitian women and a few men off to Pitcairn, resulting in violent in-fighting and race riots, as alluded to in the ending of the Brando version of *Mutiny on the Bounty*. Outsiders' wars also intrude on the islands in many movies, like 1970's *Tora! Tora! Tora!*, about the imperial Japanese air raid on Pearl Harbor, and other World War II dramas such as 1964's *The Thin Red Line,* based on James Jones' novel about the invasion of Guadalcanal. In 1994's *Blue Sky,* starring Jessica Lange (who won an Oscar for her portrayal of an anti-nuclear, anti-military activist) and Tommy Lee Jones, atomic testing and fallout beset the isles.

In 1952's extraordinarily redbaiting *Big Jim McLain,* it is the Cold War that disrupts the lives of Islanders. John Wayne plays a House Un-American Activities investigator, Jim McLain (whose initials are the same as Senator Joe McCarthy's), who comes to Hawai'i to bust a commie spy ring. It is ironic that South Seas cinema represented Pacific paradise as a form of what Marx and Engels called "primitive communism." While modern socialism is

anathema to Hollywood, its primitive, pre-Stalin, etc. form could be celebrated in Pacific pictures, even as something superior to capitalism, as long as it took symbolic, non-Leninist form.

The "natives are restless" syndrome is a reaction to the invasion of the interlopers. This can take the form of armed, anti-colonial rebellion, and atavistic, nativistic uprisings as seen in *South of Pago Pago*, *Drums of Tahiti*, and *East of Sumatra*. In *Hawaii* Christian converts "backslide" and revert to pagan practices.

One reason for the subversion of utopianism may be related to the censorship codes of early Hollywood, which allowed Cecil B. DeMille and D.W. Griffith to show biblical orgies, as long as the infidel Egyptians and Babylonians are eventually punished for their transgressions. Edward G. Robinson in 1930's *Little Caesar*, James Cagney in 1931's *Public Enemy*, and Paul Muni in 1932's *Scarface* could strut their stuff and live the high life as gangsters who defy the law in their films as long as in the end they died, proving that crime doesn't pay.

In the same way, retribution must be exacted from celluloid South Sea characters who break Western taboos. The recurring theme of miscegenation is a case in point. Frances Farmer, with her all-American looks, may fall in love with the Polynesian Jon Hall in *South of Pago Pago*, and he may be able to lead a successful native uprising against the jilted Victor McLaglen, but the lovers must pay the ultimate price: Farmer dies for her transgressions, stepping in front of a bullet meant for Hall from a gun fired by McLaglen during the indigenous rebellion. Hall then reunites with his Polynesian lover, and the message is clear as they would later sing in another

Above

This photo shows why Maria Montez was probably Dorothy Lamour's closest competitor for the coveted Hollywood title of "the Sarong Girl." Like Lamour, Montez co-starred with exotica leading man Jon Hall in jungle and costume pics.

1

Dorothy Lamour's first starring role as a sarong girl was opposite Ray Milland in *The Jungle Princess* (1936), set in Malaysia (the word "sarong" comes from Southeast Asia; Tahitians call wraparounds "pareu," Hawaiians call them "kikepa," Samoans call them "lavalava"). Lamour and Milland reunited for *Her Jungle Love* (1938), which has an almost identical plot and cast, including Lynne Overman, who provides comic relief in four Lamour films. (Coco the Chimp had a recurring role in Lamour movies, although monkeys are not native to Polynesia.) In both *Jungle* films, outsider Milland is faced with the paradise paradigm, the great existential question pondered in many Pacific pictures: once the white man discovers Utopia, will he stay or will he go?

Hawai'i and the South Sea Isles

MYTH VS. REALITY

The thousands of atolls, isles and islands that dot that part of the South Seas known as Oceania have provided the setting for many of history's most dramatic events, as well as for some of its most romantic legends.

The Hawaiian and other Pacific Island groups have attracted adventurers, missionaries, traders, whalers, and tourists for centuries. Places like Saipan, Iwo Jima and Guadalcanal became household words during World War II. Other islands, such as Fiji, Pago Pago and Moorea, gained renown through the literary works of writers like Maugham and Michener.

Indeed, these seductive islands have been a potent fount of literary inspiration for countless authors for more than 200 years. During the late Victorian era, Robert Louis Stevenson fashioned novellas and short stories for a British public smitten with the romance of the South Seas. Samuel Clemens (Mark Twain) presented his Pacific-based works to American audiences in the mid-1800s, soon followed by Jack London, who first glimpsed the Big Island of Hawai'i in 1893, the year of the overthrow of the Kingdom of Hawai'i.

These and other writers (sometimes referred to as nesomaniacs, to coin a word used by James Michener to describe those fascinated with islands) produced a charming, though sometimes confusing, portrait of seduction and corruption, intrigue and greed, using images steeped in stereotype. Hollywood movies and, later, television perpetuated this mythology that combined fact with fiction to form a conflation of Pacific cultures.

In reality, three main—but diverse and distinct—cultural groups exist in the South Pacific: Polynesia, which includes Hawaiʻi, Samoa, Tonga, Tahiti, New Zealand, Rarotonga, and Easter Island; Melanesia, which encompasses Fiji, Papua New Guinea, the Solomons, and New Caledonia; and Micronesia, which includes Guam, the Northern Marianas, the Marshalls, Yap, Pohnpei, Chuuk (Truk), Kosrae, and Palau. All these island groups were functioning societies with their own cultural history long before their introduction to the Western world by way of sixteenth- through eighteenth-century explorers.

South Sea films made in Hollywood rarely paid much attention to the specific details of the cultural backdrop of the islanders or islands that were being portrayed. The most frequently used prototype was one centered on Polynesian practices without much distinction between the different islands and peoples of Polynesia, or between Micronesia, Melanesia and Polynesia.

Some of the more memorable distortions or myths, in retrospect, have an element of humor to them. Of course, Hollywood was not attempting to portray reality; its main focus was entertainment. Just as the western did not reflect life in the old West, South Sea films did not accurately portray island life.

Myth: Beautiful princesses were sacrificed to the volcanoes.

The actress who immortalized this myth was Dolores Del Rio in *Bird of Paradise*. Human sacrifice was rare in Hawai'i, although more frequent in Tahiti, and those accounts of it reported from the Sandwich Islands never involved royalty. Interestingly, in the movies it is generally a woman who is sacrificed to the gods in some fertility rite.

Myth: Cannibalism was a prominent Pacific Island practice.

Cannibalism, like human sacrifice, was rarely practiced in Polynesia. It usually involved a powerful enemy who was ingested for his spiritual or cosmological power. Although it was practiced in the Fiji Islands, Marquesas and in Papua New Guinea, whose inhabitants are Melanesian, not Polynesian, the stereotyped image of natives with bones through their noses cooking people in pots is a fantasy.

Myth: The Hawaiians and Tahitians were a free-loving, lazy people.

The Polynesian culture and lifestyle, totally different from that of Anglo-Saxon Protestants or French Catholics, was easily misunderstood. In Tahiti, sex was linked to the nature gods of fertility cults like the Arioi Society. Polynesians didn't always cover their bodies and they lived in a very natural state. Taro patches, aquacultural undertakings and navigational feats are indicative of a work ethic.

Above
Yvonne DeCarlo performs a "native" dance. Al Kikume stands third from the right in this scene from *Hurricane Smith.*

Above

Jocelyn LaGarde plays Queen Malama (the Hawaiian word for "light"), Julie Andrews takes time out from singing to portray missionary wife Jerusha Bromley Hale, and Swedish actor Max Von Sydow depicts a self-righteous Calvinist clergyman who is as bleak as any of the Ingmar Bergman characters that Von Sydow played over the years. Hollywood had great success adapting James Michener's novels to the silver screen, and *Hawaii* (1966) features the portion of Michener's sprawling, generational saga of the same name involving the early nineteenth century conflict between Hawaiians, missionaries, and sailors. LaGarde, who is from Tahiti, won a Best Supporting Actress Oscar nomination for her role in *Hawaii* as the strong-willed royal who turns from paganism to Christianity. In the film LaGarde speaks Tahitian, not Hawaiian.

Myth: The main industries in the islands were pearl-diving and oil production from native plants.

Pearl oysters were abundant in some islands, but not in Hawai'i. Interest in them as wealth was not developed until contact with the Europeans. Copra or coconut oil was never an industry in Hawai'i; it was developed in Fiji, Tonga, French Polynesia and the Philippines. The main industries in pre-contact Hawai'i were fishing, taro and aquaculture.

Myth: The Hawaiians had no real culture of their own.

Hawaiian culture evolved from Marquesan and Tahitian origins that go back 1,500 years. Polynesians were acknowledged seafarers and masters of the waters surrounding their islands. Polynesian culture flourished in Hawai'i. Hawaiians became successful cultivators of the land, with an elaborate system of aqueducts for water and irrigation. Hundreds of crumbling stone walls, house platforms, and temples still linger among the foliage of uninhabited valleys.

Myth: Contact with white people, beginning with Captain Cook, brought prosperity to the natives and enhanced their lives.

The oldest and most northern of the major islands of the Hawaiian chain, Kauai, became the first point of contact between Hawaiians and Westerners, when Captain James Cook stepped ashore at Waimea in 1778. He named the chain the "Sandwich Islands" in honor of his patron, Lord Sandwich, First Lord of the Admiralty.

Contrary to Hollywood mythology, the local population in Hawai'i and other South Sea Islands was almost entirely eradicated by contact with Westerners. Western diseases, beginning with the spread of venereal disease in Cook's time and continuing with the introduction of additional infectious diseases,

Below

Band leader Harry Owens, famous for composing the 1937 Oscar-winning song "Sweet Leilani" (sung by Bing Crosby in *Waikiki Wedding*), and popular Hawaiian entertainer Hilo Hattie, performing her well-known "The Cock-eyed Mayor of Kaunakakai."

nearly destroyed the entire population, which had no immunity to measles or small pox.

The *hula*, which in ancient Hawaiian times was danced mainly by men, was nearly outlawed. Surfing, known as "The Sport of Kings" (certain beaches were reserved only for Hawaiian royalty), was discontinued when the missionaries labeled it a frivolous activity. The missionaries also created the *muumuu*, which they insisted the natives wear to cover their nakedness.

Myth: During the 1920s and 1930s, Hawai'i was a popular tourist destination for all of America.

Unless you were a blueblood, a celebrity, a sailor, a merchant seaman, or in the Army, visiting Hawai'i and the South Sea Islands was only a dream. Traveling that far was simply out of the financial reach of most Americans. Only the rich could afford the five-day steamship passage from a West Coast port to Hawai'i. In the movies the rich ended up staying at Waikiki's Royal Hawaiian Hotel. Waikiki became the playground of the famous, from Hollywood stars to sports figures, including Douglas Fairbanks, Mary Pickford, Charlie Chaplin, Shirley Temple, and even "The Sultan of Swat," Babe Ruth. Every starlet and pin-up girl, including such beauties as Rita Hayworth, Eleanor Powell, Movita, Esther Williams, and even little Shirley Temple, was regularly photographed in a grass skirt.

Myth: Sleek Polynesian-Hawaiian women wore sexy sarongs.

The slinky, curvaceous, sinewy lines common to the Hollywood stars who portrayed island women are stereotypical of Polynesians. In the old days, the larger the body, the more impressive the person. In Hollywood films, however, large women are usually associated with comic or matriarchal figures.

Dorothy Lamour became a sensation in a series of South Sea movies in which she played a bewitching, long-tressed Polynesian maiden dressed in a skimpy sarong and a garland of flowers. "The sarong, that little piece of cloth, was very good to me," she remarked. "Young girls all over the world would

Opposite page
Although she didn't have a drop of Polynesian blood, Dorothy Lamour epitomized America's fantasy of the sultry, sensuous, scantily clad "sarong girl." Not only did she look great in a sarong, but she could sing, too! Lamour starred in a series of jungle movies, including this remake of *Aloma of the South Seas* (1941), as well as a series of "Road" films with Bob Hope and Bing Crosby. *Aloma* ends, literally, with a bang, as a volcano explodes; natural disasters are a staple of Pacific "flicks."

Above
Even little Shirley Temple donned the grass skirt.

Following pages, left (clockwise)
Dorothy Lamour
Reiko Sato
Alice Faye and Betty Grable
Movita Castenada
Katherine DeMille

Right (clockwise)
Yvonne DeCarlo
Sophia Loren
Maria Montez
Dolores Del Rio
Rita Hayworth
Shirley Temple

Typhoon (1940) is another natural calamity film. This movie starring Dorothy Lamour and Robert Preston features a colossal storm. *Typhoon* is something of a B-picture knock-off of Lamour's earlier classic *The Hurricane* (1937) under the direction of the brilliant John Ford. According to University of Hawai'i Professor Glenn Man "Utopia is subverted" in most Hollywood South Seas cinema—islanders must be punished for their innocent, sensuous way of life. Western guilt complexes demand that Adam and Eve be expelled from Eden. (*Typhoon* may be misnamed. Tropical storms with winds 75 miles per hour and greater in the Western Pacific, such as at Guam in Micronesia, are called typhoons. In the Western Hemisphere where this movie is set they are known as cyclones or hurricanes.)

wrap tablecloths and curtains around their bodies and say, 'I'm Dorothy Lamour.'"

The word sarong is Malaysian and Indonesian, not Polynesian. Nowhere in the islands were sarongs actually worn as they were in the movies. Real Hawaiian clothing, made of tapa cloth, is fashioned to make the body look impressive and large, unlike the Western European style in which the body is meant to appear underfed.

The silky, long-haired Polynesian maidens portrayed in the movies in reality often resemble Asians as imagined by Western writers and Hollywood. Genuine hair of Hawaiians and other Polynesians is sometimes curly or wavy.

Regardless, images of long-haired, sexually inviting Hawaiian girls, willowy-figured with flowers in their hair, are still used to this day to lure tourists to the islands. The stereotype of the past is mass-marketed.

Above

Eleanor Powell and other "wannabe" hula dancers in MGM's *Ship Ahoy* wear different colored cellophane "grass" skirts. As in numerous other films, because idealized Hawaiiana was a popular facet of American culture at the time, Polynesian-style musical numbers performed during nightclub sequences were often inserted into movies that had little, if anything, to do with the Pacific. *Ship Ahoy* (1942) is a World War II yarn co-starring Red Skelton and Bert Lahr, with music provided by the Tommy Dorsey Orchestra and Frank Sinatra.

Director/actor Frank Sinatra directs Japanese actors in *None But the Brave* on a Kauai beach.

Opposite page

Director Tom Gries gives instructions to Chinese actress Tina Chen, who plays Nyuk Tsin, one of the leads in *The Hawaiians*. From humble immigrant origins, the strong-willed Nyuk Tsin rises to become the head of a business dynasty in Hawai'i.

CHAPTER TWO

Filmmaking in the Islands and the Development of the Hawai'i Film Industry

The history of filmmaking in the islands goes back to 1898, when the Thomas Edison photographers on a voyage from the Orient, W. Bleckyrden and James White, spent May 10 in Honolulu making four short movies: *Wharf Scene, Honolulu, Kanakas Diving for Money* (2 parts), and *Honolulu Street Scene.* All were copyrighted by Edison on June 22 of that year.

In 1906, Thomas A. Edison Inc. copyrighted an untitled, hour-long Hawaiian documentary comprised of more than 30 earlier short films of island scenes. The World's Fair Stock Company, in February of 1913, made the first known Hawai'i-filmed Hollywood productions, Universal's *Hawaiian Love* and *The Shark God.* These were hand-colored, one-reel movies filmed on Oahu.

In 1916, Burton Holmes made a series of travel newsreel shorts for Paramount Pictures, including *The Tonga Isles,* which featured exotic South Sea Islands.

The first feature-length Hollywood film made in Hawai'i was Paramount Pic-

tures' *The Hidden Pearls* (1918), starring Sessue Hayakawa as the young King of Apu Island who returns to his people after many years in American high society. *The Hidden Pearls* was filmed in part at Kalapana and Kilauea Crater on the island of Hawai'i.

John R. Hamilton

Below

Eleanor Powell in between takes on the set of the MGM movie *Honolulu* (1939), which co-stars Robert Young, as well as George Burns and Gracie Allen in the last feature film they appeared in together.

At the turn of the century, Hawai'i photographers, such as the legendary Ray Jerome Baker, paved the way for these films. He and his contemporaries began taking photographs and filming shorts and travelogues featuring the islanders, scenic vistas and local events. Early Hawaiian filmmakers even produced features, such as the Aloha Film Company's 1916 release *Kaoluolani* and the Hawaiian Motion Picture Company's 1921 release *The Black Lily.* In 1925, Hawaiian producer William Aldrich made a travelogue called *A Trip to the Hawaiian Islands,* and in 1929 The Junior League of Hawai'i produced *The Kamaaina,* with Kinau Wilder McVay and Harold Dillingham, a silent film about life in then-contemporary Hawai'i. It was followed the next year by *Aloha Hawaii,* a local production with an all-local cast, including Lawrence Barber and Libby Keanini.

In 1923, Paramount filmed *The White Flower*, starring Betty Compson and Edmund Lowe, with Compson riding a surfboard off Waikiki Beach.

Universal's *The Chinese Parrot,* with Anna May Wong, the first in the Charlie Chan adventures (though Chan was a minor character in this one) was filmed in part in Honolulu in 1927. *His Captive Woman,* a 1929 First National release, was filmed in part on the island of Hawai'i, apparently at Kalapana.

With the introduction of sound with its cumbersome equipment and the establishment of the major studio system in Hollywood in the 1930s, location filming became comparatively rare. Most often, the director or a second unit would go off to a location to film stock material and background plates. Then the director would rely on the skill of the studio's Special Effects Art Department to simulate the necessary exteriors.

World War II, from 1941 to 1945, interrupted Hollywood location filming in the islands. Afterward, filmmakers discovered that the islands had been made more accessible by developments in air and sea transportation to accommodate wartime mobilization. In 1950, Kauai's white beaches and green palm groves doubled for Tahiti in MGM's *Pagan Love Song,* and the island of Hawai'i served the same purpose in *Bird of Paradise* in that it served as a double for a tropical island.

Technology also shortened filming times. In 1953, Columbia Pictures filmed scenes for *From Here to Eternity* in nineteen days; *Miss Sadie Thompson* was shot in twelve days; and *The Caine Mutiny* was filmed in eighteen days. *Beachhead,* a Howard W. Koch-Aubrey Schenk production, marked the first time that a Hollywood feature film was made entirely in the islands on a 21-day shooting schedule.

Above

Betty Compson stars in the Paramount movie *The White Flower* (1923). Compson also plays the title role in *The Bonded Woman* (1922), in which she follows an alcoholic first mate from Honolulu to Samoa to clear his name. Apparently both Compson films were lensed at the same time in Hawai'i.

Above

The U.S.–Japan co-production *Tora! Tora! Tora!* (1970) painstakingly re-created Imperial Japan's surprise attack on Pearl Harbor and central Oahu's Schofield Barracks and what is now Wheeler Air Force Base. However, while care was taken to authenticate the re-creation of the "Day of Infamy," Zeros are depicted flying over the giant white cross at Kolekole Pass which was not erected at Schofield until long after December 7, 1941.

Right

This scene depicting the Japanese surprise attack on Oahu in Otto Preminger's epic *In Harm's Way* (1965) was shot at Hall Street, a redevelopment area in Honolulu that no longer exists, due to urban renewal. The Japanese planes did not actually bomb downtown Honolulu; the imperial air raid targeted military sites, and off-base civilian areas.

Above

The Pearl Harbor surprise attack is reenacted at Point Hueneme, California, for the TV mini-series *The Winds of War* (1983), one of the most expensive productions ever.

Right

Fort MacArthur, near Long Beach, is another California (note the Canary Island date palms, which are common in Southern California, but not in Hawai'i) stand-in for Pearl Harbor, as well as Schofield Barracks, in the TV mini-series *From Here To Eternity* (1979), based on the James Jones' bestseller that spawned not only a movie, mini-series, and TV series based on it, but a number of imitations, as well.

Left

Schofield Barracks under attack in 1953's Best Picture, *From Here to Eternity*. According to Kaylie Jones in an interview, the daughter of *From Here to Eternity* author James Jones, the soldiers were having breakfast and eagerly awaiting their extra rations of milk—a Sunday morning treat at Schofield—when the Japanese struck. Burt Lancaster, as Sgt. Milton Warden, sprang into action, manning a machine gun atop the Barracks and firing at the attacking Zeros. *Eternity* was shot on location at Schofield, where novelist James Jones was actually based in 1941. However, Jones bunked at D Quad, while director Fred Zinnemann's crew shot at C Quad, which is more open and has better light and aesthetics (e.g., palms). (There is a dispute as to whether or not the Japanese actually bombed and strafed Schofield Barracks. What is now Wheeler Air Force Base, adjacent to Schofield, was a prime target, because the Japanese wanted to knock out the U.S. planes based there. Some contend that Schofield was hit by accidental fire aimed at Wheeler.)

COLUMBIA PICTURES presents

FROM HERE TO ETERNITY

BURT

DEBORA

From Here to Eternity (1953), about the peacetime Army on Oahu and culminating with the Japanese suprise attack, is one of only two Pacific movies to win Academy Awards for Best Picture (the other film is *Mutiny on the Bounty* [1935]). *Eternity* won a number of additional Oscars, including Fred Zinnemann for directing, Daniel Taradash for screenwriting, and Burnett Guffey for cinematography. Burt Lancaster, Montgomery Clift, and Deborah Kerr all received best acting nominations, while Donna Reed (as a hooker!) and Frank Sinatra won Best Supporting Actor/Actress Oscars. (James Jones' daughter Kaylie Jones [in an interview] claims that rumors of Sinatra winning his big comeback role via the help of gangster connections are unfounded. Sinatra, whose career was then in decline, lobbied actively for the part of Private Maggio, the Italian-American from New York, a role that Hoboken-born Sinatra knew he could play convincingly, which he amply proved in screen tests and in an Academy Award-winning performance of a lifetime.)

LANCASTER ⋅ MONTGOMERY CLIFT
KERR ⋅ FRANK SINATRA ⋅ DONNA REED

een Play by DANIEL TARADASH ⋅ Based upon the novel by JAMES JONES

Produced by BUDDY ADLER ⋅ Directed by FRED ZINNEMANN

In a 1994 interview with the author, producer Howard W. Koch recalled, "When I arrived on Kauai I fell in love with it right away. What made it great for me is that it looked the way it should be, the tropics, coco palms and white sand beaches. When I first landed on the island, I could hear the strains of the then popular musical show *South Pacific,* and I said to myself, 'If they ever do a movie of the show, this is where they should do it' . . . sure enough four years later, Kauai is exactly where they did film it."

The 1958 production of *South Pacific,* the long-running hit Broadway musical, garnered worldwide attention for the island of Kauai. Studio publicity mills were kept working overtime, and visiting journalists reporting on the film's production wrote of the island's splendors. Ben Kaddish, assistant

to *South Pacific* director Josh Logan, said in a 1994 interview with the author that Kauai was chosen because it was "green and lush and fit the whole concept of *South Pacific.*"

▼ ▼ ▼

From its inception, Hawai'i film production was regarded as something which, for the most part, would be based elsewhere. Hollywood production companies never established studios in Hawai'i, but brought all the necessary components with them: everything from cameras and trucks to crews. In the late 1960s, however, Hollywood celebrity Richard Boone began promoting the idea of a Hawai'i film industry located in Hawai'i.

The Hawaiian Islands feature an amazing variety of terrain for such a small area: from deserts and snow-covered mountains to sand dunes, swamps, river valleys, rain forests, palm-lined beaches and active volcanoes. This diversity has enabled producers to use Hawai'i as a double for Mexico *(Ten),*

Rita Hayworth stars as a disreputable woman in the title role of *Miss Sadie Thompson* (1953). This film is the third Hollywood version of Somerset Maugham's classic short story, "Rain," about an American prostitute in Pago Pago, American Samoa. Sadie has also been portrayed by Gloria Swanson in a 1928 silent film, and by Joan Crawford in an early 1932 talkie. The Hayworth version is a musical in 3D color. Sadie's encounters with missionary and military men prompt her to declare the famous line: "You men! You filthy, dirty pigs! You're all the same, all of you. Pigs! Pigs!"

the North Atlantic *(The Enemy Below),* Australia *(The Thorn Birds),* the Caribbean *(Islands in the Stream),* Italy *(Hell Below),* and Vietnam *(Uncommon Valor).*

Five weeks of location filming of *In Harm's Way* brought $2.5 million in new income to the state. For Elvis' *Paradise Hawaiian Style,* producers spent $7 million on local salaries, services and supplies. Sixty-five people were brought from California and another forty hired locally. *Hawai'i* producers spent $6 million in and around Oahu.

In response to Boone's and others' efforts to create a local industry, veteran producer Hal Wallis pointed out one key problem, however: "The necessity of bringing together the corps of technicians needed for both movie and TV production."

In the 1970s, a local support industry was created for *Hawaii Five-0*, the first television series almost completely based in Hawai'i. Growth of support services and an experienced labor force has continued since that time, not only for films and TV, but for commercials. This industry matured in the 1980s with the production of *Magnum P.I.* and the many feature films and television movies that followed. Today's industry includes trained crews, studio-type transportation specialists, actors and extras, as well as companies and individuals serving as casting and talent agents, designers and builders of sets, production coordinators and providers of production equipment and rental and supplies.

In a 1994 interview, producer Brian Frankish, whose credits include *Field of Dreams* and work on such Hawai'i-based films as *King Kong, Aloha Summer* and *Flight of the Intruder*, recalled visiting Kauai for the first time in 1974 as a young unit production manager for *King Kong*:

"There were only four helicopters on the island, and we used all four, including Jack Carter's, who was then starting what would later become known as 'helicopter tours.' There was a 96 percent occupancy rate in the hotels, and I had to house the crew in a recently bankrupt hotel, The Hanalei Beach and Racket Club. . . .

"It was barely furnished, but it worked for us and we had breakfast catered over from Princeville Resort, which had just opened. We flew into Honopū Beach on the North Shore, which was Kong's beach, every day. After shooting background plates, the main unit came over for eighteen days of shooting. Harry Yashiro of the teamsters was of tremendous help to me on every picture, and I wouldn't do a film in Hawai'i without him. I also learned to have the set and locations blessed on every film by a local *kahuna*. It's essential that any filmmaker that goes there is respectful of the culture and the Hawaiian heritage. On *Kong* the one helicopter that was late for the blessing is the one that went down later. Since then I've never had an accident on a film in Hawai'i, even on such a big film as *Flight of the Intruder*."

In 1978, the Hawai'i Film Office was established as a staff function of what is now the Department of Business, Economic Development and Tourism. The Film Office recognized that, with the sugar cane and pineapple industries on the decline, motion picture and television production would become an increasingly important economic activity for the state.

Each episode of *Hawaii Five-O* and *Magnum,* beamed week after week into millions of homes throughout the United States and the rest of the world, acted as a commercial for Hawai'i. During this period, tourism rose from 1.7 million visitors in 1970 to 5 million in 1985. Perhaps part of this increase could be attributed to these popular programs. The pollution-free film business continues to bring millions of dollars into Hawai'i each year.

"Hawai'i itself is an element of the show for our audiences," said former *Magnum P.I.* producer Charles Floyd Johnson in a 1994 interview. "They watch Selleck, but they also watch Hawai'i. That's true for *Magnum* as it was for *Five-O.*"

In a November 25, 1986 interview in the *Hollywood Reporter Special Report Hawai'i,* Jack Lord recalled that, "The best memory of the *Hawai'i Five-O* years is the feeling of really having started an industry. We took some terrible blows in the beginning. There were editorials saying we were going to ruin the image of Hawai'i because this was a crime show. A few years later the tone was reversed. That was when they found out that 25% of the tourists coming to Hawai'i said they had been influenced by *Five-O.*"

Above
The Caine Mutiny **(1954), based on Herman Wouk's Pulitzer Prize-winning novel, is one of the best movies with Hawai'i and Pacific tie-ins. From left to right are Fred MacMurray, Robert Francis, Van Johnson, and Humphrey Bogart in one of his best roles as the mad Captain Queeg.**

The World War II Naval drama *The Caine Mutiny* **featured on-location shots of Pearl Harbor. Herman Wouk's novels on war in the Pacific Theater have been adapted into outstanding big and little screen adaptations, from** *The Caine Mutiny* **(1954) to** *The Winds of War* **(1983), to its sequel,** *War and Remembrance* **(1988). The latter two are TV mini-series and among the most expensive Hollywood productions in history.**

Left

Juanita Hall as Bloody Mary sings Rodgers & Hammerstein's delightful "Happy Talk" in an effort to entice Lt. Cable (John Kerr) to marry her daughter Liat (France Nuyen), with a vision of a happy-go-lucky life in paradise in *South Pacific* (1958). The then-17-year-old Chinese-French actress France Nuyen delightfully pantomimes the words to the "Happy Talk" song. This charming sequence includes a sensuous swim scene, which is a classic convention of South Seas cinema, with sarong-clad *vahine* (often topless) cavorting in the waters of a languid lagoon, sea, or waterfall with their muscular *tane* (men). Perhaps the first example of this cliche is in the Flaherty-Murnau silent film, *Tabu* (1931).

Below

Mitzi Gaynor as the "cockeyed optimist" Nellie Forbush, in *South Pacific* (1958), directed by Joshua Logan. To the left of Gaynor is Ray Walston as the mischief-making swabbie Luther Billis. The cast is at Hanalei, Kauai, although James Michener set his *Tales of the South Pacific* in Melanesia at the then-New Hebrides, a former French-British colony that is now the independent nation of Vanuatu.

Left

Hawaii (1966) was based on a James Michener novel set in the Pacific. Here, a cast of hundreds appears at Makua Beach, on the Waianae Coast of Oahu, in the three-hour epic about the cultural collision between Hawaiians and Westerners.

Above

Director Daryl Duke and Producer Stan Marguilies join Oahu's Reverend William Kaina and the cast of *The Thorn Birds*, including husband and wife Rachel Ward and Bryan Brown on the right, for a traditional blessing.

Hawai'i is still developing its film industry today through numerous local productions. "Encouragement of filmmakers and other creative artists is something we need more of here in Hawai'i," remarked Diane Mark, the producer of the locally produced Hawaiian theatrical feature film *Picture Bride,* in a letter to the *Honolulu Weekly* printed on September 7, 1994. "As we've learned on *Picture Bride,* hometown support can make a world of difference." Various overtures have also been made to Japan, through the reduction of foreign restrictions, to increase its use of the islands for film and commercial use.

Since 1980, Hawai'i has hosted the world-class Hawai'i International Film Festival, and in 1994 the first soundproof stage was opened in the Diamond Head area of Oahu under the guidance of the Hawai'i Film Office. The Hawai'i Film Studio is a $10 million, 16,500-square-foot building. "We were the first state to develop a studio complex," says former governor John Waihee. "We are well aware of the positive impact a television series or a feature film can have on Hawai'i's economy."

Above

A second unit shot background footage in Samoa for *The Hurricane*, although the story is actually set in the Tuamotus, an archipelago (the world's largest) of low-lying coral atolls in French Polynesia. Like *Mutiny on the Bounty*, *The Hurricane* is based on a Nordhoff and Hall novel. This is actually an anti-colonial tale, as Hall faces discrimination and persecution by whites and the French authorities. In Freudian terms, as in *Mutiny*, the instinctually liberated id battles the restraints of the civilized superego. It takes the force of nature, in the form of the big blow, to set things right.

Above

Tony Curtis and Dina Merrill on the studio "island" set of *Operation Petticoat.*

Left

Tom Selleck stars as Thomas Sullivan Magnum in MCA Television's *Magnum P.I.*

Director John Ford (second from left) on outrigger canoe for *Donovan's Reef*—Kauai location.

The grandest romance ever written . . . most famous of all American plays sweeps to the screen a flaming pageant of a forbidden love. White man . . . brown girl . . . caught in the volcanic drama of life . . . on the moon drenched shores of a magic isle . . . where blood runs hot and the heart is free and man holds in fierce embrace the alluring image of elemental woman as the jealous God in the Mountain of Fire sunders the earth and splits the skies and hurls the sea to a bottomless pit because she broke the savage Taboo!

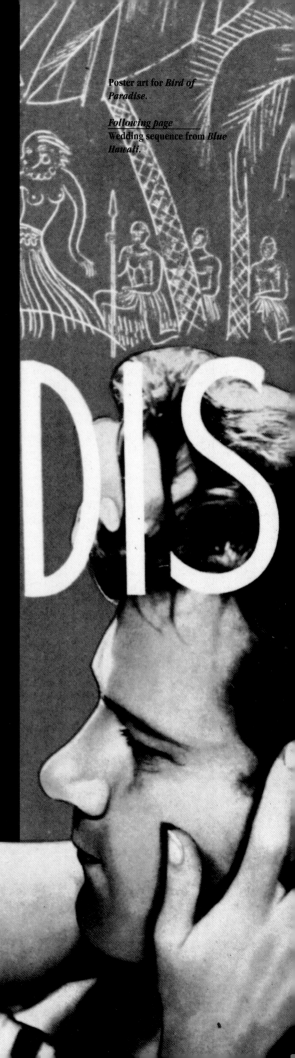

The Films

Abbreviations for the studios and releasing companies in the following chapters' film listings are:

    TCF—Twentieth Century Fox

    PAR—Paramount Pictures

    WB—Warner Bros.

    MGM—Metro-Goldwyn-Mayer

    COL—Columbia Pictures

    UA—United Artists

    U—Universal Pictures

    OR—Orion Pictures

    AIP—American International Pictures

    RKO—RKO Radio Pictures

    REP—Republic

D—Director, S—Screenplay, P—Producer, Cast

Poster art for *Bird of Paradise*.

Following page
Wedding sequence from *Blue Hawaii*.

CHAPTER THREE

Films About the Pacific Islands Made in Hawai'i

According to the late Pacific scholar and writer A. Grove Day in his *Mad About Islands*, "the Pacific or South Sea region is limited to three large island areas, distinguished mainly by the ethnic composition of their traditional inhabitants. They are called Polynesia, the place of 'many islands'; Melanesia, the 'black islands'; and Micronesia, the 'little islands.' Jointly they are termed Oceania."

Many motion pictures set in the South Seas or Pacific Islands were shot at least in part in Hawai'i. Of all the pictures filmed in Hawai'i, roughly two-thirds are actually set there, while one-third takes place elsewhere in Oceania. Almost three times more films have been shot in Hawai'i than all other Pacific Island locations combined.

Many non-Hawai'i South Sea-plot pictures were shot in Hawai'i because of geography. Hawai'i is the apex of the Polynesian triangle that includes New Zealand/Aotearoa in the southwest and Easter Island/Rapa Nui in the southeast. While Hawai'i is the only Polynesian island chain above the equator, the Aloha State has many of the attributes of other South Sea isles—rain forests, waterfalls, bamboo groves, palm trees, fragrant flowers, volcanoes, mountains, waves, sparkling seas and many of the best beaches on Earth. Hawaii's multi-ethnic community includes Polynesians, as well as Asians, who can enhance the Oceanic ambiance of casts, from leads to extras.

Hawai'i is also part of America. U.S. annexation in 1898 led to Hawai'i becoming an American territory two years later, and in 1959 Hawai'i became the Fiftieth State. Americans traveling to Hawai'i do not need passports or work visas, nor do they need to go through customs. This actually played a significant role in Hawai'i's film history. Elvis Presley's manager, Colonel Parker, was an illegal alien, and the most exotic spot he could travel to without a passport was Hawai'i. This accounts, in part, for the large number of concerts and films Presley made in Hawai'i.

New York is farther from Los Angeles than is Hawai'i, which is about 2,600 miles from Hollywood or five hours by plane, making it the nearest Pacific Island to the West Coast. Hawai'i also has available a substantial talent pool from actors to technicians, as well as major production facilities and equipment.

Hollywood is unlikely to dispatch casts and crews to work in remote isles unless the script requires it. Indeed, most Hollywood producers shoot their Shangri-las in L.A. studios. But if a South Pacific Island location is needed, Hawai'i can be used as a South Sea stand-in. Hawai'i has doubled for Tahiti in 1950's *Pagan Love Song*, for Vanuatu (formerly the New Hebrides) in 1958's *South Pacific*, and for fictitious isles and locales as recently as 1995's *Don Juan DeMarco* and *Waterworld*.

Hawai'i's combination of topography, natural beauty, development, U.S. affiliation, transport links, and proximity to Los Angeles make it attractive to filmmakers.

▼ ▼ ▼

There are more films listed in this chapter than in any of the other sections in this book because this chapter includes movies that were largely shot in Hollywood studios or elsewhere, but which have some on location Hawai'i scenes, either via a second unit camera crew, the use of stock footage, or special effects.

The reader should also note that, strictly speaking, *Made in Paradise: Hollywood's Films of Hawai'i and the South Seas* does make a few geographical exceptions. Movies set in Indonesia, for example, take place outside of Oceania proper. But the attributes of pictures like 1953's *East of Sumatra* are similar to the tropical traditions of the South Seas genre. Storytelling, not authenticity, is Hollywood's forte.

THE WHITE FLOWER
1923 PAR

D:	Julia Crawford Ivers
S:	Julia Crawford Ivers
P:	Adolph Zukor—Famous Players Lasky
Cast:	Betty Compson, Edmund Lowe

Melodrama about the daughter of a wealthy Hawaiian planter and his Hawaiian wife, who is told her one true love will be a man who gives her a perfect white flower. Newspaper ads for the movie featured star Compson riding the waves on a surfboard.

Locations were mainly in the city of Honolulu at Nuuanu Pali, Waikiki Beach and Kilauea Crater.

HULA
1927 PAR

D:	Victor Fleming
S:	Ethel Doherty, Titles; George Marion Jr., Adaptation; Doris Anderson
P:	Adolph Zukor, Jesse L. Lasky
Cast:	Clara Bow, Clive Brook, Agostino Borgato, Duke Kahanamoku (uncredited)

Clara Bow plays "Hula" Calhoun, the daughter of a fun-loving rancher. She is instantly attracted to a debonair British engineer who has staked his future on the construction of an irrigation dam on the rancher's vast Hawaiian holding.

Fleming became one of MGM's top directors. Among his many credits are *Red Dust*, *Captains Courageous*, *The Wizard of Oz* and *Gone with the Wind*.

Motion Picture News on September 16, 1927, wrote, "Having been established that Clara Bow is the 'it' girl of the screen, what would be sweeter

Above

Betty Compson is under a breadfruit tree here in 1923's *The White Flower*. Including 1922's *The Bonded Woman*, Compson appeared in at least two made-in-Hawaiʻi silent films, emerging as one of the South Seas genre's first stars. Paramount publicity for *Flower* proudly proclaims: "You'll see Betty riding the surf, shocking us all with her *hula*!"

or neater than having her demonstrate that appeal in a romance of the South Seas—one of the type of pictures where girls go native? Which means they are decorated with beads and shredded wheat costumes."

Right

The Roaring Twenties' "It Girl," Clara Bow, starred in the title role of *Hula* **(1927), based on a novel by Hawai'i writer Armine von Tempski. In this scene, Clara Bow, as Hula Calhoun, dances an ersatz hula during a *luau* at her father's ranch in order to make a man jealous. The film opens with Bow swimming nude in a pond; she is then stung by a bee. Olympic swimming champion and Hawaiian beachboy Duke Kahanamoku has a small role as a ranchhand who warns of a flood.**

FEET FIRST

1930 PAR

D: Harold Lloyd

S: John Grey, Alfred A. Cohn and Clyde Bruckman

P: Harold Lloyd

Cast: Harold Lloyd, Barbara Kent, Robert McWade

A clerk in a Honolulu chain store who dreams of becoming an important man is instructed to deliver a pair of shoes to his boss's wife on a ship bound for the West Coast. Through a series of comic mishaps, he becomes an unintentional stowaway, meets his boss and a secretary on board, and delivers a bid for a contract to Los Angeles by way of mail plane.

Portions of *Feet First* were shot on board the SS *Malolo* en route to Hawai'i in 1930. The only identifiable scenes of actual Hawai'i are the Honolulu dock sequences. The Honolulu street scenes appear to have been filmed in Los Angeles.

Above

Silent film comedian and director Harold Lloyd, best known for hanging from building ledges and giant clocks, plays a clerk in the early talkie *Feet First*.

THE BLACK CAMEL

1931 TCF

D: Hamilton MacFadden

S: Barry Conners and Philip Klein adapted by Hugh Stange

P: Hamilton MacFadden

Cast: Warner Oland, Sally Eilers, Bela Lugosi, Robert Young

The Black Camel was one of the earlier films in the popular Charlie Chan series made in Hollywood. It was also partly filmed on location in Hawai'i, the setting for the story, and Warner Oland starred as the great Chinese Honolulu detective.

The film, which begins with travelogue–style footage of Hawai'i, concerns the murder of an actress while working on a film in Hawai'i. Actor Bela Lugosi found stardom one year later in the title role of Universal's *Dracula.*

Robert Young, after much time spent as a contract player, found fame 25 years later as the star of two television series, *Father Knows Best* in the mid-1950s and *Marcus Welby M.D* in the late 1960s.

Some of the location scenes were filmed in and around the Royal Hawaiian Hotel and Waikiki Beach.

BIRD OF PARADISE

1932 RKO

D: King Vidor

S: Adapted by Wells Root, Wanda Tuchock and Leonard
       Praskins from the play by Richard Walton Tully

P: David O. Selznick

Cast: Dolores Del Rio, Joel McCrea, John Halliday, Lon
       Chaney Jr.

A boatload of fun-loving U.S. travelers drop in at Tahiti and one of them, Johnny "Bake" Baker (McCrea), stays and makes love to a native princess, Luana (Del Rio). He kidnaps her to another island and builds a native hut, where they live until a volcano erupts on her home island. The schooner with Baker's friends comes back in time, but Luana decides to stay on and sacrifices herself to the volcano.

After looking at travel brochures, it was decided to film the movie in Hawai'i, because it was closer to California—the trip to Tahiti took several weeks each way by boat. When the Hollywood troupe arrived in Hawai'i, they were hit by *kona* weather, which brought wind and rain for weeks on end. It was the worst weather the islands had experienced in many years.

If the skies cleared for a few hours, the troupe would gather over a hundred Hawai'i extras and rush out with all the filming equipment to get in as much footage as possible. Due to the inclement weather, Vidor asked producer David O. Selznick if he could return to Hollywood and finish the picture on Catalina Island, off the California coast, and at the RKO-

Bird of Paradise has a number of scenes that were shot on location on Oahu, such as at Kahala Beach, with Koko Head crater in the background. Here, Joel McCrea is at Kaneohe Bay, on the windward side of Oahu.

Pathe studios in Culver City. Selznick agreed. Exterior location footage was photographed by Clyde De Vinna.

In his book *A Tree Is a Tree*, King Vidor claimed that when he was first offered the picture, Selznick told him, "I don't care what story you use so long as we call it *Bird of Paradise* and Del Rio jumps into a flaming volcano at the finish." Dolores Del Rio executed a topless *hula* during a native dance sequence. Two small pieces of adhesive tape provided assurance that the lei covering her bosom wouldn't stray too far from its place.

The king is played by Napoleon Pukui; the medicine man, by Agostino Borgato; and the old medicine woman, by Sophie Ortego.

Below
Scene from *White Heat* a/k/a
Cane Fire filmed on Kauai.

WHITE HEAT A/K/A CANE FIRE

1934 SEVEN SEAS FILM CORPORATION

D: Lois Weber

S: Lois Weber and James Bodrero

P: Seven Seas Corp. Production

Cast: Mona Maris, David Newell

Melodrama about a sugar planter and his bored society wife. Mona Maris played Leilani, an island girl.

Filmed in 1933 on Kauai at the old Knudsen place and at Waimea Mill, many Kauai residents had bit roles, including Kamaunani Achi, Peter Hyun, Nohili Noumu, Nani Pasa and Kolimau Kamai.

Christian finds release from his responsibilities as leader of the mutineers in the arms of Maimiti, beautiful native girl.

MUTINY ON THE BOUNTY

A Metro-Goldwyn-Mayer PICTURE

MUTINY ON THE BOUNTY

1935 MGM

D: Frank Lloyd

S: Talbot Jennings, Jules Furthman and Carey Wilson,
       based on the book by Charles Nordhoff and James
       Norman Hall

P: Irving Thalberg and Albert Lewin

Cast: Clark Gable, Charles Laughton, Franchot Tone, Mamo
       Clark, Movita

Mutiny on the Bounty is the story of the 1789 uprising by the sailors of HMS *Bounty,* led by Fletcher Christian, against Captain William Bligh.

The HMS *Bounty* set sail from England in 1787, bound for Tahiti. In charge was Captain Bligh (Laughton) a harsh taskmaster. Storms lengthened the voyage, food ran low and, as Bligh's temper shortened, he raged at his underfed and embittered crew. The golden days that followed their arrival in Tahiti temporarily quieted his men, but tempers flared again soon after the start of the return voyage.

Above

A lobby card for *Mutiny on the Bounty* featuring Clark Gable as first mate Fletcher Christian and Mamo Clark as his Tahitian lover, Maimiti. Mamo Clark was a Hawaiian actress and authoress, who wrote *Except Their Sun*. The film also co-starred Mexican actress Movita. Interestingly, Movita later married Marlon Brando who played Fletcher Christian in the 1962 version of *Mutiny on the Bounty.*

Bligh's tyranny brought rebellion to the breaking point and the men rose in mutiny. Adventures followed that have been without equal in naval history: Bligh and eighteen seamen sailing 4,000 miles in an open boat; escaped mutineers seeking refuge with their native wives; Bligh's return and the capture of several of the mutineers; another shipwreck and Bligh again in an open boat at the mercy of the sea; the final court-martial back in England at which the tyrannical captain is denounced by midshipman Roger Byam (Tone).

The 1935 version became as much of a legend in itself as did the original tale. It won the Oscar as the Best Picture of 1935, and was a masterpiece of the late great producer Irving Thalberg. Clark Gable's popularity in his role led to his being chosen by the public as "The King." Rarely has a movie character been more imitated by nightclub mimics and television impersonators than Charles Laughton's Captain Bligh.

Director Frank Lloyd took a production company of record size on a 14,000-mile voyage to Tahiti to photograph exterior background scenes for *Mutiny on the Bounty*. Lloyd hired 2,500 men, women, and children in Tahiti as extras, and they inhabited the picture's two native villages, constructed to appear as they would have in the 1700s.

More than 150 actors and crew members, together with tons of equipment, were transported to the isthmus at Catalina Island off the Southern California coast, where the majority of the film was shot. Among the equipment transported on barges were three generating plants, two boom trucks, automobiles, studio lamps, props, a 100-foot Tahitian war canoe, fifteen outriggers, 24 palm trees and as many breadfruit trees, eight interior studio sets, and complete makeup and wardrobe departments. Some scenes were also shot at the MGM studios in Culver City, California.

WAIKIKI WEDDING

1937 PAR

D: Frank Tuttle

S: Frank Butler, Don Hartman, Walter De Leon and Francis Martin based on a story by Butler and Hartman

P: Arthur Hornblow Jr.

Cast: Bing Crosby, Bob Burns, Martha Raye, Shirley Ross, Leif Erickson, Anthony Quinn

Crosby, who played Tony Marvin, a singing press agent for a Hawaiian pineapple cannery, introduced the song "Blue Hawaii," which was made more famous almost 25 years later by Elvis Presley in *Blue Hawaii.* The other song introduced in the film, "Sweet Leilani" by Harry Owens, won an Oscar as Best Song of 1937 and became Crosby's first million-selling record.

Waikiki Wedding was filmed at Paramount Pictures studios in Hollywood, but in a September 1936 pre-production trip, Crosby and a small film crew led by Robert C. Bruce went to Hawai'i and shot backgrounds and process shots.

Prince Lei Lani, Nalani de Clerq, Kuulei de Clerq and George Kalunana are featured Hawaiian performers. Young actor Anthony Quinn, in one of his first film roles, played a Hawaiian native. Over his fifty-year career, with more than 200 feature film credits, Quinn would win two Academy Awards as Best Supporting Actor in *Viva Zapata* (1952) and *Lust for Life* (1957), becoming one of the finest international actors of his generation. Quinn is perhaps best known as the earthy Zorba, a role with which he came to be identified, from the film *Zorba the Greek* (1964).

Garbed in grass skirts, the "Big Mouth," Martha Raye, and Shirley Ross flank co-star, crooner Bing Crosby, in *Waikiki Wedding* (1937). Crosby warbles the *hapa-haole* hits "Sweet Leilani," which won band leader Harry Owens an Oscar, and "Blue Hawaii." A quarter century later, another pop singer, Elvis Presley, starred in a film that used the name of the song as its title—*Blue Hawaii*.

HAWAII CALLS
1938 RKO

D: Edward Cline
S: Don Blanding from his novel *Stowaways in Paradise*
P: Sol Lesser
Cast: Bobby Breen, Pua Lani, Ward Bond, Mamo Clark, Ned Sparks

This musical comedy tells the story of two boys, Bobby and his little Hawaiian friend Pua, who stow away on an oceanliner in San Francisco bound for Honolulu. On their arrival in the islands, they embark on a series of hilariously amusing adventures that culminate when they become the central figures in a dramatic search for a band of criminals.

Larry Duran, who when he was 11 years old played Banana, told the author in a 1994 interview that, except for background shots, the film was based at RKO in Hollywood.

HAWAIIAN BUCKAROO
1938 TCF

D:	Ray Taylor
S:	Original story and screenplay by Dan Jarrett
P:	Sol Lesser
Cast:	Smith Ballew, Evelyn Knapp, Harry Woods, George Regas

A standard horse opera, hyped with the injection of Hawaiian romance and personified by hip-shaking *hula* dancers, steel guitars and leis.

Photo courtesy of the DeSoto Brown Collection.

A cowboy buys a pineapple plantation, which turns out to be worthless land located on the corner of a lava bed. He meets the daughter of the owner of the largest cattle ranch on the island and rescues her from bad men.

Hawaiian Buckaroo was filmed in California, and many Hawaiians living in Los Angeles were employed on the production, among them Princess Luana, unbilled in a small speaking part. Albert Von Tilzer, Eddy Grant and Harry MacPherson wrote three tunes for the movie, including "Hawaiian Memories" and "I Left Her on the Beach at Waikiki."

Some background scenes were filmed at Parker Ranch on the island of Hawai'i.

HAWAIIAN NIGHTS

1939 U

D: Albert S. Rogell

S: Charles Grayson and Lee Loeb

P: Max Golden

Cast: Johnny Downs, Constance Moore, Mary Carlisle

The son of a hotel magnate ignores business responsibilities to organize a band. Sent by his father to Honolulu to assist with a hotel, he takes his entire band along, which results in musical comedy complications.

Hawaiian Nights was filmed in Hollywood on a modest budget. Hawaiian specialty dancers featured included Satini Puailoa and Augie Goupil. There are, however, Waikiki location background shots.

Above

Constance Moore is serenaded in *Hawaiian Nights*, which was predominantly made in Hollywood, although there are Waikiki background shots.

HONOLULU

1939 MGM

D: Edward Buzzell

S: Herbert Fields and Frank Pastor

P: Jack Cummings

Cast: Eleanor Powell, Robert Young, George Burns and Gracie Allen

Romantic musical comedy in which a movie star changes places with a look-a-like Hawaiian plantation owner, becoming involved in embezzlement and with the wrong girl.

The final spectacularly staged production number, "Hymn to the Sun," is part of the show-within-the-movie, set in the Fiesta Room, a mythical Honolulu night club. Eleanor Powell performs three dances to a medley of traditional Hawaiian music played by Andy Iona's Islanders.

Clad in a *hula* skirt and a lei, she combines tropical movements with modern tap styles to create a unique dance blend. Powell performs a so-called native drum dance and hula barefoot, then puts on her tap shoes for her version of a native dance.

MGM sent Powell and Andy Iona's Islanders (sometimes billed as Andy Iona's Hawaiians) on a cross-country personal appearance tour to promote the film, which exhibits a studio-bound Hawai'i with a few stock exterior shots.

SOUTH OF PAGO PAGO
1940 UA

D: Alfred E. Green

P: Edward Small

S: George Bruce

Cast: Jon Hall, Victor McLaglen, Frances Farmer

A group of seafaring adventurers, including a scheming blonde beauty named Ruby (Farmer), set out to find a fabulous pearl bed somewhere south of Pago Pago. When the ship reaches Manoa, the natives of the island greet them in friendship. By devious methods, the crew forces the natives to dive for pearls. Eventually they realize what is going on and, led by their chief Kihane (Hall), they drive the plunderers away from their island.

Background shots were made at Kalapana and on the Kona Coast.

Below

At the end of *South of Pago Pago*, Jon Hall and Olympe Bradna embrace and embark on their honeymoon in an outrigger canoe. Frances Farmer has died (shot by Victor McLaglen), and Hall has returned to his native lover. The moral of the story: stick to your own kind. However, Polynesians learn at least one valuable thing from Westerners—the art of kissing. When Hall tries to rub Bradna's nose in this scene, she kisses him instead, as the film ends.

Photo courtesy of the Ed Rampell Collection.

Right

Right to left: Victor McLaglen, Jon Hall, and Olympe Bradna in *South of Pago Pago*, one of the more interesting offerings from Hollywood's heyday of South Seas cinema. Victor McLaglen is a freebooting captain who tricks and forces the indigenous islanders of Manoa to dive for pearls. Part-Tahitian actor Jon Hall plays Kihane, the chief who eventually leads a native uprising against the oppressive whites. In a South Sea switcheroo, sarong boy Hall, a brown man, has a passionate affair with Ruby, portrayed by Frances Farmer, who looks like an all–American girl. Actual Samoan words, dances, etc., are used in this adventure movie (Pago Pago is a harbor in American Samoa) with socially conscious undertones.

HONOLULU LU

1941 COL

D: Charles Barton
S: Eliot Gibbons, Paul Yawitz
P: Wallace MacDonald
Cast: Lupe Velez, Leo Carrillo, Bruce Bennett, Adele Mara

The film, made before and released just days after the attack on Pearl Harbor, rather incongruously deals with life in Honolulu among boisterous all-American sailors. Audiences were not in the mood for this silly little comedy after the disastrous "Day of Infamy" on which so many young American sailors lost their lives.

Lupe Velez plays a burlesque queen, Honolulu Lu, who is out to win an island beauty contest. She assumes the identity of a society girl, Consuelo, the niece of her excitable con man uncle, Don Esteban Cordoba (Carrillo). Velez sings the Sammy Cahn and Saul Chaplin title song. Romance involves Bruce Bennett as a Navy man. Nina Campana appears as a stout native maid.

Filming was primarily studio-bound, with some stock exterior shots.

SONG OF THE ISLANDS

1942 TCF

D: **Walter Lang**

S: **Joseph Schrank, Robert Pirosh, Robert Ellis and Helen Logan**

P: **William LeBaron**

Cast: **Betty Grable, Victor Mature, Jack Oakie, Thomas Mitchell, Hilo Hattie**

Eileen O'Brien (Grable) is an Irish rancher's daughter returning to her Hawaiian home after six years of school on the mainland. Hilo Hattie, in her film debut as Palola, grabs every laugh in sight with her business of pursuing Oakie, as well as with her hula parodies.

Otto Bower went to Kalapana and the Kohala Coast on the island of Hawai'i and to the South Seas as the head of a special unit to film backgrounds and exteriors.

Most of the film was shot at Twentieth Century Fox studios. The whole two acres of Stage 14 were turned into a Hawaiian landscape, complete with towering coconut palms, small forests of Hawaiian trees, ferns and tangled tropical greenery and exotic flowers. Muralists working on 10,000 square feet of canvas painted green valleys, full waterfalls and purple mountains on a vast cyclorama that enclosed the stage.

"On Ami Ami Oni Oni Isle" and "O'Brien Has Gone Hawaiian," comedy numbers sung by Grable, culminates in a lavish ensemble of dances featuring her and two troupes of island "natives." Hermes Pan, who staged the dances, gave the hula a hilarious punching by weaving it with an Irish jig, and also created an exuberant mass dance finale. The film features music by Mack Gordon and Harry Owens and his Royal Hawaiians.

The February 4, 1942 *Hollywood Reporter* described the film as a "Tuneful girl and Poi Affair...in a lushly Technicolor musical attraction... Name if you can, a better setting for escapist entertainment than the South Sea Islands of song and fable."

Popular Hawaiian entertainer Hilo Hattie makes her screen debut as Palola in *Song of the Islands*. This scene is from the end of the film, as Hilo Hattie sings "The Cockeyed Mayor of Kaunakakai" (which refers to the main town on the Hawaiian Island of Molokai) at the St. Patrick's Day *luau*.

MILLION DOLLAR WEEKEND

1948 EAGLE LION

D: Gene Raymond

S: Charles S. Belder

P: Matty Kemp

Cast: Gene Raymond, Francis Lederer, Stephanie Paull

A young San Francisco businessman escapes to Honolulu on a commercial airliner (United Airlines is prominently featured) with his company's funds. On the plane he meets a widow who is running away from a murder charge. An associate steals the funds from the businessman's Honolulu hotel room and threatens both him and the widow with blackmail. The young businessman chases the associate back to San Francisco, where he recovers the money and returns the funds without anyone knowing they were missing. He and the widow promise to meet each other in Honolulu to start their lives anew.

Paul Ivano's background shots of Hawai'i are spectacularly beautiful in this low-budget programmer. Some filming took place in Honolulu at the Royal Hawaiian Hotel, Waikiki Beach, and the airport. There is an exciting car chase through the Nuuanu Pali, and the film features the Royal Hawaiian Serenaders and a song, "Heaven Is in Blue Hawai'i," by Paul Koy.

Above

A scene from the mystery yarn *Million Dollar Weekend*.

Howard Keel and Esther Williams star in *Pagan Love Song;* the Tahiti setting is perfect for the nautical feats Williams is known for.

Below
Five-year-old Larry Ramos and his ukulele are the center of attention in this scene from the MGM musical *Pagan Love Song*.

PAGAN LOVE SONG
1950 MGM

D:	**Robert Alton**
S:	**Robert Nathan and Jerry Davis**
P:	**Arthur Freed**
Cast:	**Esther Williams, Howard Keel, Minna Gombell, Rita Moreno, Charles Mauu**

A retired Ohio schoolteacher finds love in Tahiti, where he has inherited a plantation.

Pagan Love Song features beautiful technicolor Hawai'i on-location exterior photography in which Kauai doubles for Tahiti. Locations include Ahukini Harbor, Nawiliwili, Lydgate Park, Hanalei Bay, and the Wailua River.

The extra players were hired locally on Kauai; 27 Hawai'i residents were

selected to participate with Miss Williams in an aquatic hula—12 came from Honolulu and the remainder were residents of Kauai. This was Miss Williams' first salt-water ballet, as it was filmed actually in the waters off Kauai, and she sang "Singing in the Sun," while swimming in triangle formation. Most of the undersea ballets were shot in a freshwater tank on a soundstage at MGM Studios.

Location work on the production attracted newsworthy attention, when Williams narrowly escaped injury during a canoeing sequence, especially since she was expecting a baby at the time. She worked on the film until her sixth month of pregnancy.

Tahitian Charles Mauu, who plays an important role as Tavae, came to Hollywood on a vacation trip and remembered his father's advice to call on Joseph Cook of MGM's production department, with whom Charles' father had become friends during the filming of *Mutiny on the Bounty* some 15 years before, when Charles was just a growing boy. On a visit to the studio commissary, Arthur Freed saw Charles and promptly persuaded him to play the second male lead.

Future Academy Award winner Rita Moreno (*West Side Story*, Best Supporting Actress 1961) had an important small role as a native girl.

"Its main asset apart from the two leading players is scenery. The picture was photographed in Hawai'i, which doubled for Tahiti and a tropic mood prevails over all."—Edwin Schallert in *The Los Angeles Times*, December 30, 1950.

Above

From right to left, Esther Williams, Rita Moreno, and Charles Mauu wave in an outrigger off Kauai in the Tahiti-set *Pagan Love Song*. In this early scene in the picture, the Tahitian characters in the canoe are greeting the ship that brings Howard Keel to their isle. While Mauu is really Tahitian, Rita Moreno is another Latino actress fobbed off as a Polynesian. The Puerto Rican thespian portrayed a Thai in *The King and I* (1956) (directed by *Song of the Islands'* Walter Lang) and won a Best Supporting Actress Oscar portraying a Puerto Rican in 1961's Best Picture, *West Side Story*.

Left

Howard Keel finds out that Esther Williams is far more sophisticated than he first suspects in the love story *Pagan Love Song*, set in Tahiti, but made on Kauai.

BIRD OF PARADISE
1951 TCF

D: **Delmer Daves**

S: **Delmer Daves**

P: **Darryl F. Zanuck**

Cast: **Jeff Chandler, Debra Paget, Louis Jourdan, Maurice Schwartz, Everett Sloane, Prince Leilani, Jack Elam, Otto Waldis**

Twentieth Century Fox's *Bird of Paradise* is a romantic tragedy of 19th century Polynesia filmed in Technicolor, starring Jeff Chandler, Debra Paget and Louis Jourdan, and written and directed by Delmer Daves. Filming took place in the Hawaiian Islands and employed 200 locals, several in important speaking, dancing and singing roles.

Bird of Paradise, written in 1911 by Richard Walton Tully, was a perennial stage favorite for a quarter of a century, and at one time or another starred old-time favorites such as Laurette Taylor, Lenore Ulric and Carlotta Monterey in the tragic love lead. In 1932, the play was made into a movie by RKO and starred Dolores Del Rio.

Darryl Zanuck, Vice President in charge of production at Twentieth Century Fox, decided that the title, the locale and one dramatic highlight of the play—the sacrifice of a maiden to a volcano—were the essential ingredients for a successful motion picture. The rest of the story, he said, was too dated for modern audiences. He called on ace writer-director Delmer Daves, fresh from his success with *Broken Arrow,* a story of American Indians and the white man, to submit an original screenplay. He was so pleased with the script that Daves turned in that he gave the production an immediate go-ahead.

Andre, a Frenchman (Jourdan), tires of civilization and seeks paradise among the natives of a Polynesian village. He falls in love with a chief's daughter, Kalua (Paget), against the wishes of the people's holy man, or *kahuna* (Schwartz). The girl's brother Tenga (Chandler) befriends the Frenchman, encourages the romance and helps him to try and understand the ways of the islanders, all the while threatening to kill him if he fails the girl. Try as he may, the white man cannot cope with the religion and beliefs of the natives. He is shocked beyond belief when Kalua follows the traditional ritual of walking on fire, a feat she performs harmlessly because she has faith. Ultimately, he loses his dream of paradise and his bride when she serenely sacrifices herself in a volcano to appease the goddess of fire.

Actor Prince Lei Lani, born in Hilo, Hawai'i, traced his lineage to King Lunalilo. Leaving the islands as a young man, Leilani toured the U.S. with his "Royal Samoans" and appeared as the *kahuna* in the original stage version of *Bird of Paradise*. In the film, the tall, stately actor plays a native chief. Also featured is Mary Ann Ventura, a beautiful Hawaiian woman, regarded as one of the most talented exponents of ancient Polynesian dancing in Hawai'i. Dance movements were created by Iolani Luahine, reputedly the greatest teacher of ancient Hawaiian dances in the islands at

Photo courtesy of the Ed Rampell Collection.

the time. The *Bird of Paradise* music score included native tunes and chants by the elderly "Mama" Bray, wife of "Daddy" Bray, both of whom sang songs from memory. "Daddy" was well known and respected in Hawaiian society as one of the few men in the territory who knew the old religious chants.

The director created a composite Polynesia for the picture, "telescoping" three islands separated by 350 miles of Pacific Ocean and ten locations into a tightly compressed, one-half-square-mile Polynesian village. To create one idyllic locale, Daves photographed Jourdan and Chandler sailing a boat into Hanalei Bay, on the island of Kauai, and jumping off to greet natives swimming toward them who had been shot south of Hilo on the island of Hawai'i. From there, the film cuts to surfing scenes at Waikiki and sunset on the fabulous Kona Coast. Miss Paget's sacrifice to Mauna Loa appears only a hop and a skip away through a flowery jungle. Two-time Oscar-winning cameraman Winton Hoch captured the island vistas in Technicolor.

Art director Al Hogsett built a functional Polynesian village comprised of twenty stilted, thatch-roofed dwellings in a coconut grove on Hawai'i for the film. Three of these, along with a native outrigger canoe camp, were destroyed in a hurricane that hit the set only two hours after the principals had finished work there. But for Hogsett's foresight in using heavy coconut logs, tied and bolted, the entire village might have been destroyed by the 75-mile-per-hour winds.

The production was also marked by a near-accident, when a car transporting Paget, Chandler and Jourdan skidded on the road of a pineapple-covered mountain on Kauai. In addition, Everett Sloane broke his toe and lacerated his left leg after stumbling against glass-sharp lava while launching an outrigger canoe in heavy surf.

"*Bird of Paradise* is one of the most beautiful motion pictures ever made," reported the March 21, 1951 *Hollywood Citizen News*. "All the charm of the Hawaiian Islands where the new 20th Century Fox picture was made has been captured by the Technicolor cameras."

Opposite page
Louis Jourdan as the Frenchman Andre and Debra Paget as the indigenous Kalua are the sarong-clad—if doomed—interracial lovers in *Bird of Paradise*.

801

Below

Note the studio lights shining on the tops of the cars, indicating that this scene in *Operation Pacific* showing the arrival of the USS *Thunderfish* submarine at Pearl Harbor was probably shot on a Warner Bros. sound stage. The Pearl Harbor background seems to be a cyclorama.

Opposite page

Operation Pacific includes background shots which were taken at what is now Camp H.M. Smith and a Honolulu police station. In this scene, John Wayne and his crew are jailed after a wild night on the town in Honolulu. Superstar Wayne made many Hawai'i and Pacific-related films.

OPERATION PACIFIC
1951 WB

D: **George Waggner**

S: **George Waggner**

P: **Louis F. Edelman**

Cast: **John Wayne, Patricia Neal, Ward Bond, Philip Carey**

A story of the United States submarine operations in the Pacific during World War II and the sailors who manned the ships. The submarine USS *Thunderfish* is led by Lt. Commander Duke Gifford (Wayne).

No evidence was found that the picture was filmed in Hawai'i except for some second unit photography. Research indicates that it was filmed at a Warner Bros. studio, largely on a sound stage where an interior and exterior replica of a submarine was built. Stills from the film indicated that the stage was equipped with a huge water tank, a blue sky cyclorama, and a Pearl Harbor exterior stage backdrop.

BIG JIM MCLAIN

1952 WB

D: Edward Ludwig

S: James Edward Grant

P: Wayne Fellows Productions

Cast: John Wayne, James Arness, Nancy Olson

Big Jim McLain was one of the the first modern motion pictures filmed in post-war Hawai'i, traditional site of the South Sea Island period and costume sagas.

A company of seventeen Hollywood actors and actresses and 51 technicians was flown to and from the islands for six full weeks of intensive shooting. The Hollywood cast, headed by Wayne, his co-stars Nancy Olson, James Arness and Alan Napier, was augmented by a score of Hawai'i residents in featured and bit parts and upwards of 500 islanders in atmosphere parts. From beachboy to banker, Honoluluans and their neighbor islanders were willing volunteer actors.

Some of the most prominent and influential citizens of Honolulu accepted feature parts to add to the picture's ring of authenticity, and they acquitted themselves well. With the permission of the City Police Commission, Honolulu's island-born Chinese police chief, Dan Liu, portrayed himself and shared considerable key footage with Wayne. Vernon "Red" McQueen, dean of Hawai'i's sportswriters and for many years sports editor of *The Honolulu Advertiser*, turned actor to play the familiar role of a newspaperman. Also adding local flavor to the film were Linko "Lucky" Simunovich, heavyweight wrestling champion of Hawai'i, who was cast in the apt role of a muscle man; Professor Joel Trapido of the University of Hawai'i faculty; Bishop Kinai Ikuma, a Shinto priest; Sam "Steamboat" Mokuahi; Charles "Panama" Baptiste and Rennie Brooks; and businessmen Akira Fukunaga and Ralph Honda.

No picture of Hawai'i, past or present, would be complete without a *luau*. *Big Jim McLain* featured one that was a lulu. Al Kealoha Perry, musical director of the "Hawai'i Calls" radio program, turned out his nationally famous "Singing Surfriders" to provide the music. Twelve of the most talented *hula* girls in all the islands, individually selected, did the dancing. The *luau* was staged in the unsurpassably beautiful Hawaiian gardens of the Queen's Surf, a famous old Waikiki estate turned nightclub. Locations included the Honolulu police station; Kukui Street; Waikiki; the Royal Hawaiian Hotel;

the Edgewater, which served as company headquarters; and the Outrigger Canoe Club, all of which opened their doors and turned over their grounds to the Wayne Fellows company. Wayne also played scenes at Kalaupapa Settlement for Hansen's disease victims on Molokai, which required permission of the territorial government. A scene in the film has Wayne and Arness making a pilgrimage to the USS *Arizona* Memorial, where the shattered wreckage of the great battleship lies entombed and enshrined with 1,102 members of her crew. The two drop flower leis upon the sea graves.

Throughout the location, Wayne worked a killing schedule. Morning calls were at 6:30, and shooting never stopped until 6 p.m. Then production meetings were held and daily rushes viewed. Arness later found fame on television in the role of marshall Matt Dillon on the long running western series *Gunsmoke*.

Burt Lancaster and Deborah Kerr in *From Here to Eternity* at Halona Cove, southeast Oahu, in one of the most famous scenes in cinema history. Lancaster plays Sgt. Milton Warden, who is having a torrid affair with his commanding officer's wife, Karen Holmes (Kerr). As waves surge over the embracing couple, Kerr moans: "I never knew it could be like this!" This scene is so popular that there have been many spoofs of the seaside lovemaking by Sid Caesar and Imogene Coca, former Oahu resident Carol Burnett, the movie *Airplane!*, et al. James Jones originally didn't like the film version of his novel (which won screenwriter Daniel Taradash an Oscar), but later changed his mind as he came to realize that films and novels are different mediums. The passionate beach scene is arguably better on screen than it is in the book.

FROM HERE TO ETERNITY

1953 COL

D: **Fred Zinnemann**

S: **Daniel Taradash, from the novel by James Jones**

P: **Buddy Adler**

Cast: **Burt Lancaster, Montgomery Clift, Deborah Kerr, Frank Sinatra, Donna Reed, Ernest Borgnine, Philip Ober, Mickey Shaughnessy, Harry Bellaver, George Reeves , John Dennis**

The culmination in 1953 of more than two years of preparation after the purchase of James Jones' best-selling novel by the same name, *From Here to Eternity* was Columbia's star-studded film of the brilliant and powerful story of soldiers and soldiering.

Montgomery Clift won the role of Prewitt, the independent and unregimented G.I. which every important male star had coveted. Burt Lancaster played Warden, the first sergeant who manages his company with the dedication of a saint while engaged in a love affair with the commanding officer's wife. Deborah Kerr, as Karen Holmes, was selected for the part after almost every other top Hollywood name had been reported as seeking it. After more than fifty actresses tested for the envied role of Alma, Prewitt's girlfriend, Columbia contractee Donna Reed won the part. Frank Sinatra's persistence in applying for the off-beat role of private Maggio (to the extent of traveling 27,000 miles from Africa and back for a screen test), got him the part of the violent and funny and sour Italian-American. Stage and screen actor Ernest Borgnine, who had recently appeared on Broadway with Helen Hayes in "Mrs. McThing," was signed for the role of Fatso Judson, the sadistic sergeant of the stockade. Philip Ober, film actor and a familiar figure on Broadway for more than twenty years, played Captain Holmes, the pompous commanding officer whose infidelity causes his wife (Deborah Kerr) to seek romance with the sergeant (Burt Lancaster).

The drama, which depicted the emotional pressures that filled the vacuum of life in the pre-Pearl Harbor Army, was faithfully adapted for the screen by Daniel Taradash, who met the challenge of fulfilling the obligation to the millions of readers who expected an accurate translation of the novel. One of the most eloquent virtues of *From Here to Eternity* is the believable characters, including their brass hats. They are human within the subhuman anonymity of the military machine.

After completion of the filming of interiors in Hollywood, the cast and crew of about 100 persons flew via chartered plane to the Hawaiian Islands, where all of the exteriors were photographed at the identical locale of the novel. Approximately three weeks of shooting occurred at Schofield Barracks, the Royal Hawaiian Hotel, Waikiki Beach, Diamond Head, on the streets of Honolulu and on the Waialae Golf Course. It took three days to film the famous love scene on the beach between Burt Lancaster and Deborah Kerr.

Several pre-production trips were made to scout the film sites by Zinnemann, Taradash, Adler, art director Cary Odell, cinematographer Burnett Guffey and Columbia location manager Hal Fisher.

Because the period of the story involved the peacetime Army uniform and weapons between World Wars I and II, wardrobe and prop problems had to be tackled to ensure strict authenticity. Old-style arms and clothing for 400 men, including canvas leggings, campaign hats, blue two-piece fatigues with pullover tops and out-of-date caps, and flat steel helmets were packed and shipped to Hawai'i. Also sent were 400 1903 Springfield rifles, 20 Thompson submachine guns, 20 BARs 15.45 pistols, and approximately 55,000 rounds of ammunition. Eight hundred soldiers from the Hawai'i Infantry Training Center appear in the film.

In addition to the wardrobe and weapons, tons of equipment such as generators, cameras, lights, reflectors, cables, sound trucks, etc., were shipped several days before the personnel flew out from Hollywood to ensure they would arrive in time for immediate shooting.

Opposite page
On location at Schofield Barracks, Montgomery Clift, as Private Robert E. Lee Prewitt, gets the sadistic "treatment" in *From Here To Eternity*. Suggesting the duality of man, Prewitt is both a gifted bugler and pugilist. However, since he has blinded a man in the ring, Prewitt refuses to box in the Army championship bouts. In an effort to break him and force him to put on the gloves, Captain Dana Holmes (Philip Ober) orders that Prewitt be given the "treatment"— grueling exercises, excessive KP, and the like. The sensitive Method actor Clift was *Eternity* author James Jones' first choice for the role of the individualistic infantryman who is finally gunned down by the Army. The role won Clift an Oscar nomination for Best Actor; Donna Reed, who played opposite him as Prewitt's lover, won the Academy Award for Best Supporting Actress for playing a prostitute (called a "hostess" in the movie) before going on to play a squeaky-clean TV mom in *The Donna Reed Show*.

One of the most exciting action sequences ever filmed by Hollywood cameras was the strafing of Schofield Barracks by Japanese Zeros. This re-creation of a phase of the attack on Oahu, in which the Army installation was riddled by machine gun fire as the Japanese pilots made their bombing runs on the Navy ships, was photographed at the locale of the disaster as described by novelist Jones.

A group of planes of the 199th Squadron, Hawai'i Air National Guard, bearing the familiar red "meatball" insignia of the Japanese fighters, participated in the simulated attacks and the mock battle scenes featuring Burt Lancaster, the featured players, and the men of the Hawai'i Infantry Training Center.

The stars of *From Here to Eternity* played significantly different roles from their accepted screen personalities. Burt Lancaster, a war veteran of three years' service with the famous Fifth Army, played an Army man for the first time in seventeen starring film roles. Despite his Army service, he had to learn to use the outmoded equipment of the pre-Pearl Harbor Army as though he were a recruit.

Montgomery Clift played the individual regular Army sol-

dier, a boxer, bugler and romantic figure. Under the tutelage of former welterweight champ Mushy Callahan, Clift did roadwork, boxing and worked out on punching bags and other body-building devices to develop his muscles. He also spent several hours each day with a 30-year man, Master Sergeant Siegfrid Snyder, who taught the actor drilling and the manual of arms, including the breakdown and assembling procedure of the rifle, use of the bayonet and close-quarter knife fighting.

Frank Sinatra, who played Clift's soldier buddy, underwent the same type of military training for this nonsinging dramatic role, which was strictly offbeat for him.

Deborah Kerr completely changed her pace for this part as the captain's wife. Kerr's hair was restyled by Columbia's hairdressing expert Helen Hunt, and the color was changed from her normal ginger red to topaz blonde. She also worked at losing her British accent with a voice coach who specialized in this type of control. Movie audiences, who for the first time saw Kerr in a bathing suit and shorts, found the charming lady's figure a pleasant sight indeed.

Donna Reed was an established actress who usually portrayed the faithful wife or girlfriend of the leading man in such films as *It's a Wonderful Life*. In *From Here to Eternity,* as Alma, Donna played a completely different type.

Almost thirty years later, the December 11, 1981 "Rambling Reporter" column of the trade paper *The Hollywood Reporter* declared that Deborah Kerr's surfside smooch in *From Here to Eternity* with Burt Lancaster was the most famous love scene in film history. Kerr remarked, "All I remember is that after a full day's filming of the scene, with all that sand in my bathing suit, my skin was rubbed raw!"

The film was awarded eight Oscars, including Best Picture, Supporting Actor (Frank Sinatra, in his comeback role), Supporting Actress (Donna Reed), Director, Screenplay, Cinematography, Film Editing and Sound Recording. Other nominations went for Best Actor (Lancaster and Clift), Best Actress (Kerr), Dramatic Scoring, and Costumes.

"Out of *From Here to Eternity*, a novel whose anger and compassion stirred a post-war reading public as few such works have, Columbia and a company of sensitive hands have forged a film almost as towering and persuasive as its source," reported A.H. Weiler in the August 6, 1953 issue of *The New York Times*. "Although it naturally lacks the depth and fullness of the 430,000 words and 850 pages of the book, this dramatization of phases of the military life in a peacetime army…captures the essential spirit of the James

Jones study. And, as a job of editing, amending, rearranging and purifying a volume bristling with brutalities and obscenities, *From Here to Eternity* stands as a shining example of truly professional movie making."

"As may be surmised, credit for the metamorphosis cannot be localized. The team of scenarist, director, producer and cast has managed to transfer convincingly the muscularity of the basically male society with which the book dealt; the poignancy and futility of the love lives of the professional soldier involved, as well as the indictment of commanding officers whose selfishness can break men devoted to soldiering. They are trapped in a world they made and one that defeats them. Above all, it is a portrait etched in truth and without the stigma of calculated viciousness."

MISS SADIE THOMPSON

1953 COL

D: **Curtis Bernhardt**

S: **Harry Kleiner, based on a story by W. Somerset Maugham**

P: **Jerry Wald**

Cast: **Rita Hayworth, Jose Ferrer, Aldo Ray, Russell Collins, Diosa Costello, Harry Bellaver, Wilton Graff, Charles Buchinsky (Bronson).**

Miss Sadie Thompson is Somerset Maugham's 1921 classic short story about a carefree young prostitute avoiding criminal charges in San Francisco by working out of Honolulu and other South Pacific ports. When first published, the short story created a minor literary sensation, and it was dramatized in 1922 by John Colyon and Clarence Randolph in their play *Rain*, starring the late Jeanne Eagles. *Rain* became the great dramatic event of that memorable Broadway season and ran for two more years on the road. In 1935, *Rain* was revived briefly on Broadway with Tallulah Bankhead playing Sadie and again in 1944, when a musical version starring June Havoc was produced.

The two other films that *Rain* inspired were a silent version, made in 1928 and directed by Raoul Walsh and starring Gloria Swanson, and a sound version in 1932, starring Joan Crawford.

As the story goes, Miss Sadie Thompson (Hayworth), easygoing nightclub entertainer with

a cloudy reputation, is en route from Honolulu to New Caledonia when a ship's quarantine strands her on a tropical island; her hotel is immediately besieged by the women-hungry U.S. marines stationed on the tiny isle. Sgt. Phil O'Hara (Ray) leads the pack. Sadie's uninhibited behavior disturbs Mr. and Mrs. Davidson (Ferrer and Converse), the former a fanatical reformer dedicated to keeping evil out of the islands. Both lonely people, O'Hara and Sadie find happiness together, despite Davidson's

desperate vendetta against the girl, until Davidson finally bares Sadie's Honolulu past. Davidson persuades Sadie to seek salvation by returning to San Francisco and facing her punishment; Sadie even turns down O'Hara's repentant offer to smuggle her to Sydney, where he can join her. It is then that Davidson is no longer able to repress his passion for Sadie; he attempts to make love to her. Next morning his body is found in the surf. Unable to face himself and his own hypocrisy, he has committed suicide. O'Hara finds Sadie her old self, flamboyant and breezy and willing to accept his proposal of marriage and a new life together.

Featured player Charles Buchinsky became superstar tough guy Charles Bronson in the late 1960s.

When Columbia Pictures decided to film *Miss Sadie Thompson* in Technicolor and 3-D, it felt that only an actual tropical island would serve as background for the picture. Accordingly, stars Rita Hayworth and Jose Ferrer, featured player Aldo Ray, director Curtis Bernhardt, and a crew of eighty journeyed to the island of Kauai in the Hawaiian Islands, where the story was filmed against the natural splendor of lagoons and beaches and the tropical luxuriance of hills and valleys. Most of the film's exteriors were shot around the Coco Palms Resort Hotel and near the Wailua River.

Above

Jose Ferrer plays the repressed married moralist Mr. Davidson, who tries to convert Rita Hayworth as Sadie Thompson from her promiscuous ways; on location at Kauai in *Miss Sadie Thompson*. Ferrer's character later commits suicide at the same Kauai beach, after Sadie repulses his sexual advances.

Jose Ferrer fishes with local Kauai kids in the Coco Palms Hotel lagoons during location filming of *Miss Sadie Thompson*.

THE CAINE MUTINY

1954 COL

D: **Edward Dmytryk**

S: **Stanley Roberts, from the novel by Herman Wouk**

P: **Stanley Kramer**

Cast: **Humphrey Bogart, Fred MacMurray, Jose Ferrer, Van Johnson**

This film of mutiny against a psychopathic captain aboard an American fighting ship during World War II was based on the 1951 best-selling Pulitzer Prize-winning novel by Herman Wouk.

The filming was completed in 54 days, with locations shot at Pearl Harbor, in San Francisco and Yosemite National Park, and interiors at Columbia Studios. During the filming at Pearl Harbor, an alert young Navy rifleman saved Van Johnson from a possible shark attack. In one scene, Johnson dived from the minesweeper USS *Doyle* to retrieve a line. He was pulling it in when a shark's fin cut the water ten yards away. Gunner Mate Fisher, aboard a camera tug, stopped the shark in its tracks with a burst from his M-1 rifle. It disappeared, leaving a trail of blood, and Johnson was hauled out of the water.

Left

Van Johnson in a scene from *The Caine Mutiny*.

Location shooting aboard a Naval ship with Tom Tully and Humphrey Bogart in the World War II court-martial drama *The Caine Mutiny*. Bogart was rarely better as the demented Captain Queeg; nobody can ever forget his nervously rolling those metal balls around in his hand when Queeg sat in the witness stand!

HELL'S HALF ACRE

1954 REP

D: John H. Auer
S: Steve Fisher
P: Herbert J. Yates
Cast: Wendell Corey, Evelyn Keyes, Elsa
        Lanchester, Marie Windsor, Nancy
        Gates, Jesse White, Keye Luke

In this low-budget crime melodrama, Chet Chester (Corey) is a restaurateur in Honolulu being blackmailed by an old buddy threatening to reveal his past as a sailor in the Navy in 1941 who was presumed missing in action after the Pearl Harbor attack. Chester's girlfriend (Gates) kills the blackmailer, and Chester takes the blame for the shooting. A tip from a popular song written by Chester brings the wife he left behind (Keyes) back to Hawai'i where they meet again.

In supporting roles are Elsa Lanchester, who as Lida O'Reilly is an Omaha school-teacher turned Honolulu cab driver. Keye Luke played the Honolulu Chief of Police.

The title *Hell's Half Acre* was taken from the former crime-filled skid row section of Honolulu, which was razed in the late 1960s to make way for new buildings. The black-and-white film was shot partly on location in and around Honolulu, much of it at night. The song "Polynesian Rhapsody," by Jack Pitman, is sung by the Kaumakapili Choir.

Wendell Corey and Evelyn Keyes in what is possibly a publicity picture for *Hell's Half Acre*. (Keyes in never seen in a grass skirt in the film.) Shot on location at various Honolulu slum sites, this B picture had an air of gritty realism and authenticity missing in most "Hawai'i-wood" productions.

Above
The Kaumakapili Choir sings "Polynesian Rhapsody" in *Hell's Half Acre*. The song plays a key role in the plot of this B picture.

Left
Wendell Corey as Chet Chester, and Nancy Gates as his girlfriend in *Hell's Half Acre*. They are at his nightclub, Chet's Hawaiian Retreat, which was actually filmed on location at Don the Beachcomber's on Kalakaua Avenue, Waikiki. Gates has just shot a bad guy in the office and returned to a table in the club.

BEACHHEAD

1954 UA

D: Stuart Heisler

S: Richard Alan Simmons, based on the novel *I've Got Mine* by Richard G. Hubler

P: Howard W. Koch

Cast: Tony Curtis, Frank Lovejoy, Mary Murphy, Eduard Franz, Skip Homeier, John Doucette, Alan Wells, Sunshine Akira Fukunaga, Dan Aoki, Steamboat Mokuahi

Four U.S. marines on an island near Bougainville during World War II are sent to find a planter who is believed to have sent a message detailing the location of Japanese minefields just before a large American assault on the island.

Two marines are killed. The planter and his daughter are found and the information in the message verified. The planter is killed in a skirmish with the enemy and the remaining marines and the daughter must escape the island to save themselves.

Shot in August of 1953 in 21 days near Hanalei on the island of Kauai, the film had a budget of $400,000.

Producer Howard W. Koch, in a 1993 interview with the author, recalled that "We looked all over for the location for the story, an island in the Pacific. We went down to Florida, then someone suggested the Hawaiian Islands. On Oahu, we told someone in the territorial office we needed an area that looked like Bougainville, and they suggested I go to Kauai. They said 'it will give you the feel that you want, jungle and all.' Upon my arrival on Kauai, the picture came to life right in front of me. I returned to L.A., worked on the script and returned to shoot the picture. We put all the equipment on a boat and got it right over there. Walter Smith led us to all the great locations. We made the picture in 21 shooting days, every foot shot on the island." Years later Koch talked Frank Sinatra into using Kauai as a location for his film *None But the Brave*.

Time magazine, in April 1954, wrote that "The enemy...keep the lovebirds as well as the action on the wing through the full colored, gorgeous jungle on Kauai in the Hawaiian Islands where *Beachhead* was filmed."

The February 5, 1954 issue of *Variety* added, "As a standard war actioner, *Beachhead* is well equipped with the names and exploitation angles that should put it over as a popular entry in the regular market. With Tony Curtis and Frank Lovejoy heading the war heroics and the Hawaiian islands in Technicolor, the picture has enough commercial value to take care of any general booking."

Above

Kauai doubled for Bougainville in the World War II action film *Beachhead*, starring Tony Curtis and Frank Lovejoy, seen here at Hanalei.

THE SEA CHASE
1955 WB

D: John Farrow

S: James Warner Bellah and John Twist based on the bestseller by Col Andrew Geer

P: John Farrow

Cast: John Wayne, Lana Turner

Suspenseful action drama of a 26,000 mile sea pursuit of an outlaw German freighter by the British Navy on the eve of World War II and the torrid romance between the ship's renegade captain and a blonde international adventuress.

The production troupe of 110 was headquartered at Kailua on the big Island of Hawai'i and most of the picture was photographed at sea along the Kona Coast and at Kealakekua Bay for nearly seven weeks of location filming.

The north shore of Kealakekua Bay appears in the movie as the Auckland, New Zealand shipwreck station as well as the mythical island of Pom Pom Gaili.

The studio chartered an old freighter for the film which during production served double duty. Above water the ship was the setting for countless camera set ups for scenes in the film. Below deck it became a floating film studio complete from cameras to costumes.

"Much of the picture was shot in and around Hawaii. There are a number of picturesque settings, and in WarnerColor. In fact, the settings and the fine photography, are what makes the film interesting." *Hollywood Citizen News,* June 7, 1955

MISTER ROBERTS

1955 WB

D: John Ford, Mervyn LeRoy

S: Frank Nugent, Joshua Logan, from the play by Joshua Logan and Thomas Heggen and the novel by Thomas Heggen

P: Leland Hayward

Cast: Henry Fonda, James Cagney, Jack Lemmon, William Powell, Ward Bond

Beneath the blazing Pacific sun, the USS *Reluctant* carries cargo along the forgotten seaways of World War II. The crew is going crazy. Somewhere beyond the horizon, the real war is passing them by. Mr. Roberts struggles against a dictatorial captain on board a supply ship in the South Pacific, all the while longing for more active duty.

Mister Roberts was one of the greatest successes in Broadway history, and Henry Fonda became absolutely identified with the role, playing it over 1,600 times on Broadway and on tour. He won Broadway's coveted Tony award as Best Actor for the role.

Fonda had been away from movies almost seven years when producers began casting *Mister Roberts,* and Warner Bros., which owned the screen rights, offered the lead to William Holden, then a recent Oscar winner and the hottest actor in films. Holden turned it down on the moral ground that Fonda owned the part. Still believing that Fonda was too old and that the public had forgotten him, Warners gave the part to Marlon Brando, then the next biggest star

in movies, having received an Academy Award for *On the Waterfront.* Brando actually accepted the role. In the meantime, however, John Ford had been signed to direct the film, and Ford, remembering the many brilliant performances Fonda gave in their joint masterpieces as *Drums Along the Mohawk,*

Below

In a scene oft-repeated in Pacific pictures, a flotilla of islanders paddles out to greet the arrival of the white man's ship in *Mr. Roberts*. This sequence was shot on location at Kaneohe Bay, on the windward side of Oahu. Olympic champ, surfer, and bit-part player Duke Kahanamoku appears as an indigenous chief in *Mr. Roberts*, one of the last features of his Hollywood career that spanned more than 30 years.

Young Mr. Lincoln, The Grapes of Wrath, My Darling Clementine and *Fort Apache* (in 1948, Fonda's last starring role before his long sojourn on Broadway), insisted on Fonda for *Mister Roberts*.

Warners wanted the stage play opened up for the screen, and thus sought Naval cooperation to film at Naval bases and with Naval ships. The Navy refused, on the grounds that the captain character was detrimental to its image. Ford, who still had enormous influence with the Navy due to his extraordinary documentary work during World War II, simply went to the Chief of Naval Operations for help. The Navy immediately relented, giving Warners the use of the cargo ship USS *Hewell* and permission to film at Naval bases on Midway and in Hawai'i.

Most of the film's exteriors were shot in Kaneohe on the island of Oahu. Former Olympic swimming champion Duke Kahanamoku had a bit role as a native chief who boards the ship when it enters an island port.

Interiors were filmed at Warner Bros.' studios in Burbank, California.

When illness sidelined John Ford, Mervyn LeRoy took over direction of the film, and Joshua Logan did some uncredited work on the film.

Mister Roberts restored Fonda's screen career, and Jack Lemmon won his first Academy Award for his role as Ensign Pulver, who doubled as Officer in Charge of Laundry and Morale. By this, his fourth, film role, Lemmon had mastered the comic delivery and mannerisms that would become his trademark. His Oscar for Best Supporting Actor was the film's only prize, though it was nominated for three Academy Awards, including Best Picture.

FLIGHT TO HONG KONG
1956 UA

D: Joseph M. Newman

S: Leo Townsend, Edward G. O'Callaghan

Cast: Rory Calhoun, Barbara Rush, Dolores Donlon, Soo
       Young

An international crime syndicate boss decides to give up his life of crime, escaping through the Far East and the Pacific, and runs afoul of the gang and the police.

In addition to Hong Kong, the camera picks up scenes in Macao, Tokyo, Honolulu, Tangier, Lisbon and San Francisco.

Above
Rory Calhoun aboard a Pan American Airways plane in the smuggling yarn *Flight to Hong Kong*.

THE REVOLT OF MAMIE STOVER

1956 TCF

D: Raoul Walsh

S: Sidney Boehm, from the novel by William Bradford
        Huie

P: Buddy Adler

Cast: Jane Russell, Richard Egan, Agnes Moorehead

The story of an avaricious and ambitious woman who became the star of Hawai'i's best-known brothel, organized activities there on an assembly-

line basis, made a fortune and invested it in real estate during the war and became one of the richest women in the islands.

The Revolt of Mamie Stover presented similar problems to those of producer Buddy Adler in *From Here to Eternity:* the translation of the raw, realistic stuff of the novels (meaning sex) to the more circumscribed medium of the screen. By coincidence, both stories took Honolulu as their setting at almost identical times before and after the Japanese attack on Pearl Harbor.

The novel is a social commentary about the established order of Hawai'i and its economic feudalism that was shattered by the millions of Armed Forces members who poured through the islands during World War II. The catalytic agent for much of this change was Mamie Stover, whom Huie described as "the Henry Ford of harlotry." She is a composite character taken from several individuals who flourished in Honolulu's red-light district that was finally closed down during the war.

Mamie (Russell) falls in love with writer Jim Blair (Egan) aboard a ship bound for Honolulu after she is kicked out of San Francisco for illegal activities. In Honolulu she gains employment as a dance hall hostess, and Blair objects to her way of life, though she becomes a success through her driving ambition to use her charms to make money.

It's a wonder the studio attempted to make *Mamie Stover* at all, considering the intolerable dramatic impasse forced on it by the Johnston Morals Office censors. An unbelievable ending, because of everything that had gone before, was tacked on in which Mamie returns to her hometown in Mississippi, having given away all her hard-earned money.

Ninety percent of the exterior settings in *The Revolt of Mamie Stover* was shot on location in and around Honolulu. A cast and crew of sixty people were flown to the islands and remained there for a month of shooting. A variety of the area's world-famed beauty spots appear in the picture, including Waikiki Beach, the terrace of the Halekulani Hotel, the Pali, Ala Moana Park, Punchbowl, the view from Kamehameha Heights, and the Waialae Country Club.

In the beginning, the company feared that because parts of the film dealt with the seamier side of life in Hawai'i, the community cooperation necessary for the production would not be forthcoming. These fears were groundless. Hawai'i residents cooperated in full for the reenactment of the Pearl Harbor bombing.

Opposite page
One of Hollywood's great directors, Raoul Walsh, with bathing suit-clad Jane Russell and Richard Egan on Ala Moana Beach, with Waikiki and Diamond Head in the rear in all their glory, in the days before high-rises. *The Revolt of Mamie Stover* **was shot on location in Honolulu.**

A movie company on location is always sensitive to weather, but, despite the fact that this troupe went to Hawai'i in what was considered its rainy season, the company lost only three days to weather, right at the end of the location stay.

For the shipboard sequences, the company went aboard the Matson Line freighter *Hawaiian Educator* for three days.

Attending a *luau* one night, director Raoul Walsh and his stars heard an amusing *hula* song sung by Sterling Mossman, a police lieutenant by day and entertainer at night. "Keep Your Eyes on the Hands," written by two local songwriters, Mary Johnston and Tony Todaro, was purchased on the spot and used in the movie.

Jane Russell was stopped by a Honolulu police officer when he spotted the buxom, curvaceous star riding her bicycle around Waikiki in her bathing suit.

Philip K. Scheuer, reporter for *The Los Angeles Times*, wrote on May 9, 1956 that "The Cinemascope cameras naturally make the most of the Hawaiian land and seascapes, particularly under Raoul Walsh's direction, in depicting the December 7 bombing of Pearl Harbor and the flight of terrified civilians that followed."

Above

Punchbowl serves as the background in this scene from *The Revolt of Mamie Stover*, with Mamie (Jane Russell) and Jim Blair (Richard Egan) at his palatial hilltop Honolulu home.

BETWEEN HEAVEN AND HELL

1956 TCF

D: **Richard Fleischer**

S: **Harry Brown, based on the novel by Francis Gwaltney**

P: **David Weisbart**

Cast: **Robert Wagner, Terry Moore, Broderick Crawford, Buddy Ebsen**

The story of a company of soldiers comprised of southern boys, landowners and sharecroppers during World War II who became known as the "Hell Fighters of the Pacific."

Many of the war scenes in *Between Heaven and Hell* were filmed on location on Oahu, where some of the cast took part in amphibious landings staged by more than 700 U.S. Army and Navy troops stationed in the islands.

JUNGLE HEAT
1957 UA

D: Howard W. Koch

S: Jameson Brewer

P: Aubrey Schenck

Cast: Lex Barker, Mari Blanchard, Glenn Langan, James Westerfield, Miyoko Sasaki

A romantic triangle and melodrama develop in pre-Pearl Harbor Hawai'i when a doctor stationed on an outer island fights native unrest and labor agitation created by a plantation owner and Japanese infiltrators.

This low-budget thriller was filmed on Kauai back-to-back with *Voodoo Island*. The plot, which revolved around Japanese sabotage in the Hawaiian Islands during World War II, caused considerable controversy. No incident of sabotage or treason among Japanese or Hawaiian-born Japanese residents of Hawai'i ever occurred during the war.

Right

Lex Barker, who had also played Tarzan, returned to the tropics in *Jungle Heat*, co-starring Mari Blanchard. Here, they stand in front of a Fijian-style *tapa* (bark cloth).

Photo courtesy of the DeSoto Brown Collection.

gle heat

starring LEX
BARKER · BLANCHARD · GLENN LANGAN
JAMES WESTERFIELD
SASAKI · BREWER · Baxter · KOCH · SCHENCK · BEL-AIR · United Artists

97

also starring
BEVERLY TYLER · MURVYN VYE
with ELISHA COOK · RHODES REASON
JEAN ENGSTROM · FREDERICH LEDEBUR
RICHARD LANDAU · Music by LES BAXTER
LE BORG · Produced by HOWARD W. KOCH
Executive Producer AUBREY SCHENCK
BEL AIR Production · Released thru UNITED ARTISTS

VOODOO ISLAND
1957 UA

D:	Reginald LeBorg
S:	Richard Landau
P:	Howard W. Koch
Cast:	Boris Karloff, Beverly Tyler, Murvyn Vye, Elisha Cook, Rhodes Reason

A hotel chain, interested in building a resort on a Pacific island, sends delegates to scout possible locations. The delegates disappear, and the native islanders are discovered to use voodoo and carnivorous woman-eating plants to keep outsiders at bay. Boris Karloff played Phillip Knight, a writer with an avid interest in voodoo who is hired by the hotel to investigate the disappearances.

This low-budget thriller was filmed on the island of Kauai in seven days, immediately preceding the filming of *Jungle Heat,* which was shot in the following eight days.

Left

A title card for *Voodoo Island,* a Boris Karloff horror film set in the Pacific—even though voodoo is practiced in the Caribbean, not Oceania.

NAKED PARADISE A/K/A THUNDER OVER HAWAII

1957 AIP

D:	**Roger Corman**
S:	**Charles B. Griffith and Mark Hanna**
P:	**Roger Corman**
Cast:	**Richard Denning, Beverly Garland, Lisa Montell, Leslie Bradley**

Toy manufacturer Zac Cotton, his world-weary Girl Friday, Max, and his two Bronxite assistants, Stony and Mitch, charter the boat of an easygoing adventurer named Duke for the outward purpose of a business pleasure cruise among the islands.

Their real purpose, however, is to rob the local pineapple plantation owner. To this end, Mitch and Stony set the plantation on fire and, while the natives fight it, the two take the money and the group leaves the island. Duke decides to part company with the rest when he discovers the truth (at this

point they are staying on another island), and Max leaves with him. The pair have fallen in love.

While Zac and his boys are waiting on the island for another boat to take them to Honolulu, a storm forces Duke and Max to return. The boat Zac has been waiting for is lost in the storm, so he takes Duke's boat, making Duke and Max his prisoners, and brings along an island girl in whom Mitch has become interested. In the end, Duke and Max manage to do away with Zac, Mitch and Stoney. The native girl returns to the island and Max and Duke sail away together.

Naked Paradise, American International's action thriller starring Richard Denning and Beverly Garland, was the company's first picture shot entirely on location in Hawai'i in color. The entire company, cast and crew, flew to the island of Kauai for filming. At first they stayed at the Coco Palms Hotel, then Corman moved them to a Boy Scout camp at the other end of the island. The film was shot back-to-back with the company's *She Gods of Shark Reef* to save transportation costs.

Floyd Crosby, one of Hollywood's top cameramen and an Oscar winner, filmed the scenic beauty of the natural locations, includ-

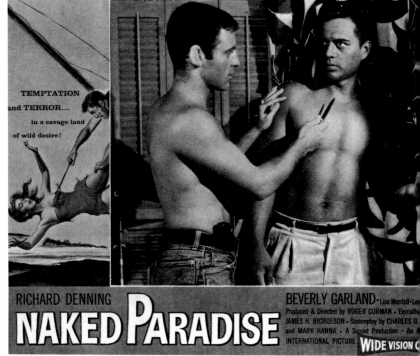

Photo courtesy of the DeSoto Brown Collection.

ing some underwater action and a thrilling sugar field fire. Denning returned to Hawai'i years later to play a recurring role as the governor on the long-running television series *Hawai'i Five-O.* Hawaiian lyrics and other songs were written by Alvin Kaleolani. Producer-director-writer Roger Corman, through his American International pictures, was responsible for a string of profitable youth-oriented, slickly and shrewdly produced and marketed low-budget films during the late 1950s through the 1960s. He introduced a new generation of distinguished film talent, including Jack Nicholson, Martin Scorsese, Francis Ford Coppola, Ron Howard, Robert DeNiro and Jonathan Demme.

Retitling occurred when the film was reissued in 1960.

Opposite page
Local fashions get a plug from Aloha shirt-clad mobsters in *Naked Paradise.*

Above
Roger Corman, the king of exploitation pictures, directed and produced *Naked Paradise,* aka *Thunder Over Hawaii.* Either way, this grade B flick has a quintessential Corman title. Cameraman Floyd Crosby, who won an Academy Award for Cinematography for 1931's *Tabu,* lensed *Naked* and is the father of one-third of Crosby, Stills & Nash.

Photo courtesy of the DeSoto Brown Collection.

FORBIDDEN ISLAND

1959 COL

D:	Charles B. Griffith
S:	Charles B. Griffith
P:	Charles B. Griffith
Cast:	Jon Hall

The story of a skindiver hired to find a precious emerald in a sunken ship in the South Pacific.

Underwater scenes were filmed at Florida's Silver Springs and above-water scenes were filmed in Hawai'i.

Left

Jon Hall, looking a bit more weathered than in his sarong days of the 1930s, reclines wearily in *Forbidden Island*.

Below

Lahaina is the backdrop as passengers are rowed out to embark on their fateful Pacific journey aboard a leaky boat in *Twilight for the Gods*.

TWILIGHT FOR THE GODS
1958 U

D: Joseph Pevney

S: Ernest K. Gann based on his novel

P: Gordon Kay

Cast: Rock Hudson, Cyd Charisse, Arthur Kennedy, Leif Erickson

A routine sea adventure drama of a group of fugitives from life's various troubles thrown together in an unseaworthy sailing vessel en route from a remote Pacific Island to Mexico.

Hudson plays the captain of the vessel, and Charisse plays a Honolulu call girl running from authorities, a la Sadie Thompson.

The film was photographed on location in the Hawaiian Islands, including scenes at Honolulu Harbor and Waikahalulu Falls.

Below

Cyd Charisse portrays a character derived from Miss Sadie Thompson, while Rock Hudson is the archetypal sea captain in *Twilight for the Gods*.

SOUTH PACIFIC
1958 Magna/TCF

D: **Joshua Logan**

S: **Paul Osborn**

P: **Buddy Adler**

Cast: **Mitzi Gaynor, Rossano Brazzi, Ray Walston, Juanita Hall, John Kerr, France Nuyen**

An interesting, but overblown, translation to the screen of the Richard Rodgers and Oscar Hammerstein II Pulitzer Prize-winning musical *South Pacific.* Ezio Pinza and Mary Martin starred in the stage musical, which opened in April 1949 at the Majestic Theater on Broadway and became one of its longest running (1,925 performances) and most popular shows.

South Pacific is the love story of U.S. Navy nurse Nellie Forbush from Little Rock and middle-aged French planter Emile DeBecque on a South Pacific island during World War II. Paralleling this romance is another between young Lt. Cable and Liat, the beautiful Tonkinese daughter of Bloody Mary.

The musical *South Pacific* contained story elements unusual for the time, including a middle-aged male star, Ezio Pinza; a wartime setting; and the central issue of racial tolerance.

The music from *South Pacific* constitutes a unique part of American musical stage history. All the great tunes of the stage success are present in the film version, including "Some Enchanted Evening," "Bali Ha'i," "I'm Gonna Wash That Man Right Out of My Hair," "Younger Than Springtime," "I'm in Love With a Wonderful Guy," and "Happy Talk."

Film director Joshua L. Logan was the co-author, co-producer and director of the musical, as well. In keeping with the Hollywood tradition of replacing original musical actors with film actors, MGM musical star Mitzi Gaynor and Italian heartthrob Rossano Brazzi took over the roles of Nellie Forbush and Emile DeBecque; only Juanita Hall as Bloody Mary and Ray Walston as Luther Billis were retained from the stage.

A large movie troupe of 178 cast and crew members went to Kauai, the beautiful Garden Isle in the Hawaiian Islands, for nine weeks to film most of the $6.5 million production. Four shiploads of cameras, lights, grip equipment, costumes, rolling stock, construction material and properties were brought to the island. Although Kauai proved to be scenically ideal, a tidal wave on March 10, 1957, and rainy weather posed numerous problems.

At Haena Beach, which was used as the Bali Ha'i Village, a pier was built for the landing of Lt. Cable and Billis, but only after dynamiting the solid coral bottom of the harbor could piles be driven to anchor the pier. The Birkmyre Estate was chosen as the film's DeBecque plantation home.

The fabulous view-commanding promontory above Hanalei Bay was an ideal setting for the "Some Enchanted Evening" romantic scene and others between Forbush and DeBecque. The company transformed a tin-roofed home there by adding a thatched roof, widening the verandahs, adding lush trees and foliage, and creating a rock pool and rock-terraced levels at the promontory's edge.

At Bali Ha'i Village, cranes, derricks and bulldozers removed 100 live coco palm trees, each 50 feet high or more, and replanted and repositioned them as needed for the cameras.

The first two days of shooting at Lumahai Beach, which was used as the nurses beach where Mitzi Gaynor, as Nellie, sings "I'm Gonna Wash That Man Right Out of My Hair," were unbearably hot and humid, but then the rains came…and lasted for three weeks. Director Josh Logan and cinematographer Leon Shamroy shot scenes between downpours and lost only one day to a storm. That torrential rain, however, eventually complicated the moving of equipment from Lumahai Beach to the Birkmyre Estate.

The Bali Ha'i seen on the screen is a composite of numerous Fiji Island and Kauai scenic spots, including the beautiful Allerton Gardens. Robert Allerton and John Gregg had developed their estate into a fabulously beautiful place complete with canyons, formal gardens, running water streams, bamboo forests, walls of maidenhair ferns, and vines with turquoise orchid-like blooms. The estate was originally a country retreat for Hawai'i's Queen Emma.

Cinematographer Shamroy and a camera crew traveled five weeks in the Fiji Islands taking pre-production shots from planes and boats for the Bali Ha'i sequence. They returned with 16,000 feet of film, and many of the choicest shots were incorporated into the final montage.

Previous page

Racism is a recurring theme in *South Pacific*, based on the James Michener Pulitzer Prize–winning novel *Tales of the South Pacific*. Mitzi Gaynor as the U.S. nurse Nellie Forbush and Rossano Brazzi as the French planter Emile DeBecque are at his plantation, shot at exquisite Hanalei Bay, Kauai. Nellie initially rejects DeBecque because the widower has half-Polynesian children, a racial taboo for the nurse from Little Rock, Arkansas. (Ironically, a huge integration struggle took place at Little Rock in the 1950s.)

One thousand marines and several hundred sailors had a field day acting as an audience for Mitzi Gaynor, Ray Walston, Jack Mullaney and Fred Clark in an actual amphitheater on the forty-acre campground. The director had Mitzi and all the cast don their costumes and do enough of the camp show so that he could get real reaction shots. Actual Marine and Naval maneuvers near Barking Sands on Kauai were filmed for a war sequence in the film's story line.

The entire company was quartered at the Coco Palms hotel on Kauai situated beside a lagoon and a grove of coconut trees. Every location was a minimum of an hour's drive from the hotel, and shooting was from sunup to sundown. The cast and crew had calls as early as 4:30 a.m.

Logan wanted his screen Liat, France Nuyen, to slide down the Waipahee slippery slide, swim underwater in the pool with Lt. Cable and

Opposite page
In this scene from the World War II musical *South Pacific*, Lt. Cable (John Kerr) and Luther Billis (Ray Walston) are greeted at the pier as they arrive for the exotic boar's tooth ceremony at "your special island... where the sky meets the sea": Bali Ha'i, a mythic Pacific paradise supposedly set in Vanuatu (formerly the New Hebrides). This scene was shot on location at Haena Beach, Kauai.

Race is also an issue for the lovers Lt. Cable (John Kerr) and Liat (France Nuyen) in *South Pacific*. Here, in a scene shot on Kauai's North Shore, U.S. Navy nurse Nellie Forbush (Mitzi Gaynor) consoles Liat after Cable's death, as Liat's entrepreneurial mother, Bloody Mary (Juanita Hall), looks on. Although Cable loves Liat—as expressed in songs like "Younger Than Springtime"—the Pennsylvanian cannot bring himself to marry Liat because she is not white. In this liberal movie that came out during the heyday of the Civil Rights movement, Nellie overcomes her prejudice and Cable's fellow island lookout—the French planter Emile DeBecque (Rossano Brazzi), Nellie's lover, who has part-Polynesian children—survives. But Lt. Cable does not—he must pay for his bigotry. Liat, by the way, is not an indigenous Pacific Islander. She is identified as a Tonk, which means that she's from the Gulf of Tonkin, in North Vietnam. (Vietnamese contract laborers worked on the plantations of the New Hebrides—now Vanuatu—where *South Padific* is set. Incidentally, the real Bali Ha'i isle is named Ambae, which author James Michener could see from the New Hebrides island of Santo, where he was stationed during World War II.) Ironically, one of Hollywood's most passionate love affairs takes place between a North Vietnamese woman and an American military officer. Just a few years after *South Pacific* was released in 1958, America and North Vietnam were at war. Also note that the Vietnamese Bloody Mary spouts anti-French, anti-colonial lines just a few short years after the Viet Minh defeated France at Dien Bien Phu.

come to its rocky shore for the "Happy Talk" number. The construction crew, however, could not think of a way to get the studio's heavy camera equipment through the torturous three-mile narrow trail through dense brush to Waipahee. The art director found a more accessible waterfall above the Kilauea River, access to which required construction of only a half mile of road. The construction crew and art department built a water slide to the director's specifications.

The Bali Ha'i sequence, which was filmed in nine days, required 350 local people as extras. Choreographer Leroy Prinze auditioned Hawaiian dancers both on Kauai and in Honolulu, and many then-notable Kauai residents were recruited as guests for the DeBecque plantation party, including the Keith Testers of the Lihue Plantation; the David Larsens of the Kilauea Plantation; the Fred W. Laurences of Grove Farm; the Laurence Holbrook Goodales of Kipu Ranch; the Wayne Ellises, owners of Lihue Building Supply; and Mrs. Henry Birkmyre, owner of the estate.

Five pretty airline stewardesses who were visiting the island and had made their way to the location were hired on the spot by assistant director Ben Kadish to act as Nellie Forbush's nurses. They took a short leave of absence from their jobs to appear in the film. For years on end these unknown nurses were prominently featured in the poster art for the film, especially in England.

The only interiors in the picture are the Service Headquarters and Liat's hut, both built and filmed at the Twentieth Century Fox studio, along with the camp and the bamboo forest for the Boar's Tooth ceremony.

The subtle changes in color during the musical numbers was an idea of Logan's. In an effort to duplicate the lighting changes that occur in the theater onto film, he attached a crank with a piece of colored glass across the lens of the camera during the shooting. The color was shot as is, right on the negative. Producer Buddy Adler tried to convince Logan to shoot it as it would look normally, arguing that the special color filter effects could be done later in the laboratory. But Logan would not change his mind and, since he was coming off the hit film *Bus Stop,* he had the power to get what he wanted. Ultimately, the effect marred the film.

South Pacific was a tremendous worldwide financial success, grossing $30 million, but most critics said it was a disappointing cinematic excursion.

Mitzi Gaynor, who made seventeen films prior to *South Pacific,* was born in Chicago and brought up in Detroit. Her mother took her to Los Angeles at the age of twelve, where she joined the Los Angeles Civic Light

Opposite page
The magnificent DeBecque plantation, with Hanalei Bay forming a glorious backdrop. Lushly beautiful Kauai is nothing less than a co-star in the Rodgers & Hammerstein musical *South Pacific*. Here, the adorable half-Polynesian children of French planter Emile DeBecque (Rossano Brazzi) meet with Nellie Forbush (Mitzi Gaynor), who, at first, has reservations about their indigenous heritage.

Opera. Gaynor made her film debut in *My Blue Heaven*, with Betty Grable, in 1950. After her movie career lapsed in 1961, she invented the one-woman Vegas-style revue show.

"I didn't think I was very good," she said of her film career in a 1966 *Toronto Star* interview. "I was adequate. I do think I danced well…As for *South Pacific,* how could anyone fail in that role?" The 63-year-old singer-dancer is still performing in major venues across the United States.

Rossano Brazzi, the one-time Italian screen idol, studied law before becoming an actor. In addition to *South Pacific,* his American films include *Little Women, Three Coins in the Fountain* and *Light in the Piazza.* Brazzi returned to Hawai'i in 1977 to guest-star in a segment of the long-running television series *Hawai'i Five-O.* Brazzi died in Rome, Italy, at the age of 78 on December 24, 1994.

Ray Walston stepped into the role that has become forever identified with him, the hustling Luther Billis, when he joined the touring company and the London production. He reprised the role in the film version. His

A lobby card advertising a reissue of the classic musical *South Pacific* (1958), based on James Michener's Pulitzer Prize-winning novel *Tales of the South Pacific.* Enhanced by a sumptuous Rodgers & Hammerstein score and location shooting in Fiji and on Kauai, *South Pacific* arguably is one of the rare exceptions when the movie is better than the book. The story about love and prejudice is set against World War II's island-hopping campaign in the Pacific Theater.

creation of another great part, the devil in *Damn Yankees,* was later acknowledged with Broadway's coveted Tony award. Walston is perhaps most recognized by a generation of television fans as Bill Bixby's extraterrestrial Uncle Martin in the 1960s hit *My Favorite Martian.* Walston's career spans over half a century; most recently, he has been seen in a recurring role as Judge Stone in the 1992 CBS television series *Picket Fences.*

Director Joshua Logan also directed the Broadway musical *Annie Get Your Gun* and the play *Mister Roberts,* starring Henry Fonda. Although Logan was known primarily as a stage director, he also directed a number of film versions of Broadway successes, including *Picnic, Bus Stop, Camelot* and *Paint Your Wagon.* Logan died on July 13, 1988 at the age of 79.

The Birkmyre Estate no longer exists. The filming site was first turned into a hotel, then a few years later into a Club Med. It was next purchased as the site of a condominium development, which went broke soon after construction began.

HAMMERSTEIN'S

PACIFIC

by DE LUXE

SONGS!

DITES-MOI • A COCKEYED OPTIMIST • SOME ENCHANTED EVENING • BLOODY MAR
MY GIRL BACK HOME • THERE IS NOTHIN' LIKE A DAME • BALI HA'I • I'M GONNA WAS
THAT MAN RIGHT OUT OF MY HAIR • A WONDERFUL GUY • YOUNGER THAN SPRIN
TIME • HAPPY TALK • HONEY BUN • CAREFULLY TAUGHT • THIS NEARLY WAS MI

featuring

SHE GODS OF SHARK REEF

1958 AIP

D: Roger Corman

S: Robert Hill and Victor Toloff

P: Ludwig H. Gerber

Cast: Don Durant, Lisa Montell, Bill Cord

The story of two American brothers who, while escaping from the police, shipwreck near a Pacific island inhabited by pearl-diving island women.

She Gods of Shark Reef was filmed on Kauai in color by cameraman Floyd Crosby.

Beautiful Maidens in a LUSH TROPICAL PARADISE ruled by a HIDEOUS STONE GOD

WIDE VISION COLOR

SHE GODS OF

Above

With sharks, scantily clad women in sarongs, and pagan gods, South Seas cinema was ripe for Roger Corman's American International Pictures exploitation pics.

SHARK REEF

Starring
DON · LISA · BILL
DURANT · MONTELL · CORD

Produced by   Directed by
LUDWIG H. GERBER · ROGER CORMAN

Screenplay by
ROBERT HILL and VICTOR STOLOFF

AN AMERICAN INTERNATIONAL PICTURE

GIDGET GOES HAWAIIAN
1961 COL

D:	Paul Wendkos
S:	Ruth Brooks Flippen
P:	Jerry Bressler
Cast:	Deborah Walley, James Darren, Michael Callan, Carl Reiner, Peggy Cass

The story of irrepressible teenagers and madcap parents on the beaches of Waikiki formed this sequel to *Gidget,* the popular and highly successful film about the teenage tomboy heroine affectionately nicknamed by a group of surfers. She is a crazy girl who loves swimming, soaking up the sun and surfing.

James Darren plays Moondoggie, the number one boy in Gidget's life with whom she has a fight when her parents take her on a trip to Hawai'i. Romantic complications result when another boy enters the picture. Darren became a teen idol in his role as Moondoggie in the 1960s *Gidget* surfing movies. He attempted serious acting in such films as *Diamond Head, Let No Man Write My Epitaph,* and in *The Guns of Navarone,* and went on to star in two television series, *Time Tunnel* and *T.J. Hooker.*

The production was located for two weeks in Hawai'i at such sites as Waikiki Beach, the Royal Hawaiian Hotel and the Queen's Surf nightclub.

SEVEN WOMEN FROM HELL

1961 TCF

D: **Robert Webb**

S: **Jesse Lasky Jr. and Pat Silver**

P: **Harry Spaulding**

Cast: **Patricia Owens, Cesar Romero, Denise Darcel, John Kerr**

A handful of defiant American women escape from a Japanese prison camp during World War II. They encounter an injured flier and an unscrupulous businessman in their journey across tropical jungle terrain on an enemy-held island.

Seven Women From Hell was filmed on the island of Kauai.

Above

A scene from the World War II action film *Seven Women From Hell*, which co-stars John Kerr and is set at what is now Papua New Guinea.

THE WACKIEST SHIP IN THE ARMY
1961 COL

D: **Richard Murphy**

S: **Richard Murphy adaptation by Herbert Margolis and William Raynor, based on a story by Herbert Carlson**

P: **Fred Kohlmar**

Cast: **Jack Lemmon, Ricky Nelson, John Lund, Chips Rafferty, Tom Tully**

Lt. Rip Crandall (Lemmon), a peacetime yachtsman, joins the Navy during World War II and is given a schooner to skipper. Much to his consternation, he has to teach the crew members about the operation of a sailing ship. Disguised as a native trading craft, the vessel and its crew is sent on a secret mission to a Japanese-held island. The idea for the film came from an actual wartime mission on a sailing vessel under orders from Army Gen. Douglas MacArthur in 1943, which explains the title.

The production on location in Hawai'i was beset with delays. The Screen Actors Guild strike occurred midway through production, which delayed shooting for a month and a half, and then weather delayed shooting even further.

"It rained practically all the time on Kauai where we did most of our shooting," Jack Lemmon recalled in a February 11, 1961 interview with Dick Williams in the *Los Angeles Mirror*. "Finally, in desperation Richard Murphy (the writer-director) decided to go ahead and shoot in the rain. So what happens? The sun came out the next afternoon and to match our shots we were obliged to bring in rain machines. This must be the first time this ever happened in Hawaii."

When the company moved to Honolulu, they expected to find the harbor full of the necessary Navy craft. The fleet, which had been there the entire time the company was on Kauai, sailed out the night before they arrived in Pearl Harbor.

Below

Once again, a natural disaster—in the form of an earthquake and volcanic eruptions—threatens a Pacific Island in *The Devil at Four O'Clock*. Here, people gather on a pier to be evacuated, and a rescue ship appears off the Maui coast, which doubles for an island in French Polynesia.

the native islanders refuse to help. After some bullying, the convicts respond and lead the kids through the hell of fiery lava. Each man works out his own special redemption.

Sinatra's first movie in Hawai'i since *From Here to Eternity* in 1953 brought back dramatic and happy memories. At the time, eight years previously, he had been in the depths of artistic adversity and had offered to play the role of Private Maggio for nothing. He eventually did it for $8,000, won an Academy Award for the part, and made one of the most remarkable comebacks in show business.

The Devil at Four O'Clock was filmed on the island of Maui. Lahaina underwent an elaborate facelift to become the French Polynesian port town of the story: a huge prison compound was constructed adjoining the south end of the county building and covered Lahaina's Wharf Street next to the Kamehameha II School, and studio technicians painted cracks on the County Building-Post Office-Courthouse to convert it to the French colonial governor's building. Two plastic cannons decorated the front of the edifice,

BLUE HAWAII

1961 PAR

D: Norman Taurog

S: Hal Kanter, based on a story by Allan Weiss

P: Hal Wallis

Cast: Elvis Presley, Joan Blackman, Angela Lansbury, Roland Winters

Chad Gates (Presley), just out of the U.S. Army, is the rebellious son of a pineapple tycoon who wants to make his own way in life. Undaunted by his father, he sets up a tourist guide service and takes a group of pretty school girls around the islands. Romantic complications ensue out of misunderstandings between Gates and his Hawaiian-French girlfriend, who is also a business partner.

Elvis Presley shared starring honors with the natural wonders of the fiftieth state in this, his eighth film and his fourth for producer Hal Wallis. *Blue Hawaii* was Elvis' biggest box-office hit, grossing $4.7 million through 1962.

Hawai'i had just joined the Union in 1959 and was as eager for the exposure of a major Hollywood film as the producers and actors were to shoot there. Among the locations used were Waikiki Beach, Mount Tantalus, Diamond Head, Ala Moana Park, Lydgate Park, Hanauma Bay, Punchbowl, the Wailua River and the Coco Palms Resort Hotel on Kauai. Further filming took place at Paramount Studios. Earlier that year, in March of 1961, Elvis had visited Hawai'i to raise $67,000 for the USS *Arizona* Memorial.

The original title of the film was *Hawaii Beach Boy*. The song "Blue Hawaii" was introduced and sung by Bing Crosby in the 1937 Paramount film *Waikiki Wedding*.

The *Blue Hawaii* soundtrack album marked the thirteenth gold record

Above
Elvis goes Hawaiian—although *Blue Hawaii* was made on location on Oahu and Kauai, this is a studio shot of Elvis Presley and Joan Blackman with a Diamond Head backdrop.

for Presley when it passed the million-dollar mark in U.S. sales. An additional half-million copies were sold throughout the rest of the world.

Paramount's promotion banners had proclaimed, "You'll Want to Visit Hawaii, After You See *Blue Hawaii*." They were absolutely right; the film introduced a generation of Americans to the beautiful sights and wonders of modern Hawai'i. In the movie, Chad (Presley) tells his pineapple-growing tycoon father that tourism is the future of the islands—a prediction that came true in real life.

The script called for Elvis, the island-raised tour guide, to include in his eye-filling itinerary all manner of scenery, native customs, songs, dances, *hukilaus* and *luaus*. Along with the rest of the company, Elvis tried most of the foods identified with Hawai'i. As for these traditional foods, Presley said those homesick Hawaiians who wanted to go back to fish and *poi* were welcome to it. "*Poi* is the only thing I don't like about Hawai'i," he stated in press notes for the film. Nobody in the principal cast liked *poi,* but all agreed that freshly picked pineapple was the greatest.

Angela Lansbury (MGM alumna and future television star of *Murder, She Wrote*) played Elvis' mother. Hilo Hattie made a brief appearance in the film. A quartet of beachboys was played by Frank Atienza, Lani Kai, Jose de Vega and Ralph Hanalei. Roland Winter, who played Elvis' father, was one of six actors to portray Charlie Chan in the movies. He starred in six Chan features for Monogram in the late 1940s. Flora K. Hayes, who played Mrs. Manika, Maile's grandmother, was a former member of the Territorial House of Representatives.

Presley made two other films in Hawai'i: *Girls!Girls!Girls!* in 1962, co-starring Stella Stevens in a romance about a tuna boat skipper who moon-

Above

Here, in 1961's *Blue Hawaii*, Elvis as tour guide Chad Gates leads four horseback girls along Kauai's Wailua river, where scenes from many famous movies, such as *Raiders of the Lost Ark*, were filmed. In 1937's *Waikiki Wedding*, another crooner, Bing Crosby, sang "Blue Hawaii."

lights as a nightclub entertainer; and *Paradise Hawaiian Style* in 1966, a musical about an out-of-work pilot who starts his own helicopter charter service. Neither film was as successful as *Blue Hawaii*.

Nadine Edwards, in a November 24, 1961 critique of the film for the *Hollywood Citizen News* wrote, "As for the story, it is little more than a lush travelogue of our 50th state with its tropical greenery and swaying palms and foam flecked waters with a couple of plush hotels thrown in for good measure. Most film singers sooner or later get around to warbling on a tropical island, so why not Elvis Presley..."

"The hip swinging rock and roller goes through his vocal and physical convolutions this time against the colorful backdrop of the Hawaiian Islands in *Blue Hawaii*."—John L. Scott, *Los Angeles Times* 11/24/61

Below

As *Blue Hawaii* is an Elvis film, Presley sings and dances in as many scenes as a screenwriter could conjure up. Here, he performs in a nightclub, shortly before a brawl breaks out. The "King of rock 'n' roll" and the "Royal Isles" proved to be such a popular combination that Elvis shot several other big and little screen productions on location in Hawai'i. *Blue Hawaii*, however, was his most successful Hawai'i-made feature and remains one of the best of the 30-odd films Elvis starred in.

DONOVAN'S REEF
1963 PAR

D:	John Ford
S:	Frank Nugent and James Edward Grant, from a story by Edmund Beloin
P:	John Ford
Cast:	John Wayne, Lee Marvin, Jack Warden, Elizabeth Allen, Cesar Romero, Dorothy Lamour

Life on a South Pacific Island where two ex-Navy men, "Guns" Donovan (Wayne) and Dr. Dedham (Warden), have remained following World War II. Donovan operates a bar and nightclub known as Donovan's Reef, and widower Dr. Dedham has married a lovely Polynesian princess, raised a family and carried on his medical practice. Another shipmate, "Boats" Gilhooley (Marvin) arrives later, and he and Donovan continue their brawling friendship. Trouble comes with the arrival of a beautiful, haughty proper Bostonian, Amelia Dedham (Allen), ostensibly to find her father, but also to uncover information that might warrant his being left out of the family will.

Dr. Dedham's friends, including sultry singer Fleur (Lamour), an entertainer at Donovan's Reef, plot to save his reputation. The results are dynamic, often hilarious and always heartwarming.

Exteriors of *Donovan's Reef* were filmed during four weeks on the island of Kauai. Wayne and Marvin had previously co-starred for director John Ford in the Western *The Man Who Shot Liberty Valence*. Thanks to Ford's peripatetic filming, approximately two-thirds of Kauai's fascinating coastal area enhance *Donovan's Reef*. Such tourist attractions as the Wailua River, Hanamaulu Beach, Makahuena Point, Nawiliwili Harbor, Waimea Canyon and Kalihiwai Bay are prominent in the backgrounds.

A native village of 31 grass shacks was built by Paramount construction crews among the palm trees at Hanamaulu Beach, where the company worked for three days. Adding decoratively to this setting were seventy of the most beautiful girls of Polynesian blood to be found on Kauai and in Honolulu. Also brought to Kauai to perform a ceremonial dance were 22 teenage Hawaiian girls from Honolulu.

John Wayne, long a big favorite in the Hawaiian Islands where he was married in 1954, was made an honorary member of the Kauai Canoe and Racing Club and presented with an official shirt bearing the club's insignia on front and back. Wayne promptly began wearing it on the set whenever he wasn't working, to the delight of the islanders. While on Kauai, John Wayne lived on the lavish Poipu Beach estate of Lowry McCaslin of Los Angeles, a former University of Southern California All-American football player. The estate was used in the picture to represent the home of Cesar Romero and includes a swimming pool built on rocks, which the surf smashes against.

Making her screen debut in the film was director John Ford's 110-foot *Araner*, which he kept in Hawaiian waters, where it was a conversation piece for tour guides. The *Araner*, portraying Wayne's trading ship in the picture, was made available by Ford to the Navy during World War II and served as the U.S.S. *Araner* from January 1942 to July 1944. Co-star Lee Marvin actually saw duty as a U.S. Marine in the South Pacific, and Dorothy Lamour single-handedly popularized the native attire called a sarong in a series of films for Paramount in which she first gained stardom.

Cast members of *Donovan's Reef*, including John Wayne, Elizabeth Allen, Lee Marvin, Dorothy Lamour, and Cesar Romero in an outrigger canoe. *Donovan's Reef* was the swan song for sarong girl Dorothy Lamour, who plays the nightclub singer Fleur in her last feature with a South Sea setting.

DIAMOND HEAD

1963 COL

D:	Guy Green
S:	Marguerite Roberts, based on the novel by Peter Gilman
P:	Jerry Bresler
Cast:	Charlton Heston, Elizabeth Allen, Yvette Mimieux, George Chakiris, James Darren, France Nuyen

Richard "King" Howland (Heston), an announced candidate for the U.S. Senate, is the often ruthless head of an agricultural dynasty. He seeks to halt the marriage of his beautiful young sister Sloan (Mimieux) to the full-blooded Hawaiian Paul Kahana (Darren). Blind to hypocrisy and disclaiming racial discrimination, Howland also carries on a clandestine love affair with the lovely Chinese Mei-Chen (Nuyen), who is to bear his son. These elements fuse into personal disaster for them all, and Howland learns that there are some things he cannot manipulate or defeat.

With the exception of a short period of time on the Columbia lot for tight interiors, *Diamond Head* was made on Kauai, the island of Hawai'i, and in Honolulu.

The advance party of *Diamond Head* jetted to Hawai'i in late February and cameras rolled early in March. On the second day of filming, a Kona storm piled up on the island of Kauai, depositing eight inches of rain in six hours, an omen of what was to come for weeks ahead. Throughout the long rough location, the company battled weather conditions.

Left

According to France Nuyen, who plays Mei-Chen, the love interest of politically connected plantation owner Richard "King" Howland (Charlton Heston) in *Diamond Head*, Howland is based on a member of a *kamaaina* large landowner family. Nuyen describes *Diamond Head* as "a love story with a racist. White men could sleep with Asians and give children, but they could not marry them." The insightful Chinese-French actress, who portrays Liat in *South Pacific* and, more recently, co-starred in *The Joy Luck Club*, has this to say on sexual stereotypes: "There's a mystique; the white man idealizes and totally dismisses the human being. Polynesian women are a fantasy of primal passion. Asians are more of a possession, like jade, a gemstone. The white man has a difficult time seeing women in general, especially women of color. Liat [and Mei-Chen are] part of that fantasy."

Cameramen trucked through burning cane fields on Kauai and climbed the summit of Kilauea on the Big Island. They shot from the decks of the SS *Lurline* at sea off Diamond Head, and caught action from the docks of a then strike-bound Honolulu harbor. The latter forced a complete dependence on air travel for both cargo and passengers.

No set was built for the locations in Hawai'i. Bar scenes took place in a small club called The Jetty in the village of Nawiliwili; ranch scenes were shot on the rolling grasslands of the famed Rice Ranch on Kauai. The house of Mei-Chen still stands on a road near Lihue, also on Kauai. The huge pineapple processing plant used in the film was in operation while film technicians worked their own trade with the cameras. Manoalani, the kingdom of "Howland," was in reality the Case Estate, a sprawling agricultural combine that dates back to 1870, and the Rice Ranch.

The production was full of real-life action and consequences. Actress Elizabeth Allen was thrown by a horse and actor George Chakiris, who didn't know how to swim, was upset when he was dunked underwater while riding in an outrigger canoe. Nuyen had made a visit to Kauai only four years previously to play Liat in *South Pacific.* Director John Ford visited the location and cast Elizabeth Allen for the female lead in his upcoming *Donovan's Reef* opposite John Wayne.

The American premiere of *Diamond Head* was held on January 30, 1962 at Honolulu's Waikiki Theatre.

Right
In a scene celebrating the return of Hawaiian Paul Kahana (James Darren) from school on the continent, he performs a Polynesian-style dance with *haole* Sloan Howland (Yvette Mimieux) in *Diamond Head*, a torrid potboiler about interracial love in Hawai'i.

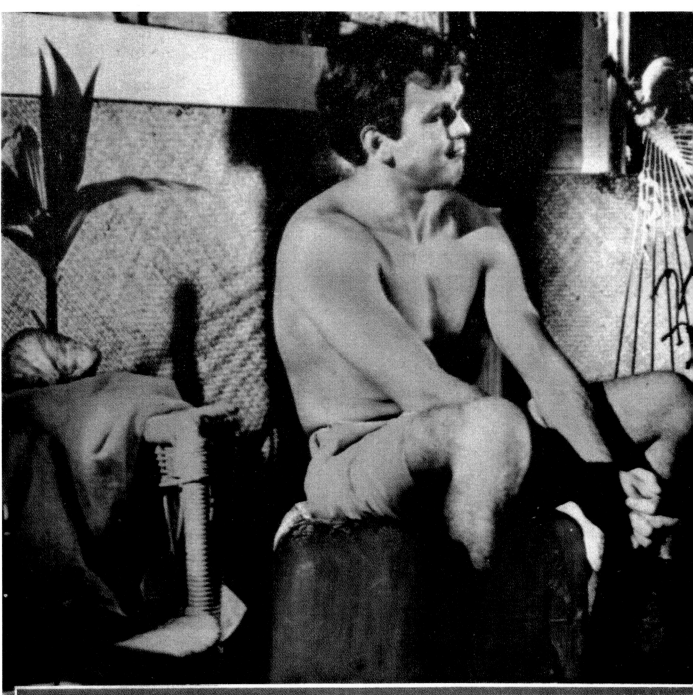

RIDE THE WILD SURF

STARRING
FABIAN · **SHELLEY FABARES** · **TAB HUNTER** · **BARBARA EDEN** · **PETER BROWN** · **ANTHONY HAYES** · **SUSAN HART**
and **JAMES MITCHUM** as Eskimo · Written & Produced by JO and ART NAPOLEON · Directed by DON TAYLOR · A Jana Film Enterprises Picture
A COLUMBIA PICTURES Release · in **COLOR**

Left

Teen heartthrob Fabian and Shelley Fabares in the 1964 Hawai'i-set beachboy flick *Ride the Wild Surf*. Jan and Dean sing the title song.

RIDE THE WILD SURF

1964 COL

D:	Don Taylor
S:	Jo and Art Napoleon
P:	Jo and Art Napoleon
Cast:	Fabian, Tab Hunter, Peter Brown, Shelly Fabares, Barbara Eden, Jim Mitchum, Dave Cadiente

Take a half dozen up-and-coming young stars with teenage appeal, put them in bathing suits against a backdrop of Hawaiian beaches, where the surf is mountain high, and you have the ideal youth picture. In *Ride the Wild Surf,* a group of young surfers from the mainland go on vacation to Hawai'i to tackle the giant waves at Waimea Bay. A climactic surfing battle at Waimea Bay occurs between Jody Waller (Fabian) and Eskimo (Jim Mitchum) to prove their superiority over the waves.

Filmed on location at Waimea, Kawela Bay, and Kahuku, courtesy of the Estate of James Campbell, this was one of the first films to feature extraordinary on-location surfing footage.

Above

Teen idol Tab Hunter dons an Aloha shirt for *Ride the Wild Surf*, which co-stars Susan Hart.

NONE BUT THE BRAVE
1965 WB

D: **Frank Sinatra**

S: **John Twist and Katsuya Susaki**

P: **Howard W. Koch**

C: **Frank Sinatra, Clint Walker, Tatsuya Mihashi, Tommy Sands, Brad Dexter, Sammy Jackson, Phil Crosby, Laraine Stephens, Takeshi Kato**

Poignant and perceptive story set on a tiny, forgotten South Pacific island inhabited by a Japanese garrison, where a transport plane bearing U.S. combat marines is shot down by enemy planes and crash lands, during World War II. After a few brief skirmishes, friendship and enmity alternate between the two sides until a fateful, but inevitable, conclusion.

None But the Brave is Frank Sinatra's only film as a motion picture director. He hadn't planned to turn director, but the story stirred him so strongly that he decided to transfer it to the screen himself, rather than entrust it to another. Sinatra also took a small role and produced.

The film was a Sinatra Enterprises production for Warner Bros. It was unique in that it is the first joint filming venture of American and Japanese companies to be made in the United States. It was a co-effort of Artanis Productions and Tokyo Eiga Co., the latter a division of Toho Films.

Through the Tokyo partnership, Sinatra and executive producer Howard W. Koch were able

to obtain 12 of Japan's outstanding actors to portray Nippon soldiers. Sinatra's co-stars are Clint Walker, Tommy Sands, Brad Dexter and Tony Bill, and in the major Japanese roles are Tatsuya Mihashi, Takeshi Kato, Homare Suguro and Kenji Sahara. The film introduces Laraine Stephens as the sole American girl in the cast.

The story was by Kikumaru Okuda and the screenplay, by John Twist and Katsuya Susaki. William Daniels was associate producer. The photography by Harold Lipstein was in Technicolor and Panavision.

Sinatra believed the dramatic effect of his narrative would be heightened if the Japanese soldiers always remained completely in "character"—that is, if they didn't speak English. So only Mihashi has English dialogue and then only when conversing with Americans in the story. The Japanese dialogue is translated in subtitles over the scene.

Exteriors representing the South Sea island were filmed at Pilaa beach on Kauai, Hawai'i. It was an unspoiled coastline near the area where *South Pacific* and other pictures, praised for their beautiful natural backgrounds, were photographed. A troupe of 150 worked four weeks at the location.

The wrecked plane shown in the picture was a C-47 brought as surplus property by Sinatra and transported by barge and truck to the beach shooting location. The studio built roads from the high lava cliffs above to this set and the beach area of the Japanese camp.

While filming on location on Kauai, Sinatra almost drowned on a Sunday morning while relaxing on a beach off the Coco Palms hotel. He went for a swim and got caught in a riptide and was rescued in time by some off-duty marines.

IN HARM'S WAY

1965 PAR

D: Otto Preminger

S: Wendell Mayes, based on the novel by James Bassett

P: Otto Preminger

Cast: John Wayne, Kirk Douglas, Patricia Neal, Tom Tryon, Paula Prentiss, Brandon de Wilde, Jill Haworth, Dana Andrews, Henry Fonda

The devastating attack by the Japanese on Pearl Harbor, and the men and women who were dramatically involved in the United States' subsequent efforts to build a new Pacific fleet from the ruins, came vividly to life in Otto Preminger's bold and dramatically absorbing film treatment of *In Harm's Way*. The screen presentation, filmed in authentic locales, was a frank exposure of the heroism, as well as the brutality, of war. Through its many stories, *In Harm's Way* dealt in depth with the struggles, disappointments, triumphs and tragedies of many participants.

Above
Kirk Douglas as Commander Paul Eddington and Jill Haworth as nurse Annalee Dorne, on location near Chinaman's Hat (glimpsed in the rear, on the right) at Kaneohe, on the windward side of Oahu, just before the dramatic rape and murder scene in *In Harm's Way*.

The courage and determination of a newly commissioned Admiral Rockwell Torrey (Wayne), who is charged with the responsibility of mounting the counteroffensive, is presented in striking contrast to his duty, his relationship with his son Ensign Jeremiah Torrey (de Wilde), and his romantic attachment to Lt. Maggie Haynes (Neal). An executive officer, Commander Paul Eddington (Douglas), plagued by a personal tragedy with his wife (Prentiss) and strained by self-torment, takes out his interior rage by brutally raping a young nurse, Annalee Dorne (Haworth), in a horrifyingly realistic scene. To redeem himself, he performs a necessary suicide mission in a daring act of heroism. Also revealed with an investigative eye are the lives of two oppositely oriented personnel: Lt. William McConnel (Tryon), dedicated to the cause, and Admiral Broderick (Andrews), dedicated to himself.

Historically eclipsed by the Japanese attack on Pearl Harbor, the Navy air base at Kaneohe Bay on the Hawaiian island of Oahu, now a Marine Corps air station, was bombarded at the same time, with equally tragic results. Twenty-three years later filmmaker Otto Preminger moved in cast, crew and cameras to photograph scenes for *In Harm's Way.* Preminger established a motion picture studio in the Ilikai Hotel in Waikiki, transporting more than 100 staff and technical crew, a cast of 50 and three boatloads of equipment, wardrobe and supplies to Hawai'i.

Kaneohe was only one of 22 Hawaiian locations utilized by Preminger, some of which were made to resemble advance naval bases during the Pacific conflict, including the Makapuu beach area and the Pearl Harbor Officers Club. Other scenes were shot on Naval bases in San Diego and San Francisco, as well as aboard fleet ships at sea. Scenes portraying an aircraft-observer's post and involving John Wayne as an admiral and Paula Prentiss as a lieutenant's wife were shot in a sugar cane field commanding a full view of Kolekole Pass, the break in the Waianae mountain range through which the Japanese planes swept for their surprise blow. Nearby are Hickam Field, Schofield Barracks and other Pearl Harbor points devastated in that bombardment.

Preminger's re-creation of the bombing of Pearl Harbor was staged in

Above
Burgess Meredith, Kirk Douglas, and John Wayne in Otto Preminger's sprawling WWII epic *In Harm's Way.*

Pearl Harbor itself with U.S. Navy assistance. The opening sequence of the attack was filmed in the summer of 1964, and U.S. Navy ships were bombed and strafed. On film, not one Japanese plane is seen; the illusion of the infamous attack was created by sound and other special effects. The filming of the burning of several buildings in Honolulu took place in the city proper, with Preminger destroying pre-selected slum areas, including a part of the famed Hell's Half Acre in downtown Honolulu. Several large private estates were used as filming sites, including the Damon and Dillingham homes. The huge Walker estate overlooking Honolulu was also used as a filming site.

The Battle of Leyte Gulf was filmed with scaled-down models and miniatures back at Paramount studios in Hollywood. It took a crew of 40, $1 million, and a month of shooting to film this sequence, which runs about five minutes on the screen.

Below
John Wayne as Admiral Rockwell Torrey, and Patricia Neal as Lt. Maggie Haynes, in a party scene from *In Harm's Way* shot at the Damon estate, a private hilltop property near Honolulu. Salt Lake, which is seen in the background of this scene, no longer exists, due to urban development.

In this scene from *Hawaii*, a double-hulled canoe bearing *ali'i* (Polynesian royalty) and *kahili* (royal feather standards) is paddled out to greet the arriving boat of New England missionaries, in early nineteenth century Hawai'i. This scene was filmed at Makua Beach, on the leeward coast of Oahu.

HAWAII

1966 UA

D:	George Roy Hill
S:	Dalton Trumbo and Daniel Taradash, based on the novel by James A. Michener
P:	Walter Mirisch
Cast:	Julie Andrews, Max Von Sydow, Richard Harris, Gene Hackman, Jocelyn Bredin LaGarde, Manu Tupou, Ted Nobriga, Torin Thatcher, John Cullum, Lou Antonio

The Polynesians who followed the stars hundreds of miles in their canoes, the stern missionaries who came from cold New England, the hard-working Chinese and Japanese, the colorful Portuguese and Filipinos who shaped and molded Hawai'i—they are all part of the story—but Hawai'i is the heroine, the enchantress, the spellbinder.

Hawaii is filled with the dramatic conflicts and love affairs that grew out of the meeting of two great cultures, the Hawaiian and the Anglo-Saxon Protestant.

From the beginning, it was evident that the major challenge in the filming of *Hawaii* was the James A. Michener novel itself. The monumental book by the opulent and expansive Michener contained such a wealth of potential film fare in the 946 pages of its multiple stories that it was soon determined that filming the entirety would time out to eleven hours on the screen.

The screenplay, written by Academy Award winners Dalton Trumbo and Daniel Taradash (*The Brave One* and *From Here to Eternity,* respectively) was aimed at retaining the essential flavor, while concentrating on the heart of the novel—the story of the early missionaries traveling across stormy seas from New England to far-off Hawai'i to bring Christianity to "pagan" natives.

The task of transforming the book into a motion picture spread itself to four parts of the world. Costumes and props came from such diverse places as Hong Kong, Denmark, Australia, Japan, and the Philippines. As part of this global concept, an international cast was assembled, including British Julie Andrews, Swedish Max Von Sydow and Irish Richard Harris.

To fill the pivotal roles of islanders, the filmmakers went directly to the islands, selecting a collection of personalities that truly depicted their forebears. Many had never acted before and one spoke no English, making the filming infinitely more difficult. Jocelyn LaGarde, a 300-pound Tahitian of royal blood, was selected to play Malama, the *alii nui* and chief spokesperson for the islanders. Her vivid performance was honored with an Academy Award nomination as Best Supporting Actress. Manu Tupou, a Fijian employed in London by the BBC, became Keoki. The role of Noelani, daughter of Malama, went to Elizabeth Logue, the Hawaii Visitors Bureau poster girl and former employee of Hawaiian Airlines. Another islander, Ted Nobriga, was found to play Keolo.

Filming was accomplished in four phases. The initial pre-production phase got underway in February 1965, off Bodo, Norway, 150 miles from the Arctic Circle, with sequences depicting the missionaries' boat, *Thetis*, sailing through the Straits of Magellan. The second phase, marking the start of principal photography involving Julie Andrews, Max Von Sydow and other leading cast members, took place in April 1965 in Massachusetts. Scenes involving both the Hale farmhouse and the Bromley mansion were filmed in Old Sturbridge Village, where a complete early New England town was meticulously constructed as a permanent historical project.

Moving to the third phase and to Hollywood, another seven weeks were spent on sound stages filming various interiors and shipboard scenes, for which a full-sized duplicate of the *Thetis* was constructed.

In June 1965, the troupe flew to Hawai'i for the fourth and lengthiest phase, some four months of filming, principally at Makua Beach, forty miles from Honolulu. A quarter-mile-long village consisting of 107 buildings was constructed and continuously aged to represent the town of Lahaina on Maui as it existed between 1820 and 1848. A former Navy warehouse at Pearl City, Oahu, was converted by film technicians into a fully equipped sound stage.

Opposite page

The film *Hawaii* is an adaptation of a portion of James Michener's sprawling generational saga. The motion picture focuses on the conflicts between indigenous islanders and Westerners, who are mainly missionaries and whalers. Interestingly, this script so critical of missionaries was co-written by Dalton Trumbo, one of the Hollywood 10, who helped break the McCarthy era blacklist. In this scene, Irish actor Richard Harris plays Rafer, the headstrong captain of a whaling ship. Tahitian actress Jocelyn LaGarde and Hawaiian actor Ted Nobriga portray brother and sister *ali'i*, Queen Malama and Keolo, who have an incestuous relationship frowned upon by the Christian missionaries. LaGarde's performance was nominated for an Oscar.

Research continued, much of it at the Bishop Museum in Honolulu, to ensure the authentic look of the area during the time depicted. The film's craftspeople found it necessary to import thatch from Japan, since the pili grass normally used for thatching huts in the era of the story was difficult to find in the Hawaiian Islands. For the colorful costumes, rooster feathers were imported from the Philippines, red and gold royal cloaks from Hong Kong, imitation tapa cloth from Ireland, silk maile leaves from Japan, straw mattings from Mexico, boar's tooth necklaces and bracelets from India, and original tribute silk from Taiwan. All of it represented materials used in Hawai'i when the missionaries first arrived, but none of the originals were available to the filmmakers.

At the newly constructed replica of 1820 Lahaina, 150 mainly Native Hawaiian extras formed a village population. Kids played hide and seek in some two dozen grass houses constructed for the film. Other reminders that the date was actually 1965, not 1820, were evident: an elderly Hawaiian leaning comfortably against his grass shack reading *The Honolulu Advertiser*; the ever-present Hawaiian taro patch sporting plastic plants; modern haircuts covered by black wigs; actress Elizabeth Logue's false Polynesian nose.

Hawaii brought mixed reviews. "The film's main problem (there are others) is its lack of a compelling central character. That is one who creates keen interest, or moves us to relate to him, for better or worse through affection, hatred, pity or horror, or simply his tantalizing complexity as a dramatic figure," wrote Giles M. Fowler in the February 19, 1967 *Kansas City Star*.

On the other hand, *Box-Office* reported on October 10, 1966 that "The Mirisch Corp. has brought forth a scenically beautiful, fascinating and always absorbing production which in every sense of the word rates the classification as a road show picture."

Opposite page
Elizabeth Logue plays Queen Malama's daughter, Noelani, and Manu Tupou depicts her brother, Keoki, in *Hawaii*. An early convert to Christianity, Keoki inspires the New England missionaries to come to Hawai'i and spread the gospel. But in the course of the film, Keoki "backslides" and reverts to heathen ways, including having sex with his sister. Note that the highly stylized Hawaiian-like costumes and Tiki image are not authentic. Logue went on to become a Hawai'i Visitors Bureau poster girl and appeared in a promotional travelogue.

PARADISE, HAWAIIAN STYLE

1966 PAR

D: Michael Moore

S: Alan Weiss and Anthony Lawrence

P: Hal B. Wallis

Cast: Elvis Presley, Suzanna Leigh, James Shigeta, Donna Butterworth, Irene Tsu, Philip Ahn, Robert Ito

Filmed on location in Honolulu; on Kauai (Hanalei Plantation Resort); on Maui (Maui Sheraton Hotel); and on the Kona Coast. Jack Regas, who staged the film's musical numbers, was a choreographer at the Polynesian Cultural Center where part of the movie was shot. During filming on Oahu, Elvis stayed at the Ilikai Hotel.

KONA COAST

1968 WB

D: Lamont Johnson

S: Gil Ralston

P: Richard Boone

Cast: Richard Boone, Vera Miles, Joan Blondell, Steve Ihat,
         Chips Rafferty, Kent Smith, Sam Kapu Jr., Gloria Nakea

Captain Moran (Boone) is caught in the world of wild beachfront *luau* after his teenage daughter (Nakea) falls victim to a rough crowd getting its kicks from drugs. Moran runs into a band of toughs who plague him from island to island until the film's explosive conclusion.

"On *Kona Coast* we used only seven people from Hollywood… It did come in slightly under budget and was a respectable product for the price," remarked actor-producer Richard Boone after filming.

Kona Coast was filmed in authentic Hawai'i locales, including several dwellings in Kailua-Kona on the Big Island of Hawai'i, among them the home of Harold Dillingham, a member of one of Hawai'i's prominent families. Diamond Head and Honolulu on the island of Oahu were also featured.

Kona Coast, made by Pioneer Productions, was the first all-Hawai'i film production for Warner Bros.

TORA! TORA! TORA!
1970 TCF

D: Richard Fleischer

S: Larry Forrester, Hideo Oguni, Ryuzo Kikushima, based on *Tora! Tora! Tora!* by Gordon W. Prange and *The Broken Seal* by Ladislas Fargo.

P: Elmo Williams

Cast: Martin Balsam, Sol Yamamura, Joseph Cotten, E.G. Marshall, Tatsuya Mihasi, Jason Robards, James Whitmore

Tora! Tora! Tora! is a meticulous and dramatic exploration of both the Japanese plans and the American responses in the months leading up to the surprise attack on Pearl Harbor on December 7, 1941. The Japanese side is intercut with the American side, and Japanese characters speak in their language with English subtitles provided on screen. The 144-minute film is logically divided into a 79-minute first act, which crosscuts between Japan and America locales, and a 65-minute second act, which consists mostly of the masterful cinematic reenactment of one of the decisive events of the 20th century.

The title is taken from the Japanese code signal Tiger! Tiger! Tiger!, which was used to convey news of the successful attack.

Producer Elmo Williams, Darryl F. Zanuck's associate on *The Longest Day,* began preliminary work on the film in 1966, but it was not until 1967 that the possibilities and impossibilities were sorted out. Key to the concept were the re-creation of the Japanese air strike force, the building or leasing of full-sized ships, and the persuading of Japan to make its own side of the story with its own technicians and language. It took almost every day of three years of preparation to mount the production on both sides of the ocean.

The Hawai'i production of *Tora! Tora! Tora!* required logistics nearly as complicated as a war. American airplanes of pre-World War II vintage were acquired from all over the world, and Japanese planes had to be converted from other models, because no real ones had survived the war. After the surrender, Gen. Douglas McArthur had ordered the Japanese to melt down their military aircraft, and the destruction had been carried out with Japanese thoroughness. In reality the Zekes (fighters) and Kates (torpedo planes) were American-made AT-65s, and the Vals (bombers) were BT-13s. These aircraft were extensively modified to resemble the Japanese Mitsubishi Zeros. The company rented five old destroyers from the Navy, but hired the Maritime Services Division of the Dillingham Corporation in Honolulu to build a full-scale section of the USS *Arizona* at a cost of $1.5 million. Mounted on two steel barges, the 309-foot steel superstructure, fully fitted, was towed to Battleship Row to play her historic role.

"There were so many elements involved in each scene that we were lucky to get one shot a day," said director Richard Fleischer to Associated Press writer Bob Thomas in the June 14, 1969 edition of *The Los Angeles Herald Examiner.* "For instance we had 28 planes in the sky, and they had to maneuver so they could be seen in every camera. On the ground we had special effects men providing fire and smoke, and a sudden shift of wind

Opposite page

Historical accuracy is stressed in the reenactment of imperial Japan's air raid on Oahu in *Tora! Tora! Tora!*, but this scene set in central Oahu seems apocryphal. By the 1940s, pineapple plantation workers did not wear such hats as shown in the foreground, and it's unlikely that agricultural laborers would be picking pineapples early on a Sunday morning. The point of this dubious scene is that the workers carried on working, unconcerned and unknowingly, as Zeros soared overhead en route to Pearl Harbor—an indication of America's lack of preparedness for the events of December 7, 1941.

could send the smoke right into the cameras so we'd photograph nothing, or the sun would go behind the clouds and ruin the scene. We had the planes circling for an hour and a half before getting a shot."

Filming began on December 2, 1968 aboard the aircraft carrier USS *Yorktown* portraying the Japanese carrier *Akagi*. On January 20, 1969 the planes came in low over the serene, silent monument that covers the USS *Arizona* and dipped their wings in tribute to the men entombed there. This time, though, the planes were in the air to mark the opening photography of *Tora! Tora! Tora!*

It was the start of weeks of aerial and ground second unit photography headed by Ray Kellogg, Second Unit Director, whose film credits include *The Alamo* and *The Tall Men.* The aircraft, tested in California, were flown almost continuously from mid-December 1968 to late April 1969. Forty-seven experienced pilots, mostly on leave from the Air Force and Navy, comprised what came to be affectionately called The Fox Air Force.

Many other films have been made of the "Day of Infamy," December 7, 1941, when an armada of Japanese planes swooped down to attack Pearl Harbor, knocked out the American fleet, and catapulted the U.S. into World War II. The earliest film was Japanese propaganda produced for home consumption not long after the attack. Others were *Remember Pearl Harbor, Air Force* and *From Here to Eternity.* Japan produced *I Bombed Pearl Harbor,* which dealt with the time after the attack to the Battle of Midway.

"It had been a rather strange war, this second air battle of Hawai'i, chilling at times," commented Buck Buchwach, editor of *The Honolulu Advertiser* in December 1968, while watching the filming of *Tora! Tora! Tora!* "Sometimes it seemed too real. It was comforting to know those were American pilots up there this time."

Tora! Tora! Tora! was photographed at the actual locations in Hawai'i where it all took place: Ford Island, Hickam and Wheeler Fields, Kolekole Pass, Schofield Barracks, Waikiki, Aloha Tower, the Kalihi district of Honolulu, Koko Head, Opana Point, Fort Shafter, and Chinaman's Hat.

Business on the island boomed during production. More than 300 carpenters, painters, steel workers, scenic artists and cabinet makers, most of them Hawai'i residents, were employed. Huge Hangar 79, marked with bullet holes from the real attack on Pearl Harbor, along with two smaller satellite hangars, was turned into a mini-film studio that became the hub of construction and storage facilities. In place of the Navy fighter planes and dive bombers the structures once housed were racks of both American and Japanese naval uniforms. Where engines were once tuned, scenic artists painted P-40 aircraft and built bomb craters out of plastic.

Filming in Hawaiʻi went smoothly and on schedule, but in Japan problems occurred from the beginning. Akira Kurosawa, the most famous Japanese director of the time who was engaged to direct the Japanese sequences, was replaced by two Japanese directors after he contractually failed to deliver the amount of footage requested. Two of Japan's most highly regarded screenwriters, long-time associates of Akira Kurosawa, with whom they had collaborated on *Seven Samurai, Yojimbo* and *Throne of Blood,* were enlisted to work on the screenplay.

The Japanese sequences of *Tora! Tora! Tora!* were filmed at Ashiya on the island of Kyushu; at Iwanai, on Hokkaido; and in Tokyo for exteriors of the Imperial Palace and the United States Embassy. Interiors were filmed at Toei-Kyoto and the Shochiku Studios in Kyoto and also in Osaka.

The large and distinguished cast of 155 members was drawn from both film and theatrical performers. Cameras rolled on March 3, 1969 at Ashiya Air Force Base, located midway between Fukuoka and Koakura on Kyushu. On the beach was constructed a full-scale model of three-quarters of the 35,000-ton Japanese carrier *Akagi*, Admiral Nagumo's flagship for the Pearl Harbor attack. Parallel and 2,000 yards away, looming against low mountains, her prow to the sea, was the full-sized *Nagato*, flagship of Admiral Isoroku Yamamoto.

THE HAWAIIANS

1970 UA

D: **Tom Gries**

S: **James R. Webb, based on the novel by James A. Michener**

P: **Walter Mirisch**

Cast: **Charlton Heston, Geraldine Chaplin, John Phillip Law, Mako, Tina Chen, Alec McCowen, Naomi Stevens**

Based on the second half of the phenomenal best-seller *Hawaii,* this epic drama stars Charlton Heston as Whip Hoxworth, grandson of the towering Rafer (Richard Harris), a man of the sea and an avid exploiter. Geraldine Chaplin plays his wife, Purity; John Phillip Law is their son; and the Japanese Academy Award nominee Mako plays the leper Mun Ki. Tina Chen was Nyuk Tsin, the Chinese girl for sale who becomes the matriarch of a dynasty; and Naomi Stevens portrays Hawaiian Queen Liliuokalani, who stands steadfast in her defense of Native rights.

The film carries the islands from their era as a missionary settlement into a thriving, prosperous early twentieth-century. Included in this epochal family drama and panoramic picture of the islands' history is the arrival of the first Chinese and Japanese workers, whose personal and cultural contributions have made Hawai'i so unique. The development of the islands' pineapple industry, one of its mainstays, is traced, as is the political evolution from an independent kingdom to a republic.

The Hawaiians was filmed in sixteen weeks in twelve locations on the islands of Maui and Kauai. To justify the roughly 30-year scope of the story from 1870 to 1900, the Mirisch organization built a sprawling set representing Honolulu at the turn of the century. Dozens of extras were employed, and a whole fleet of contemporary vessels were built to re-enact the bustling

Below

Between takes on the set of
The Hawaiians: **Tina Chen as Nyuk Tsin and Geraldine Chaplin as Purity age through the magic of the make-up department in this film based on James Michener's generational saga.**

port scenes. Honolulu's Chinatown, circa 1900, was constructed in sugar cane fields outside of Lihue on Kauai. As a climax to the film, it was burned to the ground.

Opposite page

The Hawaiians is a less grandiose film adaptation of part of James Michener's huge novel *Hawaii* than the 1966 movie epic *Hawaii* is. *The Hawaiians* follows the subsequent generation of missionaries and other characters in later nineteenth century Hawai'i. In this scene, Charlie Chaplin's daughter Geraldine portrays the part-Hawaiian Purity, who is facing a mental breakdown; Charlton Heston plays her husband, businessman Whip Hoxworth. The Native Nationalist Purity is presented negatively presumably because she longs to return to her Hawaiian roots. *The Hawaiians* is noteworthy because it may be the only Hollywood feature to ever depict the 1893 overthrow of Queen Liliuokalani (Naomi Stevens) and the independent Kingdom of Hawai'i.

John R. Hamilton

Below

Jessica Lange, the bride-to-be, sits in King Kong's massive hand.

KING KONG

1976 PAR

D: **John Guillermin**

S: **Lorenzo Semple Jr.**

P: **Dino De Laurentiis**

Cast: **Jessica Lange, Jeff Bridges, Charles Grodin**

An exploration team is sent to the South Pacific to find an underwater oil shelf. Instead, the team finds King Kong and, realizing the commercial value of the find, the leader of the team makes off with Kong to New York.

Though it has a different story than the 1933 version, this $22 million Dino De Laurentiis production retelling the classic "Beauty and the Beast" story was filmed on locations ranging from the island of Kauai in Hawai'i to a multitude of sets on Hollywood sound stages and, finally, to the streets near New York's World Trade Center.

No major, commercial film company had gone ever before into the rugged terrain of northern Kauai, an incredibly remote area, with beautiful valleys and mountains that rise from the Pacific Ocean floor and on to the north shore. This was the area used in the filming of *King Kong*.

Four helicopters daily airflifted the 50-member company over the beautiful valleys and mountains of the Na Pali coast to the location, so inaccessible that it would have taken the company at

least two and a half days on foot. For three weeks the company shot on the Kauai coast, bringing boats through surf running as high as 12 feet to get footage of the crew from Petrox coming ashore on Skull Island to begin the dangerous search for Kong.

On one of the last days on the island, the company laid down a fog bank to create the eerie, mysterious feeling surrounding Kong's home. Tourists and natives on the beach at Hanalei Bay were startled to find their clear, sunny day disappear behind Hollywood clouds.

Above

The Dino De Laurentiis *King Kong* (1976) remake was shot on the islands of Kauai and Manhattan. Kong is found at the Na Pali coast of Kauai, which stands in for the ape's home isle; (in the 1933 original, the giant gorilla is discovered near Indonesia on Skull Island, which is inhabited by Melanesians— black Pacific Islanders). From left to right are Julius Harris, Jessica Lange, Jeff Bridges, Rene Auberjonois, and Charles Grodin. Jessica Lange made her movie debut as Kong's lovely, long-legged, blonde bride-to-be.

BIG WEDNESDAY
1978 WB

D:	**John Milius**
S:	**John Milius and Dennis Aaberg**
P:	**Buzz Feitshans**
Cast:	**Jan-Michael Vincent, William Katt, Gary Busey**

The story of a group of surfing friends growing up in California between 1961 and 1974 and how those years affect their lives.

Scenes filmed at Oahu's Sunset Beach featured top Hawaiian surfer Gerry Lopez.

Above

(left to right) Gary Busey, Jan-Michael Vincent and William Katt in *Big Wednesday*.

GOIN' COCONUTS A/K/A ALOHA DONNY AND MARIE

1978 INTERPLANETARY PICTURES

D: Howard Morris

S: William Marc Daniels, Raymond Harvey

P: John Cutts

Cast: Donny Osmond, Marie Osmond, Herb Edelman

Famous juvenile entertainers of the era Donny and Marie Osmond (playing themselves) are en route to a Hawai'i concert when they are approached by a priest who pleads with them to accept a shell necklace. When the plane arrives in Honolulu, it seems like every underworld thug wants to get his hands on the necklace.

This comedy mystery tale was filmed on location in Hawai'i. Harold Sakata, Oddjob of Goldfinger fame and Khiegh Dhiegh, Wo Fat of *Hawaii Five-O,* both Hawai'i residents, appear together as villains in the film.

Below

Among the villains who compete to do in Donny and Marie Osmond in the madcap comedy *Goin' Coconuts* are the clumsy crooks, including Khiegh Dhiegh (who played Wo Fat in *Hawaii Five-O,* and Harold Sakata (who played Oddjob in the 007 thrillers).

THE CASTAWAY COWBOY

1979 BV

D: Vincent McEveety

S: Don Tait, based on a story by Tait, Richard Bluel and Hugh Benson

P: Ron Miller and Winston Hibler

Cast: James Garner, Vera Miles, Robert Culp, Eric Shea, Manu Tupou, Gregory Sierra, Shug Fisher, Ralph Hanalei, Kahana

James Garner plays a seafaring Texas wrangler who jumps ship near the Sandwich Islands, gets tangled up with a pretty widow and her young son, and finds himself ramrodding the first cattle spread in Hawai'i. The job includes turning a bunch of happy-go-lucky islanders into hard-riding cowhands and dealing with a mixed bag of crooks.

After surveying all the Hawaiian Islands, the producers decided that Kauai presented the best opportunities for settings and backgrounds. Filming began there on September 5, 1978. In addition to 62 craftsmen from the Disney Studios in Burbank and 25 actors and assistants from Honolulu, the producers employed 150 local residents.

The Garden Isle of Kauai was "discovered" by Captain James Cook in 1778 and by numerous filmmakers thereafter. The island's profuse waterfalls, harbors, mountains, forests, pastures, meadows and unspoiled beaches make it breathtakingly beautiful.

The main setting of *The Castaway Cowboy*, the Macavoy Farm, was designed by Robert Clatworthy and built on a bluff accessible only by private road. Water-slide scenes took place at Kilauea falls, where bathers shot off a slippery lava slide into a natural pool.

The waterfront set was built at Mahaulepu at the "bottom" of the island, offshore scenes were filmed at Moloaa at the "top," and the rest were shot all over Kauai. Seven top Hawaiian performers headlined in the film, including Nephi Hannemann, a singer, composer and recording artist of Samoan ancestry, and Elizabeth Smith, a ukulele-playing singer and dancer. The farmhands who become paniolos were portrayed by Lito Capina, Kahana, Manu Tupou, Lee Wodd and Ralph Hanalei. In addition to being actors, Kahana was a fire dancer; Tupou, a teacher; Wodd, a stunt man; Hanalei, an ace golfer; and Capina, a dancer and waiter at several hotels.

Opposite page
James Garner in *The Castaway Cowboy*.

The film was originally titled *Paniolo,* the Hawaiian word for cowboy. *The Castaway Cowboy* completely misrepresents the origins of the first paniolos, who were Mexican-Californians who came to the islands to teach the Hawaiians cattle ranching in the late 1840s.

"What could have been a harmless passable film, is instead filled with racial slurs, inane dialog and a general lack of intelligence," wrote Richard Natale in the August 15, 1974 *Women's Wear Daily.*

THE LAST FLIGHT OF NOAH'S ARK

1980 BUENA VISTA

D: Charles Jarrott

S: Steven W. Carabatsos, Sandy Glass and George Arthur Bloom, based on a story by Ernest K. Gann

P: Ron Miller

Cast: Elliott Gould, Ricky Shroeder, Genevieve Bujold

The turbulent struggle for survival by four people in a rattletrap B-29 bomber loaded with farm animals. A high-living pilot is hired by an evangelist to fly the plane full of livestock to a South Pacific mission.

The Last Flight of Noah's Ark was filmed on Kauai and in the waters off Waikiki Beach.

WHEN TIME RAN OUT

1980 WB

D: James Goldstone

S: Carl Foreman and Stirling Silliphant

P: Irwin Allen

Cast: Paul Newman, Jaqueline Bisset, William Holden, Edward Albert, Red Buttons, James Franciscus, Veronica Hamel, Barbara Carrera

Also known as *The Day the World Ended* and on television as *Earth's Final Fury,* this all-star-cast disaster movie is the story of the inhabitants and guests of a newly opened super-luxury resort on a Pacific island who are caught by a volcanic eruption. Newman plays an oil driller, and Franciscus is a hotel representative who suspects an eruption but keeps the geologists' reports quiet to protect his oil and resort interests. The volcano finally erupts, causing earthquakes, tidal waves and lava flows, which wipe out a village and the hotel inhabitants.

Filming took place for one month in and around the Kona Surf Hotel on the usually sun-washed Kona Coast, which was at the time lashed by heavy rains. The crew next moved to the Hilo side of the island of Hawaiʻi, where they stayed at the Naniloa Surf Hotel. Filming occurred at Mauna Kea crater, in the rain forest, and at Peʻepeʻe Falls. Life and art nearly collided when, two days before the start of principal photography, Hawaiʻi was shocked by an earthquake registering more than five points on the Richter scale, with an epicenter at Kilauea.

BEHOLD HAWAII

1983 MacGillivray-Freeman Films

D:	Greg MacGillivray
S:	Alec Lorimore
P:	Greg MacGillivray
Cast:	Blaine Kia, Kanani Velasco, Peter Kalua, Kimo Kahoano

A spectacular forty-minute IMAX/OMNIMAX large-screen film of a young Hawaiian's magical journey through time. Set in a dreamscape among his ancient ancestors, Keola (Kia), a native Hawaiian, faces many exciting challenges and harrowing dangers as he searches for his Hawaiian heritage.

IMAX's 70-millimeter film stock is the largest ever made and is projected in special theaters on five-story-high IMAX screens. *Behold Hawaii* took that format beyond the scope of documentaries into the realm of feature films with its character-filled drama.

"*Behold Hawaii* is an historically accurate document," said producer Greg MacGillivray in production notes for the film. He and his film crew worked with the strict guidance of Hawai'i's Bishop Museum through the entire production to assure a thoroughly detailed, accurate depiction of the old Hawaiians and their life. "Weaving together Hawai'i's past and present seemed like the natural thing to do to tell a story that was uniquely Hawaiian. So the accuracy of the cultural scenes became a major aspect of the film's integrity," remarked MacGillivray.

An ancient village was constructed from local materials. Volcanoes National Park provided pili grass for the thatch; the *lauhala* (pandanus) stripping for the interiors was picked and woven in Kona; and ohia trees from the island of Hawai'i were cut for the posts and crossbeams. The village was then transported by barge to a set on Kauai.

Opposite page

Contemporary Hawaiian Keola (Blaine Kia) goes back in time in the big screen IMAX production *Behold Hawaii*, which depicts precontact Hawaiians as excessively brutal. Popular Hawaiian deejay and entertainer Kimo Kahoano is on the left; Blaine Kia is second from the right, in this scene portraying ancient Hawai'i before the arrival of Captain Cook and Europeans.

Behold Hawaii took nearly three years to complete, including a year for pre-production, five months for shooting the 300,000 feet of film, and a year of editing.

Then 18-year-old Blaine Kia, just graduated from Honolulu's McKinley High School, was selected to play Keola after a long casting search.

"Never was a landscape more suited to the Omnimax medium than Hawai'i's," wrote Karin Winegar in the January 27, 1984 issue of the *Minneapolis Star and Tribune*.

BLACK WIDOW

1987 TCF

D: **Bob Rafelson**

S: **Ron Bass**

P: **Harold Schneider**

Cast: **Debra Winger, Theresa Russell, Nicol Williamson, Dennis Hopper**

Debra Winger starred in *Black Widow* as Alex Barnes, a federal agent hunting a woman she suspects of marrying and murdering a series of wealthy men. Theresa Russell starred as Catharine, the elusive beauty whom Alex pursues.

James Hong had a featured role as a jittery Hawaiian private detective, and Danny Kamekona played another detective.

Cast and crew flew to the volcanic island of Hawai'i, where the majority of the filming took place. In the story, it is the dream of Paul Nyutten to build a unique hotel on that island. He takes Catharine to the spot where he envisions his resort, which is to be located on the captivating, unearthly bluff overlooking Kilauea, one of the world's most active volcanoes. For the last half of the film Catharine is surrounded by mountains, seascapes and erupting volcanoes, the mythic attributes of a primitive goddess.

Filming the actors against the background of a volcano in full eruption was the biggest production challenge the filmmakers faced. Producer Harold Schneider posted observers to alert him to the timing of the volcanic eruptions, which had been occurring on a fairly predictable cycle once every 24 or 28 days. Once alerted, director Rafelson broke the set where a day's filming had begun and flew his key crew members and actors Russell and Frey, to within a mile and a half of the

exploding crater. Within an hour, cameras were shooting the scene in front of an eruption that had reached its peak of 1,200 feet.

The diverse topography of the volcanic island offered other enchanting visuals, as well. The sparkling white sand beaches along the Kona Coast were a marked contrast to the black sand of Kalapana and the pastured hills of the northern ranchlands. "The easy thing to do, being in Hawai'i, would be to go into the rainforest dripping with African tulips," said production designer Gene Callahan. "We wanted to avoid that by showing places where there is a certain beauty, and which are different from North America, where the early scenes of the film are set, and we found places like that: just different enough, and attractive enough, to work."

Hawai'i's rich history also lent itself to the script. The island's first Catholic church, founded by Father Damien, known as "the leper priest" for his association with the colony for Hansen's disease patients on the island of Molokai, was used for the marriage ceremony sequence. The seaport town of Hilo, twice devastated in this century by tsunamis (the great sea waves caused by earthquakes or underwater volcanic eruptions) provided a quaint townscape that was a step back in time.

Above
Department of Justice investigator Alex Barnes (Debra Winger) confronts murderess Catharine (Theresa Russell) in *Black Widow*, shot on location on the Big Island of Hawai'i.

THROW MOMMA FROM THE TRAIN

1987 OR

D: Danny DeVito

S: Stu Silver

P: Larry Brezner

Cast: Billy Crystal, Danny DeVito, Anne Ramsey, Kate Mulgrew

Larry Donner (Crystal) is a novelist who ekes out a meager living at a two-year college in the San Fernando Valley. His ex-wife Margaret stole the book that was his life's work, sold it as her own, became the toast of the talk-show circuit and soared to the top of the best-seller list. Ever since, Larry has had a cement writer's block that extends to his libido.

Owen Lift (DeVito) is a would-be mystery writer who's under the thumb of his domineering mother. When Larry urges Owen to study the films of Alfred Hitchcock to learn how to motivate a murder mystery, Owen misconstrues the message. He assumes that if he does away with Larry's former wife, Larry will send Momma to her maker. They'll crisscross their intended victims, just as Robert Walker and Farley Granger did in Hitchcock's *Strangers on a Train*.

Unfortunately, Owen fails to communicate these ideas to his would-be partner in crime. By the time Larry gets the drift, Margaret is missing, he's wanted for murder, has no alibi and is expected to knock off a nasty old lady he's never even met.

On Kauai, the company used some fifteen different locations for Owen's inept attempts to murder Margaret. "The look of the island was just right for this film," remarked Producer Brezner. "There were clouds hanging on the mountains, a sense of doom nearby and Danny hiding ominously behind the couch on which Margaret is researching her next erotic novel with the gardener."

Above

Danny DeVito plays Owen Lift, the loser from Loserville, with the mother from hell in the Alfred Hitchcock-inspired comedy *Throw Momma from the Train*.

NORTH SHORE

1987 U

D:	William Phelps
S:	Tim McCanlies and William Phelps, from a story by Phelps and Randal Kleiser
P:	Bill Finnegan
Cast:	Matt Adler, Nia Peeples, John Philbin, Gerry Lopez, Gregory Harrison

Rick Kane (Adler) is an 18-year-old surfer from Arizona who dreams of going to Hawai'i to ride the waves of Oahu's legendary North Shore. Having won the state title on artificial swells at his neighborhood wave pool, Rick is ready for a real ocean, and heads for Oahu's North Shore, where nature's most powerful waves challenge the world's most fearless wave warriors. He spends his prize money on airfare to Hawai'i instead of college, and this rites-of-passage adventure begins.

Rick's disastrous first encounter with the waves at Sunset Beach leads to an unfortunate surfing collision with Vince (Lopez), the respected leader of the Hawaiian brotherhood, the *hui*.

Rick finds more trouble when he falls in love with Vince's beautiful cousin Kiani (Peeples), a girl whose ties to her family become entangled with her love for the young mainlander. Turtle (Philbin), a surfboard sander, becomes Rick's best friend and guide through the intricacies of life on the North Shore.

Production of *North Shore,* filmed on location on Oahu and in Palm Springs, California, began on February 18, 1987 and wrapped on April 19, 1987. Fifteen locations on

Below
Bud Browne's *The Big Surf* and *Hawaiian Memories* drew attention to surf films in the 1940s. These were followed by Bruce Brown's *Slippery When Wet* and *Surf Safari* in the 1950s. The trend continued into the 1960s, with *Ride the Wild Surf* and *The Endless Summer*, and into the 1970s with flicks like *Big Wednesday*. *North Shore* brought the surfing movie into the 1980s, and the 1991 California-set *Point Break* included location footage of Oahu's famous North Shore waves. Below are Matt Adler as Rick Kane and Nia Peeples as Kiani in *North Shore*.

Oahu and water footage covering the entirety of the North Shore provide a detailed look at island life today. In the sugar cane fields of central Oahu, a tricky scene was filmed involving a raging fire and a car full of rowdy surfers.

Other locations included several ramshackle beach houses, a sleepy plantation village and an ancient Hawaiian *heiau* (temple), an unprepossessing pile of lava rocks that nevertheless had a deeply spiritual effect on the cast and crew.

John Milius, director of the surfing drama *Big Wednesday*, provided significant aid and advice for the production, including suggesting that Gerry Lopez and Laird Hamilton, both well-known surfers and celebrities in their own right, round out the list of principals.

North Shore also boasts performances by such top professional surfers as Mark Occhulipo, Robbie Page, Shaun Tomson, Hans Hedemann and Derek Ho.

ALOHA SUMMER

1988 SPECTRAFILM

D: Tommy Lee Wallace

S: Mike Greco and Bob Benedetto

P: Mike Greco

Cast: Chris Makepeace, Yuji Okumoto, Don Michael Paul, Tia
Carrere, Andy Bumatai, Lorie Griffin, Warren Fabro,
Blaine Kia, Scott Nagawa, Robert Ito, Sho Kosugi

Aloha Summer is set in exciting and beautiful Hawai'i as it moved into statehood during the summer of 1959. Six teenage boys chance to meet in Waikiki, including 18-year-old Chuck Granville (Paul), who disembarks from a luxury liner with his parents and sister (Griffin) and immediately teams up with Mike Tohnetti (Makepeace), who has just flown in tourist class with his family. Together at Waikiki, they become friendly with Kenzo (Okumoto), a second generation Japanese-American, and his cousin (Nagawa), along with two Hawaiian beachboys, Jerry (Kia) and Kilarney (Fabro). Casually crossing cultural and economic barriers, the six guys together earnestly pursue the most memorable summer of their lives.

Chuck has his first serious romance with Lani (Tia Carrere), a lovely Hawaiian girl who is watched over by her prejudiced brother (Bumatai). Mike tries to reach far above his social status when he falls in love with Chuck's sister. Kenzo defies his domineering and stern father (Kosugi), and enjoys and adapts to American and Hawaiian customs. Jerry and Kilarney risk disapproval of their beachboy peers by befriending the newcomers.

Unexpected battles with sailors, introductions into the world of kendo martial arts, wild rides through Honolulu's red-light district, lazy afternoons and romantic evenings, and conquering the pounding surf off the islands all create a special summer for the boys. The close friends have given each other the courage to be themselves and discover that this Aloha Summer has changed their lives forever.

Above
Hawai'i's statehood summer of 1959 provides Mike (Chris Makepeace) and Chuck (Don Michael Paul) a chance to conquer the surf.

Aloha Summer is loosely based on producer Mike Greco's personal experiences in Hawai'i when he first arrived in 1958 with his parents. "Being eighteen for almost anyone, regardless of culture or economic position, is a time of idealism, a time of innocence, a time of discovery," remarked Greco, "Being in Hawai'i during that period was like being in Heaven."

One of the major tasks in the filming of *Aloha Summer* was to turn back the clock to 1959, when only a handful of small, spacious hotels graced Waikiki Beach. Restoring Honolulu and its environs to that time was not so much a question of what to film as what not to film.

The production team of *Aloha Summer* stripped nearly 30 years from Waikiki Beach through the use of period umbrellas, towels, ice chests, radios and surfboards, plus a large catamaran whose sail was used to mask off new hotels at the far Diamond Head portion of Waikiki. A site close to the famous Royal Hawaiian Hotel (the venerable "Pink Palace"), one of the first hotels ever built in Hawai'i, served as an authentic background. For a native *luau* setting, the area of Kahana Bay on the unspoiled windward side of Oahu, one of the most idyllic settings on the island, proved a perfect location. The *luau* area was surrounded with 1959 vintage automobiles, which production designers had discovered were the single most important step in effecting a transformation of the times; they found over 45 trucks, police cars, buses and private autos to dress the sets.

Other special techniques employed to restore the period included keeping cameras trained on the 50-year-old Aloha Tower for scenes at the dock, exposing original wrought iron railings used for passenger control, and adding a 1950s-style facade to a small, shocking-pink hotel on the back streets of Waikiki to create a rather tacky tourist trap for the Tohnetti family.

Producer Mike Greco filmed at the famed Hanauma Bay at dusk to avoid the swarms of tourists who have changed the scenic spot into an aquatic Disneyland, and he masked off traffic lights and concrete planters and added cheap neon to return Hotel Street to the garish quality of former times.

Above
Chuck is confronted by Lani's brother, Kimo (Andy Bumatai), who demands that the mainlander break off his romance with Lani.

One of the biggest cheats was the use of the Halekulani Hotel's lanai bar, called The House Without A Key, for a formal dance setting featuring Del Courtney and His Orchestra. The Halekulani, which was recently rebuilt in the style of the old Hawai'i resorts, featured open spaces, high ceilings and painted concrete construction. With grass mats on the stage, 1950s-style furniture, and the liberal use of potted palms and other plants to block views of numerous new high-rise hotels, the desired effect was obtained.

The changes from 1950s-era Hawai'i-style dress are subtle but substantial. Careful research was conducted by wardrobe supervisor Paula Katz in libraries, museums and with obliging clothing manufacturers, including Scott Shoe Company, Iolani Sportswear, and major Honolulu retailers such as Sun Fashions, Kamehameha Fashions, Local Motion and Reyns.

Local actors Scott Nagawa, Blaine Kia, Warren Fabro, and Andy Bumatai were all cast in the film, as was Robert Ito, who played Ted Tanaka and is best known for his role as Sam opposite Jack Klugman in the *Quincy* television series. Japanese-born Sho Kosugi, famous for his success in a series of ninja martial arts action films, plays a stern father.

Opposite page
Aloha Summer is a coming-of-age picture symbolically set in 1959, the year Hawai'i passed from territorial status to statehood. Cast members of *Aloha Summer* wear aloha shirts and leis and hold samurai swords at the end of the movie, as Jerry (Blaine Kia) goes off to college. From left to right: Yuji Okumoto, Warren Fabro, Blaine Kia, Scott Nagawa, Don Michael Paul, and Chris Makepeace. Oahu "local girl" Tia Carrere was discovered for *Aloha Summer*, and she has gone on to co-star in *Wayne's World* and appear in movies opposite stars like Sean Connery and Arnold Schwarzenegger. Assistant Director Matt Locey, who may be the only Hawaiian belonging to the Directors Guild of America, also got his start with *Aloha Summer*.

Scott Tanaka (Scott Nakagawa, left) teaches his Japanese cousin, Kenzo (Yuji Okumoto), how to surf on the waves of Waikiki.

Tom Hanks, in his best Banana Republic tropical togs, with Meg Ryan in one of her three roles in the comedy *Joe Versus the Volcano*.

JOE VERSUS THE VOLCANO
1990 WB

D: John Patrick Shanley

S: John Patrick Shanley

P: Teri Schwartz

Cast: Tom Hanks, Meg Ryan

This romantic comedy starring Tom Hanks and Meg Ryan was filmed primarily on Hollywood sound stages. Production designer Bo Welch and his artisans created over a dozen sets on a sound stage, including the great volcano that holds the Waponi Woo culture hostage.

The production company traveled to the North Shore of Oahu on July 12, 1989 for eight days of location filming. The spectacular setting for Waponi Woo, the troubled mythical South Seas paradise where Joe comes to grips with life in an awesome way, was located there.

Below

Back-to-back Oscar winner Tom Hanks plays Joe Banks (the same name as the scientist aboard Captain Cook's 1769 Tahiti expedition) opposite Meg Ryan in a triple role in *Joe Versus the Volcano*, which includes every South Seas cinema cliche: bizarre native rituals, canoe flotillas greeting foreigners, human sacrifice, natural disaster, etc. The biggest plot twist is that unlike in movies like *Bird of Paradise*, in *Joe*, a male is sacrificed to the volcano god. (Hawaiian adherents of the fire goddess Pele insist that this was never done to placate Pele.) The contemporary islanders of fictional Waponi Woo are the result of intermarriage between shipwrecked Celts and Jews and isle aborigines. They are merely an exotic backdrop for the white stars: Italian-American actor Abe Vigoda, who was in *The Godfather* and the *Barney Miller* TV series, plays a Polynesian *kahuna* (shaman). Scenes were shot at Oahu's North Shore and along Oahu's southeastern coast—as a California stand-in! Hawai'i's U.S. Congressman Neil Abercrombie's vintage taxi is briefly glimpsed.

HONEYMOON IN VEGAS

1992 COL

D: Andrew Bergman

S: Andrew Bergman

P: Mike Lobell

Cast: James Caan, Nicholas Cage, Sarah Jessica Parker, Pat Morita

Jack (Cage) a goodhearted, but rather rattled and fearful, young man, afraid of marriage (due to a deathbed promise made to his mother), takes his girl Betsy (Parker) to Las Vegas, intending to tie the knot at last. In the lobby, New York gangster Tommy Korman (Caan) spots Betsy and thinks she exactly resembles his late wife. He lures the eager Jack into a poker game, and Jack becomes so far in debt he fears for his life and has to give Betsy to the gangster for the weekend. The gangster flies her to Hawai'i, and Jack finds a way to bring her back via the island of Kauai and Vegas.

Pat Morita plays a Kauai cab driver, and Peter Boyle portrays a strange island character who sings songs from *South Pacific*.

After three and a half weeks in Las Vegas, the crew returned to Los Angeles to film interiors at Culver Studios for several weeks. Then it was off to paradise, the island of Kauai. Although considered the most beautiful of the Hawaiian Islands, it is also the rainiest. Filming took place on both sides of the island in such picturesque locales as the beach at the Princeville Hotel, Bali Hai, the North Shore mountain range, Waimea Canyon, Anini Beach, the lush Allerton Gardens of the National Tropical Botanical Gardens, the

Westin Hotel's Inn on the Cliffs, the Kauai police station and Poipu Beach.

One of the comic high points of the film is a convention of Elvis impersonators in Las Vegas. Hundreds of walking, talking images of the King of Rock and Roll constantly cruise the casino. Jack is forced to return from Hawai'i, after a futile search for Betsy, in a chartered plane full of skydiving Elvis impersonators. The soundtrack featured Elvis Presley hit songs performed by artists such as Billy Joel, Ricky Van Shelton, Travis Tritt, and Willie Nelson singing his rendition of "Blue Hawaii."

UNDER SIEGE
1992 WB

D: **Andrew Davis**

S: **J.F. Lawton**

P: **Arnon Milchan, Steven Seagal, Steven Reuther**

Cast: **Steven Seagal, Tommy Lee Jones, Gary Busey**

Killer-elite commandos hijack the USS *Missouri*'s nuclear armaments on its last voyage, overpowering the crew except for one man, Casey Rysback (Seagal), who wages his own war to regain control of the battleship.

The bulk of the film was shot in Alabama aboard the USS *Alabama*, standing in for the USS *Missouri*. The opening sequences actually took place on the USS *Missouri* at sea in Pearl Harbor, with President George Bush and the sailors on the deck in uniform.

Above

Having lost Sarah Jessica Parker to card sharp James Caan, Nicholas Cage chases the couple to Kauai in *Honeymoon in Vegas*. On Kauai, Cage is led on a wild goose chase by cab driver Pat Morita, as Mahi, who takes Cage to meet a demented Hawaiian chief played by Peter Boyle, who sings songs from *South Pacific*. In this scene, director/screenwriter Andrew Bergman is slyly spoofing Marlon Brando, who owns a Tahitian atoll and starred in *Mutiny on the Bounty*, and whom Bergman had just directed in *The Freshman* (1990).

GOODBYE PARADISE

1992 LATITUDE 20 PICTURES

D:	Dennis Christianson and Tim Savage
S:	Dennis Christianson and Susan Killeen
P:	Dennis Christainson and Tim Savage
Cast:	Joe Moore, Elissa Dulce, Pat Morita, James Hong Danny Kamekona, Megan Ward, Ray Bumatai, Dennis Chun, Richard Vales, Varoa Tiki

In the wake of urban renewal, a venerable nightclub in downtown Honolulu, The Paradise Inn, must close its doors after sixty years. The veteran manager of the club is asked to stay on for the new owners, and so must witness, with growing concern, the passing of the old and the coming of the new.

Goodbye Paradise is the first feature by filmmakers Dennis Christianson, Joe Moore and Tim Savage. It is also the first modern regional film produced in Hawaii. "We knew that we were going to have to make a 'Small' movie, and we believed something distinctive could be accomplished despite our limited resources," remarked Christianson in press notes for the film. "We thought it was worth the risk." They raised the financing for the project themselves, and in April 1991 founded Latitude 20 Pictures to produce *Goodbye Paradise.*

A temporary slowdown in local movie production provided a good opportunity to work with island film professionals who might otherwise be tied up in larger projects. Local companies offered goods and services at tremendous discounts or at no charge whatsover in order to support the film, but this also required mounting the production in a very short period of time.

"The support of our local unions and production community was critical" said co-director/co-producer Tim Savage. "It increased our production value dramatically. What we lacked in money, they helped make up in *Aloha.*"

A cast was selected and established actors Danny Kamekona, James Hong and Oscar-nominated Pat Morita agreed to join the project, working at much lower than their usual fees because they loved the project and the people involved.

Local casting for other roles turned out a well-experienced company, including: lead actor Joe Moore, renowned local news anchor on KHON-TV; Elissa Dulce; Richard Vales; Varoa Tiki; Dennis Chun; Don Nahuku; Ray Bumatai and others.

Hawaii Five-O veterans Kwan Hi Lim and Kam Fong (who was unknowingly cast to play father to his real-life son Dennis Chun) agreed to play key character roles. For most of the actors and crew *Goodbye Paradise* was a chance to finally work on a project that did not resort to island stereotypes and exotic settings.

Diamond Head Theatre, which was between seasons, was selected as a low cost sound stage where a 360-degree bar set was designed. Other locations included a rooftop set built on a parking structure in downtown Chinatown, a back alley set created in the parking lot of the theatre and the exterior of the bar (in fact a sundry store and architect's office in Chinatown). The film was shot in 17 days for a budget of under two million.

Goodbye Paradise made its world premiere screening at the opening of the 1991 Hawaii International Film Festival. It was the winner of the bronze medal at Worldfest Houston, and selected for the 1992 American Independent Showcase at The Cannes Film Festival.

"A sweet slow paced film that shows the inner beauty of a neighborhood. For moviegoers, it is a chance to see a film that portrays the people and city of Honolulu sensitively and realistically." Diane Yen Mei Wong, *The Hawaii Herald,* May 15, 1992.

Above

Actor/anchor Joe Moore plays the club manager faced with saying goodbye to Paradise Inn.

Right

Longtime Hollywood actor James Hong, who has appeared in films such as 1987's *Black Widow*, plays a tempermental cook who brings comic relief to *Goodbye Paradise*.

NORTH

1994 CASTLE ROCK/COL

D:	Rob Reiner
S:	Alan Zweibel and Andrew Scheinman, based on a novel by Zweibel
P:	Rob Reiner and Alan Zweibel
Cast:	Elijah Wood, Bruce Willis, Jon Lovitz

North is an 11-year-old boy who, feeling unappreciated by his mother and father, finds a lawyer, declares himself a free agent and searches the world for the perfect parents. In one section of the film, the young man is wooed by Hawai'i potentates Governor and Mrs. Ho (Keone Young and Lauren Tom).

Hawai'i scenes were filmed on Kauai.

PICTURE BRIDE

1995 MIRAMAX

D:	Kayo Hatta
S:	Kayo Hatta and Mari Hatta
P:	Lisa Onodera and Diane Mei Lin Mark
Cast:	Youki Kudoh, Akira Takayama, Tamlyn Tomita, Cary-Hiroyuki Tagawa, Toshiro Mifune

Inspired by the true stories of Hawai'i's pioneers during the early years of this century, *Picture Bride* is the story of Riyo (Youki Kudoh), a spirited young Japanese woman who ventures to Hawai'i as a "picture bride." In her attempt to leave behind a troubled past in Japan, Riyo exchanges photographs and letters with Matsuji (Akira Takayama), a Japanese sugar cane worker in Hawai'i, and a marriage is arranged. Upon her arrival in Hawai'i, Riyo discovers that her new husband bears little resemblance to the handsome young man in the photo, while her new world is not the paradise she expected—plantation life is grueling and hard.

A friendship with an enigmatic woman she meets in the cane fields however, helps Riyo through her first year of life in plantation Hawai'i, a time of struggle and unexpected joy. *Picture Bride* tells the moving and inspiring story of the pioneers who came to Hawai'i as plantation workers and stayed to create one of the world's most successful multiethnic societies.

Produced by Thousand Crane Filmworks, *Picture Bride* is one of the first modern local Hawai'i theatrical film productions. Hawai'i-born director Kayo Hatta wrote the script with her sister Mari Hatta. They teamed up with Lisa Onodera, a UCLA classmate, and Diane Mei Lin Mark, a Hawai'i-based writer and media specialist, who moved the film forward as producers. Legendary Japanese film star Toshiro Mifune signed on for a cameo role as the *benshi*, or silent movie narrator, through the assistance of Kauai businessman Art Umezu, a friend of the actor.

Picture Bride was filmed primarily on an actual working sugar cane plantation at Waialua on the North Shore of Oahu, as well as on the Hamakua coast of the Big Island. In addition to the cane fields, on-location shooting included the Kanraku Tea House in Kapalama (for the Japan scenes), Honolulu Harbor, and the Diamond Head Film Studio.

The I.A.T.S.E., Screen Actors Guild and Teamsters local unions were all extremely supportive of *Picture Bride*. Long-time Hawai'i residents do

Opposite page

The optically opulent *Picture Bride* is indicative of the future of South Seas cinema. In *Bride*, locals tell their own story. This is a moving slice of life about Hawai'i's Japanese immigrant past in Hawai'i, including plantation workers and their imported wives, told by Americans of Asian ancestry. Hawai'i locals came together to produce this love story about laborers at North Shore sugar cane plantations that are the newcomers' fields of dreams. The movie omitted the labor aspect of the original script (a workers' strike is only alluded to in the final version), instead playing up the love story between a plantation cane cutter and his mail-order newlywed — Youki Kudoh as Riyo, who is seen here in the Waialua sugar cane fields. *Picture Bride* makes one wonder what a full-length feature film about Hawai'i would be like if Native Hawaiians made more

Production "PICTURE BRIDE"
Scene 88A Take 1
Director K. HATTA Roll # A-43
Camera C. ROCHA
Date 7/25/93 ' ; day / EXT

the Arts, American Film Institute, National Asian American Telecommunications Association, Cecile Company, and numerous other organizations.

Picture Bride won the Audience Award for Dramatic Film at the 11th annual Sundance Film Festival in 1995.

Opposite page

Picture Bride may have competed at the box office with violent flicks starring popular action heroes, but the made-in-Hawai'i romance has a cameo by one of the great action heroes: Toshiro Mifune, who played the lead in countless classic Japanese *samurai* sagas, such as Akira Kurosawa's 1961 *Yojimbo* and 1954 *The Seven Samurai*. In *Bride*, Mifune plays a *benshi*, or narrator of silent films. Incidentally, the movie projected on a sheet in the cane fields features *samurai* swordsmen in a sly reference to Mifune's illustrious career, which includes other forays into South Seas cinema, such as the shot-in-Palau WWII drama *Hell in the Pacific* (1968). Mifune is not the only action star to make a cameo in *Bride*: Hawai'i's own Jason Scott Lee, who played Bruce Lee in the early '90s biopic *Dragon, The Bruce Lee Story*, makes an uncredited appearance as field laborer in a brief fight scene.

Above
Scenes that are supposed to be the island of Eros were shot at Oahu's North Shore, near the Turtle Bay Hilton, where Depp walks in above photo for *Don Juan DeMarco.*

DON JUAN DeMARCO

1995 NEW LINE CINEMA

D: Jeremy Leven

S: Jeremy Leven

P: Francis Ford Coppola, Fred Fuchs, Patrick Palmer

Cast: Marlon Brando, Johnny Depp, Faye Dunaway

Marlon Brando returns to the screen for his first lead role in years as a psychiatrist analyzing Johnny Depp, who fantasizes he is Don Juan, the world's greatest lover. It turns out that Depp's romanticism is contagious, and Brando's marriage to Faye Dunaway is reinvigorated by this encounter with the would-be Don Juan. Scenes that are supposed to be the island of Eros were shot at Oahu's North Shore, near the Turtle Bay Hilton. *Don Juan DeMarco* is at least Brando's third picture with one scene or more set in the Pacific Islands. The first, of course, is *Mutiny on the Bounty*. The second is *A Countess from Hong Kong*, which co-stars Brando as a diplomat and Sohia Loren as a stowaway in a Charlie Chaplin-directed film. In a scene set in Honolulu, Hawaiians dive for coins tossed into the harbor by tourists aboard an ocean liner. The same activity, by the way, was depicted in the first motion picture made in Hawai'i, Thomas Edison's *Kanakas Diving for Money*, and seen as recently as 1988 in *Aloha Summer*.

Mel Gibson plays screendom's fifth incarnation of
the born-again Christian. Here, Gibson as Fletcher
Christian stages a mutiny in *The Bounty*.

Photo courtesy of the Ed Rampell Collection.

CHAPTER FOUR

Films About the South Sea Isles Made in the South Seas

South Seas cinema had two sets of roots. From the outset there were the early ethnologists who, although lacking film training, were devoted to documenting the disappearing cultures of the Pacific Islanders. They generally made crude, low-budget, anthro-home movies. There were the New Zealand 1919-1923 McDonald films with indigenous advisers that recorded Maoridom, and Hawai'i's Bishop Museum's Dr. Kenneth Emory's documentary *Kapingamarangi*, about a Polynesian islet in Micronesia in 1947. In these amateur productions the subjects were sometimes framed with their heads cut off or out of focus. Nevertheless, the scholarly value of these visual records of aboriginal peoples in their homelands is immeasurable.

The early professionals, mainly Hollywood filmmakers, produced features with production values, scripts, actors, financing, etc. Most of these theatrical releases were made primarily outside of Oceania in studios and back lots, although second unit and stock footage from the islands were sometimes added. These features were intended as mass entertainment.

In both cases—anthro-chronicles or Hollywood flicks—the directors were not from the South Seas. Whether it was nonartist field workers such as Margaret Mead and Thor Heyerdahl, or Hollywood artists like D.W. Griffith and King Vidor—and even documentarian Robert Flaherty, the key creative people behind the cameras were Westerners.

While this book focuses on the Hollywood-made movies, South Seas cinema involves other countries and non-Westerners working outside of the Hollywood system, particularly in the last two decades.

In the 1970s indigenous islanders began to make films and/or have major creative input into features. Earlier, in 1950, Samoan screenwriter Johnny Kneubuhl directed *Damien,* a Hawai'i-produced feature about the priest who battled Hansen's disease (once known as leprosy) on Molokai, but this was an isolated effort. As Oceania matured economically, indigenous South Seas cinema began to emerge as part of a cultural renaissance.

The revival of island culture known as the "Pacific Renaissance" has spread to film and video. Instead of Western ethnologists aiming the cameras at exotic islanders, indigenous people are now taking cameras into their own hands and finding their own voices and images. In an even more artistically bold move, Pacific Islanders are writing and directing dramatic features, and an indigenous island aesthetic is being born. Production values, cinematic artistry, and technology are finally uniting with on-island location shooting of real Pacific people.

New Zealand, a major regional power, has taken the lead in the flowering of Pacifica film culture. In 1974, Maori Barry Barclay directed documentaries about Maori traditions. In 1987, Barclay's *Ngati (Tribe)* became the second full-length feature directed by a Polynesian. Maori Tama Poata wrote the screenplay about natives in a remote New Zealand village who take over a factory abandoned by white owners. In Barclay's 1990 feature *Te Rua*, Maoris try to steal sacred ancient artifacts from a Berlin museum to return them to Aotearoa/New Zealand.

Two New Zealand productions have been based on Samoan novelist Albert Wendt's books. In 1979, Kiwi Paul Maunder directed and wrote the script for *Sons for the Return Home*. Shot in Western Samoa and New Zealand, *Sons* is about a Samoan immigrant who experiences racism, interracial love, the struggle for identity, etc. Martyn Sanderson's 1989 version of Wendt's *Flying Fox in a Freedom Tree* is an existential exploration of culture clash, atheism, rebellion, and more in Samoa, and is one of this genre's best.

Maori director Merata Mita's 1980 *Bastion Point* documents a native land struggle in Auckland. Mita's 1983 *Patu!* is a riveting documentary about the controversial tour of a South African rugby team in New Zealand. Mita became the first Pacific woman to direct a feature. In 1989's *Mauri (Life Force)*, real life ex-con Anzac Wallace plays an ex-con who goes home. Also a talented actress, Mita co-starred with Wallace and Wi Kuki Kaa in one of this genre's most critically acclaimed films, 1983's *Utu*, which is a John Ford-style western in which the cowboys and Indians are replaced by *pakehas* ("whites") and Maoris.

Mike Walker's 1985 *Kingpin* deals with a New

Photo courtesy of the Ed Rampell Collection.

Zealand reform school. The screenplay was written by Mitchell Manuel, a Maori former inmate, who also plays a lead role. In the late 1980s, a series of five Maori dramas called *E Tipu E Rea* was broadcast by Television New Zealand.

Maori movies reached an apotheosis with 1994's smash international hit *Once Were Warriors*, acted, scripted, and directed by Maoris from Maori Alan Duff's novel. Director Lee Tamahori's gritty feature is an unflinching look at gangs and child/substance/wife abuse among Maoris. Combined with 1993's Academy Award winning *The Piano*, directed by Caucasian New Zealander Jane Campion, New Zealand is emerging on the world stage as a player in global cinema.

Other Pacific Islands are getting into the act, as well. In 1990, Pengau Nengo became the first Papua New Guinean director of a 35mm feature with his comedy *Tin Pis Run*, a Melanesian road picture set in Papau New Guinea's highlands.

While Native Hawaiians have not yet created a feature, there is a thriving video documentary scene in Hawai'i, epitomized by Na Maka O Ka Aina ("The Eyes of the Land"), which specializes in militantly pro-indigenous political statements. Their high-quality 1990s documentaries include *Act of War*, about the 1893 overthrow of Queen Liliuokalani, and *The Tribunal*, which documents a people's trial of America for U.S. involvement in that 1893 coup. Hawaiian musician Eddie Kamae turned to the documentary as a means of preserving the Polynesian way in his 1988 *Li'a—The Legacy of a Hawaiian Man,* about a composer.

Hawai'i contributes to the genre in other ways, as well. The Hawai'i International Film Festival is the main U.S. showcase of Oceanic pictures. Honolulu-based Pacific Islanders in Communications is a minority consortium funded by the Corporation for Public Broadcasting for the purpose of increasing public programming by and about Pacific Islanders.

South Seas cinema has come full circle. No longer are islanders the passive subjects or nonsubjects of ethnologists and Hollywood dream merchants. Today, Polynesians, Melanesians, and Micronesians are active participants in the creation of their own screen identities.

MOANA OF THE SOUTH SEAS

1926 PAR

D: Robert J. Flaherty

S: Robert J. Flaherty

P: Robert J. Flaherty

Cast: Ta'avale, Fa'Angase, Tu'ungaita

Below

Anthropology meets Hollywood: Samoans hold a crab in Robert Flaherty's classic *Moana of the South Seas*, about the daily life of Polynesian villagers in Savaii, Western Samoa.

An ethnographic documentary about Samoan life and customs framed by the story of a boy's ritual initiation into manhood.

When making *Moana,* documentarian Robert J. Flaherty lived for two years among the South Sea islanders, which he described as the greatest experience of his career. He and his family settled on the Samoan island of Savaii, where he had found a large cave with a spring of cold water in which he could develop his negatives.

On Savaii, Flaherty looked for the elements of conflict and struggle which his previous film *Nanook of the North* had taught him were essential to the dramatization of real life. This search was long and fruitless, for Savaii afforded no filmable fight for food and shelter. The Flahertys decided that their picture must record "Fa'a Samoa," the complex weave of custom, ceremony, and tabu which formed the social texture of Samoan life. In thus adhering to the truth of the locale, Flaherty presented a dramatic story of how the Samoans, free from the painful struggle with nature, inflicted pain to demonstrate their manhood. The climax of *Moana* is the application of the traditional knee-to-navel tattoo, a rite of passage from boyhood to adulthood.

THE PAGAN

1929 MGM

D: W.S. Van Dyke

S: Adapted from the short story by John Russell

P: Metro-Goldwyn-Mayer

Cast: Ramon Novarro, Dorothy Janis, Renee Adoree, Donald Crisp

This story of a South Sea half-caste and the hypocritical cruelty of a white trader contains an effective tropic love element, smashing photography and a fine production. The influence of civilization is shown to corrupt the idealistic life of the simple native.

No dialogue is used in the film, only song and sound sequences, and the title method of exposition. *The Pagan* was filmed in Tahiti and on Bora Bora over a two-month period in 1928.

WHITE SHADOWS IN THE SOUTH SEAS

1928 MGM

D: W.S. Van Dyke, Robert Flaherty

S: Jack Cunningham, Ray Doyle, based on the book by
        Frederick O'Brien

P: Irving Thalberg

Cast: Monte Blue, Robert Anderson, Raquel Torres

The legendary Irving Thalberg is supposed to have been so moved by Frederick O'Brien's account of the exploitation of the Polynesians by white traders, and so taken by the title, that he persuaded director Robert Flaherty to go to Tahiti to film the story. As a precaution, however, he also sent Van Dyke, an MGM staff director. When Flaherty quit in the inevitable quarrel over the story and artistic control, Van Dyke took over and finished the film. Photographed by Clyde de Vinna, some of the sequences retain the Flaherty influence, including stunning location photography in the Marquesas Islands complementing a genuinely effective melodrama.

Monte Blue gives a tremendous performance as a drunken doctor who finds happiness with a native woman, then meets his demise when he refuses to stoop to the level of the genocidal colonizers.

White Shadows in the South Seas was shot entirely silent, but that did not deter Douglas Shearer, a pioneer in post-production sound editing. Working in a New Jersey sound studio, Shearer synchronized sound effects, such as a father mourning his son, pounding drums, crashing surf, some dialogue and a musical score adapted from a half dozen composers to create MGM's first sound feature. The film won an Academy Award for Best Cinematography (Clyde de Vinna, George Nogle and Bob Roberts).

Left
In *White Shadows in the South Seas*, Raquel Torres is another Latino actress portraying a Polynesian. Robert Flaherty, who had an ethno-documentary-style approach to cinema, left the project over clashes with the Hollywood studio system.

Above
Raquel Torres and indigenous cast on location in French Polynesia in *White Shadows in the South Seas*. Black and white location shooting in the spectacular Marquesas Islands—still among Polynesia's most unspoiled isles—helped win the filmmakers the Best Cinematography Oscar. The film is based on Frederick O'Brien's book of the same title, which is a travelogue of the author's life and adventures in the Marquesas. However, while the "White Shadows" in the movie refer to the encroachments of Western civilization—in the form of white traders, etc., on the islanders—in the book, the title refers to something else. O'Brien believes that Polynesians have Caucasian origins and are, hence, *White Shadows in the South Seas*.

TABU
1931 PAR

D:	**F.W. Murnau and Robert Flaherty**
S:	**Friedrich Murnau and Robert Flaherty**
P:	**F.W. Murnau and Robert Flaherty**
Cast:	**Matahi, Reri, Jean, Hitu**

Tabu is the story of a Tahitian fisherman's love for a young woman whose body had been consecrated to the gods, rendering her tabu for mortal men.

Like Chaplin's *City Lights, Tabu* was planned and made as a silent film. It was also released well after sound film had arrived and silents with musical scores had become commercially obsolete. *Tabu,* often referred to as a Flaherty-Murnau production, was indeed planned as a collaboration between Robert Flaherty, the American documentarian, and Murnau, the great German master of fantasy and poetic drama. Not unnaturally, the two personalities clashed; one a realist, the other a romanticist, their approaches to film were automatically at variance. According to cameraman Floyd Crosby in an oral history, Flaherty withdrew before the film was properly underway, and what emerged was wholly Murnau's in conception and execution. Flaherty worked on the story, the opening sequences of frolicking natives, and in supervising the lab work. The precise detailed direction elsewhere was Murnau's.

Murnau's ability in editing, and the lyricism and simplicity of the tone he achieved, is what made *Tabu* a masterpiece.

A similar conflict had occurred with an earlier film, *White Shadows in the South Seas,* with Flaherty withdrawing and the film becoming the work of W.S. Van Dyke.

Tabu is an American film in that it was financed, and released, by Paramount, which had been pleasantly surprised by the box-office and critical response to Flaherty's earlier *Moana.* In the end, Flaherty sold his interest in the film to Murnau, relinquishing any control over the production.

Photo courtesy of the DeSoto Brown Collection.

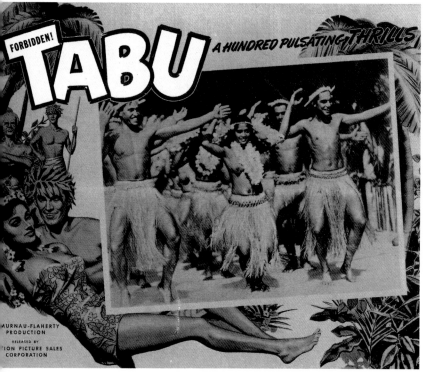

Tabu began production in Tahiti in 1930. Murnau was assisted by that fine American cameraman Floyd Crosby, whose lyricism was later somewhat wasted in American International's beach party and surfing pictures of the mid-1950s and early 1960s. Crosby, who, incidentally, is the father of singer David Crosby of the famous Crosby, Stills and Nash band, won an Academy Award for his stunning cinematography on *Tabu*.

Although the film was favored by the critics, *Tabu* was not a great box-office success, being too downbeat for the Depression years.

Above

Tabu is notable for its many ethnographic sequences, such as spearfishing, that show the daily life of Tahitians.

MR. ROBINSON CRUSOE
1932 U

D: Edward Sutherland

S: Story by Elton Thomas, adaptation by Tom Geraghty

P: Douglas Fairbanks

Cast: Douglas Fairbanks, William Farnum, Maria Alba

In order to win a bet, a man comes to survive alone on an island without tools or weapons. "Friday" in this version becomes a native girl whom Fairbanks rescues and brings back to civilization, where he puts her to work as a *hula* dancer.

Mr. Robinson Crusoe was filmed in Tahiti during a yacht cruise by Fairbanks and his crew, who lived aboard the yacht while location filming in the South Pacific.

THE HURRICANE
1937 GOLDWYN

D: John Ford

S: Dudley Nichols and Oliver H.P. Garrett, from the novel by Charles Nordhoff and James Norman Hall

P: Samuel Goldwyn

Cast: Dorothy Lamour, Jon Hall, Raymond Massey, Mary Astor, Thomas Mitchell, John Carradine

Two native lovers, Marama (Lamour) and Terangi (Hall), try to live in peace on the island of Manakoora despite relentless persecution by its stern colonial governor (Massey). A devastating storm hits the island, and the lovers paddle off to a new life.

Airplane propellers were used to create wind; crushed leaves and sulfur were mixed to simulate smoke; and sand and four 1,500-gallon tanks of water were employed to create the twenty-minute hurricane sequence. The stunning special effects were created by James Basevi, who also simulated the earthquake in *San Francisco* (1936) and the plague of locusts in *The Good Earth* (1937).

The Hurricane, directed by John Ford *(The Informer, Stagecoach, The Grapes of Wrath, The Searchers)*, established Lamour, who had made her feature debut the year before in *The Jungle Princess.* Thanks to the film's costumer, Omar Kiam, Lamour and the sarong would be forever linked, a pairing that would be as frustrating for her as it was exploitable for the studio. She always had to struggle to get dramatic acting roles outside of the jungle genre.

The entire film was made on the Goldwyn back lot and studio in Hollywood, where an entire village was built. Fresh flowers were flown in from Hawai'i. Only the second unit traveled to Samoa to photograph backgrounds and establishing shots.

Left
The island village for the fictitious isle of Manakoora in *The Hurricane* at the Samuel Goldwyn Studios was one of Hollywood's most elaborate sets during this era. The entire set was literally struck, when the Oscar-winning special effects cyclone demolished it during the making of this A picture, directed by cinema giant John Ford.

THE BLUE LAGOON
1949 U

D: Frank Launder

S: Frank Launder, John Baines and Michael Hogan

P: Frank Launder and Sydney Gilliat

Cast: Jean Simmons, Donald Houston, Noel Purcell

The story of two youthful shipwrecked castaways on a tropical island who come to young manhood and womanhood without the benefit of social rules or adult guidance. The story is based on a novel first published in 1903. *The Blue Lagoon* introduced to American audiences talented young English actress Jean Simmons, who had been seen as Ophelia in Laurence Olivier's *Hamlet.* Simmons went on to become one of the major leading actresses of the 1950s in such films as *The Robe, The Big Country, Spartacus* and *Desiree.* Donald Houston, a Welsh actor who had appeared in repertory theatre, made his debut in this film and later became an important British supporting player.

The Blue Lagoon, with a crew of 35 people, was filmed in Technicolor on a small Fijian island.

Left

Young love in paradise: Donald Houston and Jean Simmons marooned with little else to do than make love in *The Blue Lagoon,* the first of three versions shot on location in Fiji.

AMERICAN GUERRILLA IN THE PHILIPPINES

1951 TCF

D: Fritz Lang

S: Lamar Trotti, based on the novel by Ira Wolfert

P: Lamar Trotti

Cast: Tyrone Power, Tom Ewell

Story of the role played by American and Filipino guerrilla fighters in helping pave the way for General Douglas MacArthur's eventual return during World War II.

Filmed on location in the Philippines on the island of Luzon and at Subic Bay. During the war actor Tyrone Power was a Marine transport pilot in the South Pacific.

Left

Tyrone Power rides a caribou in the jungle in the WWII pic *American Guerrilla in the Philippines*. Water buffalo are still mass transit in the countryside of this Southeast Asian archipelago.

RETURN TO PARADISE

1953 UA

D: Mark Robson

S: Charles Kaufman, based on the book by James A.
       Michener

P: Theron Warth

Cast: Gary Cooper, Barry Jones, Roberta Haynes, John
       Hudson, Moira Walker

American wanderer Mr. Morgan (Cooper) arrives in 1929 on a Polynesian island which is ruled by ruthless Pastor Corbeth, with whom he clashes. Morgan falls in love with an island girl and returns years later to rescue the daughter he fathered.

Return to Paradise was filmed in Samoa.

Right

Return to Paradise is the first feature based on James Michener's fiction. Here, Gary Cooper plays the world-weary Mr. Morgan, who is forced, once again, to fight; this time, against overly repressive missionary goons on a South Sea isle. The movie was shot on location in Upolu, Western Samoa, in the beachside village of Lefaga. The villagers there capitalized on the film's fame, charging a small fee to swim at the "*Return to Paradise* Beach" Ironically, signs have been posted by the missionized villagers warning women not to wear bikinis. The American cast stayed at the famous Aggie Grey Hotel, where, to this day, there is a sign on one of the units that says: "Gary Cooper's Fale" ("hut"). One of *Return to Paradise's* Samoan co-stars, Felise Vaa, played Coop's sidekick Rori when he was about eight. Vaa's family used the money to send him to New Zealand to further his education, and Vaa eventually became the editor of *The Samoa Times* newspaper, a university professor, and a scholar. The Samoan actress Moira Walker went on to co-star in the film *Sons for the Return Home* (1979), based on the novel by Samoan author Albert Wendt.

HIS MAJESTY O'KEEFE
1954 WB

D: Byron Haskin

S: Borden Chase and James Hill, suggested by a novel by Lawrence Klingman and Gerald Green

P: Harold Hecht

Cast: Burt Lancaster, Joan Rice, Tessa Prendergast, Abraham Safaer, Archie Savage, Benson Fong, Phillip Ahn

The South Seas of the 1870s serve as the background for *His Majesty O'Keefe,* a Technicolor swashbuckler made to order for the barechested heroics of Burt Lancaster. Photographed entirely on the Fijian island of Viti Levu, the film is an eye-filling mixture of Hollywood moviemaking and authentic native scenery.

The story involves a sea captain, set adrift by a mutinous crew, who lands on a lush coconut palm-studded island. He immediately begins pondering how he can cash in on the immense copra stockpile, and he eventually engages the natives and sea traders in a strange and fierce battle over copra and Yapese stone money.

An entire motion picture production plant was set up by Warner Bros. in Fiji, nearly 6,000 miles from Hollywood. The Beachcomber Hotel, at Deuba Beach, 120 miles from the Nandi airport and 40 miles from Suva, capital city of Fiji, was taken over by the company and remodeled and enlarged to house approximately 150 people.

The entire village of Goloa, five miles west of the hotel, was rented by the studio, and twelve thatched-roof huts were erected for movie scenes. The film was made with funds frozen in Britain, which explains why it was made in Fiji, then a British colony. The studio augmented the cast with Joan Rice, a British actress; Abraham Safaer, a Burmese-born actor; Andre Morell of the British stage; Alexander Archdale, an Australian; Tess Prendergast, of Jamaica; Lloyd Berell of New Zealand; and hundreds of Fijian, Chinese and East Indian atmosphere players.

Opposite page
Burt Lancaster and a beautiful, grass-skirted Melanesian in the exciting swashbuckler *His Majesty O'Keefe.*

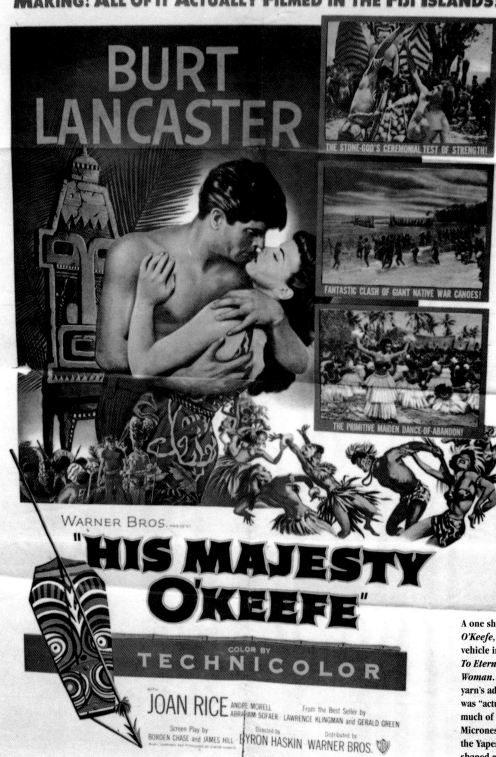

A one sheet poster for *His Majesty O'Keefe,* the third Burt Lancaster Pacific vehicle in two years, including *From Here To Eternity* (1953) and *South Sea Woman.* While this rollicking adventure yarn's advertising proudly boasts that it was "actually filmed in the Fiji Islands!", much of the story is set on the Micronesian isle of Yap and deals with the Yapese stone money—large, donut-shaped rocks that are, literally, a form of Pacific hard currency. *His Majesty O'Keefe* is loosely based on real events and characters, such as infamous buccaneer Bully Hayes and his piracy on the high seas as well as O'Keefe himself.

CINERAMA SOUTH SEAS ADVENTURE

1958

D:	Francis D. Lyon, Walter Thompson, Basil Waangell, Richard Goldstone, Carl Dudley
S:	Charles Kaufmann, Joseph Ansen, Harold Medford
P:	Carl Dudley
Cast:	Narrator Orson Welles

This documentary and travelogue, designed to showcase the Cinerama widescreen film process, focused on a South Seas adventure involving Tahiti, Tonga, Hawai'i, Fiji and New Zealand.

The filmmakers roamed the beach at Waikiki; showcased Leilani, a featured entertainer at Don the Beachcomber's; the catamarans of Honolulu, and many other sites.

Right

A Cinerama camera crew photographs Ramine of Bora Bora in this scene from *Cinerama South Seas Adventure.*

MUTINY ON THE BOUNTY

1962 MGM

D: **Carol Reed and Lewis Milestone**

S: **Charles Lederer**

P: **Aaron Rosenberg**

Cast: **Marlon Brando, Trevor Howard, Richard Harris, Tarita**

Marlon Brando decided that he would play Fletcher Christian as an English fop, and Trevor Howard played Captain Bligh as a man whose cruel and sadistic acts were those of a quiet, understandable and reasonable man.

Filmed In Ultra Panavision 70 millimeter and Technicolor by three-time Academy Award-winning cinematographer Robert Surtees, *Mutiny on the*

Bounty is filled with breathtakingly beautiful seascapes and landscapes. One such memorable scene features the *Bounty* dwarfed in the vast emerald curve of a Tahitian bay as natives by the thousands paddle their outrigger canoes across sparkling aquamarine waters. For this scene, 5,000 native extras were hired.

Filming took place almost entirely in and around Tahiti and the neighboring islands of Moorea and Bora Bora, near the actual locales where the romantic adventure took place. Tons of equipment and some 125 men and women were transported to this remote area of the South Pacific, and a small army of crew members were maintained there for almost a year.

For months during and after filming, magazines and newspapers had devoted many pages to the theme that, with the arrival of the jet (as many as eight a week began landing at the lone airport after the film was completed), Tahiti would never be the same again. The worldwide publicity blitz caused by the film did, in fact, make Tahiti a favored tourist destination.

The film unit spent more than $2 million on the islanders, 7,000 of whom were employed in the film's production. All the islanders had, in one way or another, been made immediately aware of the film's local and global impact.

To help ensure authenticity of the scenes to be filmed in the islands, Aurora Natua, anthropologist Bengt Danielsson and Leo Langomazino, recognized experts on the subject of customs and cultures of the Polynesian islands, were engaged to assist in the production. At the same time, Captain Donald MacIntyre, who had retired from the British navy after 33 years as a naval aviator and destroyer commander, was brought from England to serve as advisor on the nautical sequences.

Marlon Brando, acknowledged by many to be the finest actor of his generation, was cast as Fletcher Christian. Trevor Howard, the distin-

Below

White men can't *hula*: Tahitians' "revenge" on *popa'a* ("whites") is to force them to dance the *tamure* at public dances. Trevor Howard as Captain Bligh in *Mutiny on the Bounty* wasn't the last rhythmless Caucasian "tourist" to make a public spectacle of himself by trying to get down and boogie Polynesian-style, much to the amusement of the indigenous audience.

guished British actor, made his Hollywood debut in this film, though he is best remembered for his work in British films of the 1940s and 1950s, including Noel Coward's *Brief Encounter,* and for his Oscar-nominated performance in *Sons and Lovers.*

The producers felt from the start that a pure Polynesian should be selected to portray Maimiti, the young native girl who wins the heart of Fletcher Christian and accompanies him to Pitcairn Island. After an exhaustive search that covered several South Pacific islands and interviews with more than 200 girls, Tarita, a dark-haired 19-year-old dancer from the island of Bora Bora was chosen. Matahiarii Tami plays Chief Hitihiti, who thirty years before had played a leading role in *Tabu,* the classic Robert Flaherty film about Polynesian life.

Veteran character actor Frank Silvera played Minarii. To fill the other colorful character roles, a cast of expert performers were literally gathered from the far corners of the world. Richard Harris, then a young Irish actor, was chosen to portray John Mills, one of the mutineers who eventually opposes Christian.

Brando had a celebrated romance with Tarita and fathered two children by her. Eventually he moved to Tahiti and purchased his own private little island nearby.

TIKO AND THE SHARK

1963 MGM

D: **Folco Quilici**

S: **Ottavio Alessi, A. Frassinet and Folco Quilici, from the novel *Ti-Koio and His Shark* by Clement Richer**

P: **Goffredo Lombrado**

Cast: **Al Kauwe, Marlene Among**

This Italian international production was picked up for release by MGM. Filmed in color in French Polynesia with a Hawai'i cast, the story revolves around a young Polynesian boy, Tiko, and recounts his adventures and romances as he grows up. He raises and trains a baby shark as a pet, which he shares with his island playmate Diana. After a decade, the three are reunited, but the world has changed: Tiko and Diana have become adults; the shark, a dangerous man-eater; and the inroads of civilization have left their mark on the beautiful tropical island.

Right
Al Kauwe and Marlene Among in *Tiko and the Shark*.

HELL IN THE PACIFIC

1968 CINERAMA RELEASING

D:	John Boorman
S:	Alexander Jacobs and Eric Bercovici
P:	Reuben Bercovitch
Cast:	Lee Marvin, Toshiro Mifune

Jungle sounds, tropical downpours and pounding surf add to a credible and sharply etched portrait of men who move from animal behavior to human interdependency. A World War II Marine Corps fighter pilot, forced to ditch his plane at sea, reaches safety, then finds that the only other inhabitant is a castaway Japanese naval officer.

Hell in the Pacific was shot entirely in the Palau Islands in the Western Pacific in the Western Carolines of Micronesia.

Right

Lee Marvin and Toshiro Mifune in the anti-war World War II drama *Hell in the Pacific,* shot on location on a Rock Island (now known as "Lee Marvin's Island") in Palau, Micronesia, where major World War II battles took place in 1944.

TOO LATE THE HERO

1970 CINERAMA RELEASING

D: Robert Aldrich

S: Robert Aldrich and Lukas Heller

P: Robert Aldrich

Cast: Michael Caine, Cliff Robertson, Henry Fonda, Ian Bannen

A British army patrol and a lone American naval officer set out on a mission against a Japanese base on a South Sea island, a year after Pearl Harbor.

Filmed in the Philippines and at the Los Angeles County Arboretum.

HURRICANE

1979 PAR

D: Jan Troell

S: Lorenzo Semple Jr.

P: Dino De Laurentiis

Cast: Mia Farrow, Dayton Ka'Ne, Jason Robards, Max Von Sydow, Trevor Howard, Timothy Bottoms

In Samoa in the 1920s the young daughter of the governor of Pago Pago comes to the South Pacific to visit her father and paint, but ends up passionately in love with a young native chieftain.

This $20 million pallid remake of the original classic was filmed on location in Tahiti and Bora Bora. Five spectacular sets, with practical exteriors and interiors were built at a cost of $7.5 million. They included the town of Pago Pago, built on 40 acres; a governor's mansion; a unique French chateau; a Samoan village constructed on a 21-acre *motu* (a sand-covered coral

Above

Michael Caine and Cliff Robertson as Allied servicemen in the WWII action film *Too Late the Hero*.

reef); a cathedral with a moat so water could rise on cue and a 160-foot special effects tank used for most of the hurricane sequences in which actors were involved. Glen Robinson, then a 64-year-old veteran who worked on the special effects in the original film for John Ford, headed the special effects team for this version.

De Laurentiis constructed the Hotel Marara, which housed the 150-member cast and crew that worked on the film in Bora Bora. He shipped equipment to Bora Bora from all over the world on a freighter he purchased for that purpose.

Coming to Tahiti, French Polynesia, to film *Hurricane* was nothing unusual for British actor Trevor Howard, who had traveled all over the world to work as an actor, but who had been in Tahiti 16 years previously for his starring role as Captain Bligh in *Mutiny on the Bounty* opposite Marlon Brando. Hawai'i-born athlete and surfer Dayton Ka'Ne, with no previous acting experience, made his film debut in this movie. More than 35 French Polynesians who spoke English were given roles in the film.

This 1979 version of *The Hurricane* doesn't measure up to the 1937 classic; Samoans marched in the streets of Honolulu to protest the Dino De Laurentiis production's lack of cultural sensitivity. One big switch from the original movie is that the main love interest of the male lead (Hawaiian actor Dayton Ka'Ne, from Waimanalo, Oahu) is a white female (Mia Farrow in pre-Woody days). Ka'Ne's character actually dumps his nubile native lover for a woman about 15 years his senior (but, she has blonde hair and blue eyes). Farrow, however, is not a total stranger to the jungle genre—her mother, Maureen O'Sullivan, played Jane in the Johnny Weissmuller *Tarzan* series.

Prior to the De Laurentiis Hollywood invasion of the island, there was a previous one by American soldiers in 1942. When America entered World War II, U.S. troops established a reserve center, supply base and airstrip on the island to protect their means of communication with Australia and New Zealand, two strongholds of defense in the South Pacific.

THE BLUE LAGOON
1980 COL

D: Randal Kleiser

S: Douglas Day Stewart

P: Randal Kleiser and Richard Franklin

Cast: Brooke Shields, Christopher Atkins, Leo McKern

Latchkey kids in paradise—the insouciant innocence of Brooke Shields and Christopher Atkins discovering young love as castaways on a guiltless and parent-less isle in *The Blue Lagoon.*

What would it be like to come of age in an isolated corner of the South Pacific, struggling through the mysterious changes of puberty without the benefit or confusion of adult guidance?

That is the exciting premise with which Henry DeVere Stacpoole wrote his famous novel *The Blue Lagoon* in 1903. Two children are shipwrecked on a Garden of Eden-like island with one salty sailor who dies soon after, leaving them to find their way through the maze of physical and emotional reactions to their coming of age.

The Blue Lagoon, producer-director Randal Kleiser's second feature film, stars Brooke Shields as Emmeline and newcomer Christopher Atkins as Richard, two teenagers discovering themselves and the splendor of natural love.

The film was shot entirely on location in the Fiji Islands. The book had been made into a 1949 film, with Jean Simmons making her debut and Donald Houston playing her romantic interest, but Kleiser felt that a more successful version could be made that did not depart so dramatically from the novel and that reflected Stacpoole's intentions more clearly.

"Today, you can make a film that is much closer to what the novel was trying to say than you could in 1949, which is why they added the sub-plot of two men coming to the island and forcing the boy to dive at gun point for pearls," he remarked in the film's press notes. "It was something they had to invent to fill out time, because they couldn't really get into what really goes on when two people grow up with no supervision and no knowledge of what adolescence is about and what changes their bodies are going through."

Academy Award-winning cinematographer (*Days of Heaven*) Nestor Almendros captured the majestic lushness of Fiji, using a mostly Australian crew and shooting the film with available light. The cast and crew lived on a boat and in huts on the beach.

Below
The prisoner of war World
War II drama *Merry
Christmas, Mr. Lawrence*
was filmed in the interior
of Rarotonga, in the Cook
Islands, doubling for
Southeast Asia.

MERRY CHRISTMAS, MR. LAWRENCE

1980 U

D: Nagisa Oshima

S: Nagisa Oshima and Paula Mayersberg, based on the
        novel *The Seed and the Sower* by Sir Laurens Van
        Der Post

P: Jeremy Thomas

Cast: Tom Conti, David Bowie, Ryuichi Sakamoto

The story of a 1942 Japanese POW camp on a tiny island in Java, where culture and attitudes clash between the British prisoners of war and their captors.

For a two-month period in 1982, the cast and crew took over one of the Cook Islands, Rarotonga, where all the sets were built. The ensemble was comprised of a mix of Japanese and British filmmakers, actors, and crew.

1980 U

D: Frank C. Clark

S: Jim Carabatsos, based on the novel *Ti-Koio and His Shark* by Clement Richer

P: Raffaella De Laurentiis

Cast: Dayton Ka'Ne, Maren Jensen, Keahi Farden, Kathleen Swan, Jason Robards

The story of a boy who speaks to the great and noble spirit that lives inside a fifteen-foot tiger shark, which becomes his protector, and the native girl who is his childhood love. After ten years in America, the boy returns to find the lure and lore of the islands overpowering her.

Beyond the Reef was filmed at the same time as *Hurricane*, employing the extra crew members and star Ka'Ne on the days he was not working on the other film.

This is at least the fifth film version of the HMS *Bounty* saga, first lensed as a 1916 silent film. Mel Gibson plays the born-again Mr. Christian in *The Bounty* (1984). Errol Flynn (in his first starring role in a 1932 Australian production and who was actually descended from one of the mutineers), Clark Gable, and Marlon Brando have all depicted mutineer Fletcher Christian. Mel Gibson co-starred in good company in *The Bounty,* with Laurence Olivier as a member of the British Admiralty, Anthony Hopkins reprising the Captain Bligh role that Charles Laughton and Trevor Howard previously played, Daniel Day-Lewis as a mutineer, former nightclub impresario and tattoo artist Tavana as a Polynesian prime minister, and the charming Tahitian actress Tevaite Vernette as Gibson's indigenous love interest.

THE BOUNTY

1984 OR

D: **Roger Donaldson**

S: **Robert Bolt, based on the book *Captain Bligh and Mr. Christian* by Richard Hough**

P: **Bernard Williams**

Cast: **Mel Gibson, Anthony Hopkins, Edward Fox, Laurence Olivier, Daniel Day-Lewis**

Based on one of the most famous epic sea dramas of all time, *The Bounty* tells of the famed 18th-century voyage from England to the South Seas. Included is a dramatic, unpremeditated mutiny and the romance of the ship's first officer (and mutiny leader) with a beautiful Tahitian princess. *The Bounty* also relates the story of a close friendship between its two leading characters, Captain Bligh (Hopkins) and Fletcher Christian (Gibson) and how it altered dramatically after a four-month stay on the island paradise of Tahiti.

Photo courtesy of the Ed Rampell Collection.

Left

British actor Anthony Hopkins reprises the Captain Bligh role, formerly played with great elan by Charles Laughton and Trevor Howard, in 1984's *The Bounty*.

Bye bye Bligh: Mutineer Fletcher Christian (Mel Gibson) seizes the *Bounty* and Captain Bligh (Anthony Hopkins) is arrested. Note: Liam Neeson is a mutineer who restrains Bligh. Years later Neeson won acclaim for his portrayal of Oskar Schindler in the 1993 Steven Spielberg masterpiece *Schindler's List*. A decade after *Bounty*, both Neeson and Gibson went on to play Scottish nationalist heroes in the epic adventures *Rob Roy* and *Braveheart*.

The film was lensed in England, Tahiti and New Zealand.

From England, the cast and crew moved to Tahiti, where eight weeks were spent filming on location on Moorea, Tahiti's sister island, which is still filled with natural unspoiled beauty. The first landing and subsequent scenes of *The Bounty* were staged at picturesque Opunohu Bay, which doubled for Tahiti's Matavi Bay. This bay had also been used for previous *Bounty* films, and one elderly Tahitian woman extra had also appeared in the Charles Laughton and Clark Gable 1935 film version.

Many hundreds of native Tahitians were hired as workers and extras. A huge fleet of outrigger canoes and larger craft was built for use in the picture, and a construction crew spent four months building three native villages and the huge Coupang set.

The buildings and wharf of this coastal town in the Dutch East Indies colony of Timor were completely built to historical detail, and countless props, horses and car-

Right

From Mad Max to mutineer: Mel Gibson reprises the Mr. Christian role previously played by Errol Flynn, Clark Gable, and Marlon Brando. His depiction is a cross between Gable's he-man and Brando's foppish dandy torn by conscience.

Photo courtesy of the Ed Rampell Collection.

riages and extras were added for various scenes. After filming was completed, the set, built at a cost of $250,000, was turned over to residents of Moorea who had been left homeless by recent hurricanes. Scarce and expensive wood from the sets was used to help rebuild houses. During filming, a number of local residents actually inhabited the set when it was not being used.

Yet another Moorea bay, Atiha, served as the Tofua Island landing by Bligh and his loyalists, where they are attacked by savage islanders and one of the men is brutally killed. Extensive breadfruit groves were also an important part of the location; Fletcher Christian's hut, where Bligh interrupts his first officer in the company of the uninhibited Tahitian natives, was built near there.

Tevaite Vernette, a 19-year-old Tahitian model from Papeete, made her screen acting debut in the part of Mauatua, daughter of the King, who falls in love with Christian.

Right

In *The Bounty*, the bountiful allures of sexually liberated Tahitian *vahines* epitomized by Tevaite Vernette as Mauatua are more responsible for the mutiny aboard the HMS *Bounty* than the cruelty of Captain Bligh and his breadfruit mania. In this version of the most famous nautical revolt ever, Mel Gibson as first mate Fletcher Christian is inspired to commit high treason on the high seas as much by his desire for Mauatua as he is by Bligh's injustices.

FOR THE LOVE
OF A WOMAN,
FOR THE HONOR
OF THEIR GODS,
THEY WOULD
DESTROY PARADISE.
300 YEARS AGO EASTER ISLAND WAS CALLED
RAPA-NUI
WARNER BROS. PRESENTS

RAPA NUI

1994 WB

D: Kevin Reynolds

S: Kevin Reynolds and Tim Rose Price

P: Kevin Costner and Jim Wilson

Cast: Jason Scott Lee, Esai Morales, Sandrine Holt

Rapa Nui, an adventurous love story set and filmed on remote Easter Island, takes place in the late 1600s, during a time when social conflict and environmental hardship polarized the culture of Easter Island's two tribes. In an effort to save their home from the gods' wrath and win the loyalty of the woman they both love, two young men compete against one another in the physically and mentally grueling Birdman competition. This competition guarantees its winner leadership of the island, known to its residents as Rapa Nui.

Easter Island, a mere 65 square miles in size, is located in the middle of the South Pacific: 2,300 miles west of present-day South America and 1,500 miles east of its nearest neighbor, Pitcairn Island. But the island is not a very convenient place to shoot a movie. Officially part of Chile since 1888, life for the nearly 3,000 present-day Spanish-speaking residents remains tied to the traditions, customs and pace of its Polynesian past.

The filmmakers conducted a two-month sweep of Polynesia, looking for the perfect combination of actors to fill over 45 supporting roles which required Polynesians. This search led to New Zealand, where casting took place among the Maori people, a culture with a distinct connection with the Rapa Nui, but who speak English. Rapa Nui is primarily known for its gigantic stone sculptures called *moai*, which play an important role in this movie.

Photo courtesy of the DeSoto Brown Collection.

Opposite page

Rapa Nui **is a Polynesia-set version of Hollywood biblical spectacles with casts of thousands building pyramids and the like. Easter Island's *moai* are Polynesia's largest stone statues. Hawaiian-Chinese actor Jason Scott Lee co-starred with Anzac Wallace (star of the 1984 New Zealand hit *Utu*).**

RETURN TO THE BLUE LAGOON
1991 COL

D: William A. Graham

S: Leslie Stevens

P: William A. Graham

Cast: Milla Jovovich, Brian Kruse, Lisa Pelikan

When two young lovers lose their lives at sea, they leave a young son behind. A kind-hearted widow and her daughter rescue the orphan, but, through tragic circumstances, the children are abandoned on a deserted island. As days grow into years, the two children grow up and have to face the world as it intrudes on their island paradise.

Return to the Blue Lagoon was filmed on Taveuni, one of 300 islands in the Fiji Archipelago.

(left to right) David Cadiente, Sabu and Robert Mitchum in *Rampage* which was filmed on the Big Island of Hawai'i.

▼ ▼

CHAPTER FIVE

Films Made in Hawai'i About Other Places

Hawai'i's climate and location are key factors that lure filmmakers to the Fiftieth State to shoot stories not set in the Pacific Islands. Much of the world is tropical, and Hawai'i can be substituted for most tropical destinations. In 1979's *Ten* starring Bo Derek, Hawai'i substitutes for Mexico in some scenes. Kauai doubles for the Caribbean in 1977's adaptation of Ernest Hemingway's *Islands in the Stream*, while in 1981's *Raiders of the Lost Ark*, Steven Spielberg's movie magic transforms the Garden Isle into a South American jungle. In 1995's Dustin Hoffman vehicle *Outbreak*, Kauai is an African jungle. Kauai is also used to create Peter Pan's Neverneverland in Spielberg's 1992 *Hook*. In Spielberg's 1993 *Jurassic Park* and in 1994's *Exit to Eden*, Kauai and Lanai stand in for fictional isles somewhere off the coast of the Americas.

More than any other non-Oceanic locale, Hawai'i impersonates Southeast Asia. The Big Island is supposed to be Malaysia in 1934's *Four Frightened People* and in Robert Mitchum's 1963 big game hunter adventure picture, *Rampage*. The Indochina wars account for most of Hawai'i's Southeast Asia doubling. America may have lost the war in Vietnam off-screen, but victory has been won on screen on Hawai'i's battlefields. In 1983's *Uncommon Valor*, Gene Hackman launches an MIA rescue mission on Kauai, aka Vietnam. In 1987's TV pilot and series *Tour of Duty* and in 1991's *Flight of the Intruder*, Hawai'i's jungle terrain again doubles for Vietnam.

Hawai'i's shimmering Pacific waters are glimpsed in several well-known submarine war pictures not set in Hawai'i. *Hell Below* (1933) supposedly occurs in the Adriatic, while 1957's *The Enemy Below* is supposed to take place in the Atlantic. In 1995's sub flick *Crimson Tide*, Director Tony Scott was alerted that a nuclear submarine was leaving for sea and submerging after a few days off the coast of Pearl Harbor. The director flew to Hawai'i with a camera crew and caught the naval action as it happened, utilizing the footage in the film. And, Oahu's North Shore waves are seen in 1993's Southern California-set Point Break.

Weather plays a role in luring productions to Hawai'i. While it may occasionally rain in paradise, there is no winter nor many cloudy days. In addition to the tropics, Hawai'i's expansive environment embraces a variety of topography, including rain forests, deserts, canyons and snow-capped mountains.

Hawai'i has more than its diverse nature to offer filmmakers. As one of America's largest urban centers, Honolulu can double for Saigon and even for Manhattan (as in 1995's *Don Juan DeMarco*). Hawai'i has a wide range of architecture, from landmark buildings reflecting the nineteenth century to postmodern towers and sleek skyrises. It also has ranches, cattle herds and cowboys.

The State of Hawai'i is also set up to accommodate film and TV production. Hawai'i is the only state with a film studio built and owned by the state government. The Hawai'i Film Studio includes a state-of-the-art, 16,500-square-foot sound stage and a construction mill for building sets. The Hawai'i Film Office is an important division of the State's Department of Business, Economic Development & Tourism, dedicated to assisting movie and TV production in the Aloha State. Each Hawai'i county has a film commission. Hawai'i's extensive talent pool, from craftsmen to actors, enhances the Aloha State's status as a world-class site for location shooting of stories set almost anywhere on Earth.

Not surprisingly, Hawai'i has been the location of choice for big-budget motion pictures, such as 1976's *King Kong*, *Raiders of the Lost Ark*, *Hook*, *Jurassic Park*, and 1995's *Waterworld*. One reason for the decision to shoot in the Hawaiian Islands is that expensive movies have the financing to incorporate on-location footage of some of the most breathtakingly beautiful places in the world. Hawai'i's spectacular scenery enhances the marketability of films. *Jurassic Park* is the top-grossing blockbuster of all time, while *Waterworld* is the most expensive movie ever made, to date.

Motion pictures and television are big business for Hawai'i's economy. The year 1994 was a record year for the film and TV industry, earning Hawai'i more than $96.5 million. During the shooting of the $160 million *Waterworld*, the Kevin Costner epic pumped more than $30 million (about $250,000 per location day) into the Big Island economy.

Above
Julie Andrews, Dudley Moore and Bo Derek star in *Ten*. Selected scenes were filmed in Hawai'i, doubling for Mexico.

HELL BELOW

1933 MGM

D:	Jack Conway
S:	Adapted by Laird Doyle and Raymond Shrock, dialogue by John Lee Mahin and John Meehan, based on the book *Pigboats* by Commander Edward Elsberg
P:	Metro
Cast:	Robert Montgomery, Walter Huston, Robert Young, Jimmy Durante

The experiences of a World War I American submarine crew at a base in the Mediterranean off the coast of Italy.

The MGM unit filmed the picture at Pearl Harbor, where the remarkably clear water made possible a series of effective shots of the submerged submarine. Special cameras were used for the filming, some fastened in diving bells, some operated from portholes of submarines, and some actually slung on the submarine decks in glass-windowed boxes. For fifteen days the actors were coached by regular Navy men on how to man torpedo tubes, work the controls and otherwise live under the water at the submarine base at Pearl Harbor.

Below
Cecil B. DeMille, one of Hollywood's biggest directors, noted for his spectacles, directed one of Hollywood's top stars, Claudette Colbert, in *Four Frightened People*, made in 1934 (the same year Colbert won an Oscar for *It Happened One Night*). Here, Colbert appears with William Gargan and Herbert Marshall on location on the Big Island of Hawai'i.

FOUR FRIGHTENED PEOPLE
1934 PAR

D: Cecil B. DeMille

S: Bartlett Cormack, from the novel by E. Arnot Robertson

P: Cecil B. DeMille

Cast: Claudette Colbert, Herbert Marshall, Leo Carrillo, Mary Boland and William Gargan

The story of a group of people who escape a ship stricken with bubonic plague and make their way to the mainland of Malaysia, where they enjoy various bizarre adventures in the jungle.

DeMille announced that the production would be made on location in the Hawaiian Islands and left on the Matson ship *Malolo* in September of 1933. He and his crew checked into the Royal Hawaiian Hotel, began looking for locations, and found marvelous jungle regions and other suitable areas at Waialua and Keauohano. DeMille's final selection of locations was based mainly on the island of Hawai'i, where tractors had to be brought in to haul the sound machines, light generators and other equipment for sequences in the jungle and on the slopes of the dormant volcano Mauna Loa.

DeMille naively shot near shark-infested beaches, and the cast and crew were bothered by bugs and spiders crawling everywhere. Actress Claudette Colbert, recovering from a recent appendicitis operation, went swimming under a beautiful waterfall for scenes that took the better part of the day to shoot, and came down with intestinal influenza. The cast and crew returned home to Los Angeles via Honolulu on the *Lurline* on November 14, 1933.

THE ENEMY BELOW

1957 TCF

D: **Dick Powell**

S: **Wendell Mayes, based on a novel by D.A. Rayner**

P: **Dick Powell**

Cast: **Robert Mitchum, Curt Jurgens**

The story of a U.S. destroyer chasing a German submarine during World War II in the North Atlantic, this film won an Academy Award for special effects work by Walter Rossi.

All the ocean scenes that take place in the frigid North Atlantic were shot in Hawai'i for its clear skies and fair weather. The cold temperatures, unpredictable ocean currents and weather would have made shooting on actual locations difficult.

A near-accident occurred while shooting eighteen miles off Pearl Harbor. While director Dick Powell filmed scenes with Robert Mitchum as the captain giving orders to fire, eleven depth charges exploded prematurely off the stern of a Navy destroyer.

Above right
Robert Mitchum in the World War II submarine action film *The Enemy Below*.

Right
Curt Jurgens plays a German captain in *The Enemy Below*.

COLUMBIA PICTURES presents

DAVID BRIAN

GHOST OF THE CHINA SEA

GHOST OF THE CHINA SEA
1959 COL

D:	Fred F. Sear
S:	Charles B. Griffith
P:	Charles B. Griffith
Cast:	David Brian

A plantation owner in the Philippines escapes from the Japanese advance on the islands at the beginning of World War II. This was an early film role for Kam Fong Chun, who later played Chin Ho Kelly on the television series *Hawai'i Five-O*.

Ghost of the China Sea was a B movie filmed entirely on location in Hawai'i.

Above

David Brian stars in *Ghost of the China Sea*, another WWII action picture about the Japanese invasion of the Philippines and Yanks abroad.

GIRLS! GIRLS! GIRLS!

1962 PAR

D: Norman Taurog

S: Edward Anhalt and Allan Weiss, story by Allan Weiss

P: Hal B. Wallis

Cast: Elvis Presley, Laurel Goodwin, Stella Stevens, Jeremy Slate, Guy Lee, Benson Fong, Beulah Quo, Robert Strauss

Below
Elvis dances with Laurel Goodwin in the no-brainer *Girls! Girls! Girls!*.

Romantic drama of a tuna boat skipper who moonlights as a nightclub singer while trying to recover his father's boat.

The story is set in a warm-water port in the Hawaiian Islands. Not one shot of Diamond Head or a grass skirt was included that would have established the location, perhaps intentionally because the original story was set off the coast of Louisiana.

Girls! Girls! Girls! reunited Presley with his film discoverer Hal Wallis and director Norman Taurog, who together had made two of Paramount's biggest box-office bonanzas of the past two years, *G.I. Blues* (1960) and *Blue Hawaii* (1961).

Photo courtesy of the DeSoto Brown Collection.

13 of The Coolest Songs in RCA'S Fabulous "Girls! Girls! Girls!" Album!

ELVIS PRESLEY HAL WALLIS' PRODUCTION "GIRLS! GIRLS! GIRLS!"

Scenery almost as gorgeous as the girls in TECHNICOLOR®

STELLA STEVENS JEREMY SLATE LAUREL GOODWIN

A PARAMOUNT

RAMPAGE
1963 WB

D: Phil Karlson

S: Robert I. Holt and Marguerite Roberts, based on a novel by Alan Cailou

P: William Fadiman

Cast: Robert Mitchum, Elsa Martinelli, Jack Hawkins, Sabu, David Cadiente

A big game trapper is on an expedition in the Malayan jungle for two tigers and a fabled beast known as "The Enchantress."

Hilo, on the Big Island of Hawai'i, was transformed into Malaya for *Rampage*.

The 100-person cast and crew at times worked near the slopes of Mauna Loa. Executive producer William Fadiman collected and had transported to Hilo 50 tons of equipment ranging from a ten-ton crane to poplin tents, showers, folding wicker furniture and crystal goblets. Four Bengal tigers (not to be found in Hawai'i) were brought over from Hollywood, with lions with movie experience, a trick half leopard-half tiger and 150 Java monkeys.

Ten acres of Hawaiian jungle had to be encircled with nine-foot-high wire fencing. The camera crew was enclosed in wire cages for protection in order to film a thrilling tiger-trapping scene. The sign at Hilo Airport was repainted for an airport sequence to read "Kuala Lumpur." Forty Waikiki beachboys were cast in the picture to portray jungle beaters and trackers.

The film marked the return to the screen of Sabu, who as a young Indian actor starred in a series of "Elephant Boy" B films and in such classics as *The Jungle Book* and *The Thief of Bagdad*. He died shortly after the filming of *Rampage*.

ISLANDS IN THE STREAM

1976 PAR

D: Franklin J. Schaffner

S: Denne Bart Petitclerc, based on the novel by Ernest Hemingway

P: Peter Bart and Max Palevsky

Cast: George C. Scott, Claire Bloom, David Hemmings

The story of Thomas Hudson (Scott), a middle-aged artist living on the island of Bimini during the first year of World War II. The focus is the poignant renewed relationship with Hudson's three young sons and former wife and what happens to him when he finds himself drawn into the war and away from his self-imposed security on the island.

Most of the action of Ernest Hemingway's last published novel takes place in the Caribbean pre-World War II days.

In translating this story for the screen, however, for several practical reasons, the studio and others involved wanted to find a locale that would look similar to the Caribbean, yet have a more dramatic and pictorial quality.

Kauai, Hawai'i, was judged to be the ideal location because of its combination of remote terrain, dramatic sea and natural harbor that would not require dredging to permit the navigation of large boats. Kauai locations were chosen with the assistance of Maile Semitekol of the Hawai'i Visitors Bureau on Kauai, and Sylvia Scott, the then-coordinator of Special Services of the Hawai'i Visitors Bureau in Honolulu.

A 100-member cast and crew stayed at the Kauai Surf Hotel. On Kauai, at Kukuiula Bay, a small natural harbor and

a Bahamian village was constructed. The new buildings included a two-story hotel bar, fishing shacks, an open-air market, as well as an impressive High Commissioner's mansion. The perfect site for Hudson's house was found on an isolated virgin bluff overlooking the sea at Mahalulepu in the Kawailoa Bay area, which was accessed by cane roads on property owned by McBride Company.

The sets were removed following completion of filming and the site was returned to its previous state—a requirement of the Department of Land and Natural Resources and the Conservation District.

To simulate the geography of the low-lying, coral-based Bahamas, cameras were kept at low angles to prevent glimpses of a nearby mountain. The Wailua River on Kauai closely resembles inland rivers on some Caribbean islands, particularly Cuba, so the locale where Hudson puts the refugees ashore was changed to Cuba from the novel's Everglades. A gun battle takes place on the Wailua River between Cuban patrol boats and Hudson's boat, the *Tortuga*.

Production manager Chico Day, with four decades of filmmaking behind him, said no movie in his memory was more carefully planned in regard to sea footage. Day praised the local residents who gave the company daily technical advice about locations of dangerous coral reefs and the ever-changing violent tides.

Opposite page
George C. Scott, Michael-James Wixted, Brad Savage and Hart Bochner in *Islands in the Stream*.

Above
Jamaican village set for *Islands in the Stream*, shot on Kauai.

RAIDERS OF THE LOST ARK
1981 PAR

D: Steven Spielberg
S: Lawrence Kasdan
P: George Lucas
Cast: Harrison Ford, Karen
        Allen, Denholm Elliott

We first meet archaeologist Indiana Jones (Harrison Ford) in a South American jungle, pillaging a temple full of booby traps and blow guns, just having narrowly escaped from the Indians of Chachapoyan.

The South American scenes were shot on the island of Kauai. The first location, where the temple exterior was shot, was reached via a narrow dirt track that led down a cliff face into a hole full of mosquitoes. Other locations included Na Pali coastal mountain shots, for which donkeys were transported by helicopter, and the Huleia River on the east side of the island.

Left
Producer George Lucas and director Steven Spielberg with local actors playing South American Indians on location on Kauai, which doubles for a South American jungle.

UNCOMMON VALOR

1983 PAR

D: **Ted Kotchoff**

S: **Joe Gayton**

P: **John Milius, Buzz Feitshans**

Cast: **Gene Hackman, Fred Ward, Reb Brown, Patrick Swayze, Tim Thomerson, Robert Stack**

A contemporary action thriller about retired Marine Colonel Rhodes (Hackman), who rounds up his son's former company for a secret raid on a Vietnamese prison camp, where he hopes to rescue his son and other American M.I.A.s.

Cast and crew moved to Hawaiʻi on July 12, 1983, for the filming of the climactic Laotian sequence. After scouting locations all over Hawaiʻi, Mexico and the Caribbean, director Ted Kotchoff settled on lush Kauai as the ideal duplicate for Southeast Asia. "The landscape in Hawaiʻi, the vegetation, the red earth, was amazingly similar to what we were looking to duplicate for our scenes taking place in Laos," said Kotchoff.

The island's economy benefited enormously from the production. Over 150 cast and crew members moved into the Sheraton Coconut Beach Hotel in Kapaa town. Nearly 1,000 Hawaiʻi teamsters were hired to transport the production from the hotel to locations and back, and between locations. More than 100 locals with Asian features were hired as extras for scenes demanding large numbers of Thais and Vietnamese. During the filming of one massive battle scene, more than 275 lunches were served each day on the set by local caterers.

The Kauai skies, dark and stormy for the week preceding shooting, remained that way on the first day. Local Reverend Will Kaina visited the set that day to give a prayer ceremony asking that blessings be bestowed on the entire production. After two days, the rain disappeared and did not return until filming was nearly completed. Even tropical storm George diminished to drizzles before it reached the island.

Numerous sets were constructed on Kauai, but none was more taxing or impressive than the Viet Cong P.O.W. camp, which covered nearly ten acres in Lumahai Valley. "When I first saw it, I honestly believed for a minute that I was back in Vietnam," said veteran and technical advisor Laurence Neber. Although the set had been three months in construction, it was reduced to

Opposite page

Scenes from the war movie *Uncommon Valor*, about Vietnam vets who invade Laos to rescue Americans believed to be held captive in a P.O.W. camp.

rubble in less than three weeks after intricately choreographed bombings, explosions and strafing attacks.

Most of the company agreed that Hawai'i was an ideal place to be on location for six weeks. Families, wives and girlfriends arrived en masse from the mainland to share in the good times. Cast and crew worked during the six production days of each week, but Sunday provided a chance to sleep in, go to brunch, and explore the island. John Milius took advantage of the location to go surfing, which is one of his major passions. Ted Kotchoff went snorkeling with his son Aaron, and Buzz Feitshans took his children on a Zodiac raft trip to the wilderness area along the Na Pali Coast. Patrick Swayze went water-skiing, diving, hiking and parasailing, and spent many nights in the local disco. Gene Hackman stayed home to paint and relax. Randall "Tex" Cobb could be found on Sundays working out at the Kapaa Boxing Club.

The six weeks of Hawai'i filming ended on August 19, 1983.

KARATE KID PART II
1986 COL

D:	**John G. Avildsen**
S:	**Robert Mark Kamen**
P:	**Jerry Weintraub**
Cast:	**Pat Morita, Ralph Macchio, Danny Kamekona, Nobu McCarthy**

Sequel to the popular *The Karate Kid* of 1984, in which an American youngster, Daniel, becomes a martial arts champion under the tutelage of a Japanese-American elder, Mr. Miyagi. The picture won actor Pat Morita an Academy Award nomination as Best Supporting Actor for his role as Mr. Miyagi.

In the sequel, Daniel is not fighting for competition points in Los Angeles but defending himself and Mr. Miyagi against bitter foes bent on the destruction of Miyagi's ancestral home in Okinawa.

The production reconstructed a full-scale Okinawan village in "beautiful downtown" Kahaluu on Oahu's windward coast. A search had been conducted in Okinawa as well as Japan to find a village to portray Miyagi's roots, but producers were not satisfied until they found the scenic area on the windward coast of Oahu, twenty miles from Honolulu. The "Okinawa" location, on private property, was first spotted in an aerial survey by helicopter and was later approached by boat.

Covered with palms, the idyllic spot encompasses 43 acres of beach front, complete with a lagoon that once served as a royal fish pond for King Kamehameha III. In the land redistribution of the Great Mahele of 1848, about one-third of the land was given to the *alii* (royalty), and this property was passed to Kamehameha.

The beautiful location was owned by a retired local physician, who had substantially reconstructed the pond and retained its ingenious design. The doctor and his daughter had refused numerous offers to sell the land for commercial development, and had, in fact, formed a corporation to guarantee the site's preservation.

Closed to the public, there seemed little likelihood of the land's owners allowing a film company to come in with bulldozers to build a village and bring actors and crew to photograph a movie.

Two factors made it all possible. Actor Pat Morita, a frequent visitor and popular favorite in Hawai'i, had previously made several appearances at fund-

Opposite page
Pat Morita and Ralph Macchio appear at Kahaluu, on the windward side of Oahu, in *Karate Kid Part II*.

raisers for State Senator Duke Kawasaki, a close friend of the doctor's. Furthermore, the doctor's daughter worked for the mayor of Honolulu, one of whose pet projects was encouraging filmmakers to location in the islands. Permission was given for the village construction, which was supervised by Hank Wynands, who years ago had built the sets for *Hawaii*.

Principal photography began on September 23, 1985, after a week of rehearsals. In keeping with the milieu of the film and in deference to the fifty Okinawa-born Hawai'i residents recruited to portray the villagers, filming was preceded by a colorful Shinto ceremony. Bishop Shigemaru Miyao, who headed the Izumu Taisha Kyo Mission, and his assistant minister Jiroomi Ito blessed the health and well-being of the cast and crew.

In October, shooting was resumed at the Burbank Studios in California.

ISLAND OF THE ALIVE
1986 WB

D: Larry Cohen

S: Larry Cohen

P: Paul Stadus

Cast: Michael Moriarity, Ann Dane, Karen Black.

This film was a follow-up to the successful monster baby films created by Larry Cohen in the 1970s. It went directly to video release.

Island of the Alive was filmed for two weeks on Kauai on the property of Jules Kanarek in Waipouli, which stood in for Florida and Cuba.

POINT BREAK
1991 TCF

D: Kathryn Bigelow

S: W. Peter Liff from an original story by Rick King

P: Peter Abrams and Robert L. Levy

Cast: Keanu Reeves, Gary Busey, Patrick Swayze

F.B.I. Agent Johnny Utah (Reeves) is assigned to investigate a near-perfect string of bank robberies. Taking a lead from his partner (Busey), Utah goes undercover among the maverick fringe who surf off the Southern California coast. There he meets his match, the mystical mastermind Bodhi (Swayze).

Surfing sequences were filmed in Southern California as far north as the Ventura County line and as far south as Manhattan Beach. The crew traveled to Hawai'i to shoot key sequences on Oahu's North Shore, south of the famed Banzai Pipeline.

Below

Keanu Reeves (who is part-
Hawaiian) and Patrick Swayze in
Point Break; some surf
sequences were lensed at Oahu's
North Shore.

FLIGHT OF THE INTRUDER

1991 PAR

D: John Milius

S: Robert Dillon and David Shaber based on the novel
       by Stephen Coonts

P: Mace Neufeld and Robert Rehme

Cast: Danny Glover, Willem Dafoe, Brad Johnson, Rosanna
       Arquette

Set on an aircraft carrier in the South China Sea and in enemy airspace above North Vietnam in 1972, *Flight of the Intruder* is a wartime action-adventure film about three U.S. Navy men.

Danny Glover plays the squadron leader, Commander Frank Camparelli; Willem Dafoe is the bombardier, Lt. Cmdr. Virgil Cole; and Brad Johnson is the pilot, Lt. Jake "Cool Hand" Grafton.

Hawai'i was chosen as the film site after a lengthy location search by producer Mace Neufield and executive producer Brian Frankish. The islands' tropical jungle terrain is similar to that of Southeast Asia and the Philippines, and a flight crew tactical squadron from the U.S. Navy based in Hawai'i could be on hand for the duration of the filming.

All over the island of Kauai, filmmakers transformed rustic towns and tropical terrain into Vietnamese villages, war zones and Philippine towns of the 1970s.

Principal photography for *Flight of the Intruder* began October 16, 1989 at Pearl Harbor, Hawai'i, which became NAS Cubi Point in the Philippines, with Barbers Point NAS becoming the home of three A-6 Intruders, three A-4 Skyhawks and one B-53 Sea Stallion helicopter.

The location for the first of three phases of principal photography would be the islands of Oahu and Kauai, with a remote area of Kauai providing the appropriate landscape to recreate a Vietnamese terrain for scenes involving a crashed A-6 Intruder.

Kauai locations were also used for such settings as the Philippine red-light district of Olongapo City, which was re-created in the town of Hanapepe with 250 local extras. The officers' clubs and quarters were filmed at the U.S. Navy Pacific Missile Range facility on Kauai's west shore.

Eight days of filming took place near the base of Kauai's Waialeale, one of the wettest locales on earth, which receives approximately 444 inches of rainfall annually. While filming here, A-6 Intruders and A-1 Skyraiders were flown as low as fifty feet above the ground at close to 200 miles per hour.

Because the location in ancient times was inhabited by Hawaiian royalty, executive producer Brian Frankish left nothing to chance, bringing in a Hawaiian *kahuna* to bless the crash site and those who worked there. "I filmed here in 1976 on *King Kong,* and I was warned to have everything blessed," says Frankish. "We blessed everything except for one helicopter which broke down during filming (no one was hurt). So this time I was taking no chances." Following the blessing, the weather cooperated with the production schedule; it rained for only three hours during the eight days of filming.

One A-6 Intruder was assembled by crane after being transported in sections over roads made through sugar cane fields. Because of the inaccessibility of the area, the journey of the plane had been started a month earlier in St. Augustine, Florida, where it had been hauled in sections onto four wide-load trucks and driven to Long Beach, California. From there it had been shipped to Honolulu and then Kauai. Frankish brought 135 crew members, 3 U.S. Navy jet bombers, and 48 Navy personnel on location for the month-long shooting schedule. Many locals were also assigned to the production, which left behind more than $2 million in revenues on the island.

The second phase of the production entailed filming at sea aboard the Navy aircraft carrier USS *Independence.* The third phase of filming was done on stages at Paramount Studios.

JURASSIC PARK

1993 U

D: Steven Spielberg

S: Michael Crichton and David Koepp, based on the novel
        by Michael Crichton

P: Kathleen Kennedy and Gerald R. Molen

Cast: Sam Neill, Laura Dern, Jeff Goldblum, Richard
        Attenborough

Jurassic Park is the highest-grossing film ever, at just over $900 million worldwide. It was the winner of three Academy Awards, including Best Visual Effects. The island of Kauai, which played a starring role in this recor-breaking box-office hit, could revel in the worldwide attention the film garnered.

Imagine that you are one of the first visitors to Jurassic Park, a melding of scientific discovery and visual imagination. You arrive as a child would, free of preconceptions and ready for anything. Your adventure is about to begin.

Entering the gates of the park, your senses are overwhelmed by the world that surrounds you: the sounds, the smells, even the feel of the earth is curiously different. Somewhere in the distance, you hear the movement of huge animals; the ground shakes with their passing. You are a stranger in an alien world.

You look into the night sky, at stars whose light was born before humans ever existed; born when a different race of beings walked the planet— swift, powerful animals, rulers of the earth for 160 million years.

The Jurassic period has left only faint traces of itself in fossils, footprints, and in relics of blood cells encased in amber, which form a time capsule that has remained closed for countless millennia. Now the time capsule has been opened, and man and dinosaur, the two rulers of the earth, will meet for the first time.

All our scientific resources have been dedicated to bringing Jurassic Park to reality; it is now the ultimate amusement park. But someone forgot to tell the dinosaurs.

Meeting them in their environment, we realize they are not monsters, but animals far more agile, intelligent and dangerous than we guessed. We can give birth to dinosaurs, but nothing can prepare us for what will happen afterward. Jurassic Park is where science ends and the unpredictable begins.

Directed by Steven Spielberg and taken from the best-selling book by Michael Crichton, *Jurassic Park* stars New Zealander Sam Neill as Dr. Allen Grant, a renowned paleontologist who is asked to inspect a spectacular amusement park. Laura Dern plays his colleague, Dr. Ellie Sattler, and Jeff Goldblum plays a brilliant but eccentric mathematician whose Chaos Theory explains the dangers inherent in the project. Sir Richard Attenborough plays John Hammond, the park's ambitious developer, and Ariana Richards and Joseph Mazzello are Hammond's young grandchildren.

When *Jurassic Park* began principal photography on the island of Kauai on August 24, 1992, exactly two years and one month had passed since the start of pre-production. For more than eighteen months before filming began, an award-winning design team had been conceiving and creating the live-action dinosaurs that would inhabit the unique park.

The lush green resort land near Lihue was an ideal setting for the exteriors. Locations included Manawaiopuna Falls in Hanapepe Valley, The Blue Hole, Hanapepe Falls and the base of Waialeale crater. The Okolele Valley, carved centuries ago, can be reached only by air, so the production built a helipad there.

After three weeks of filming under the tropical sun, a real-life drama overshadowed the movie, as Hurricane Iniki slammed into Kauai. As the hurricane approached, the crew was asked by Westin Hotel management to pack their suitcases and fill their bathtubs with water in case of future power outages and water shortages. Next, they were instructed to pack a day bag and meet in the ballroom on the basement level.

By 9 a.m. the storm was headed straight for the island. "We started pulling all our supplies into the ballroom, and the camera crew was quickly packing their things in the trucks," recalled Kathleen Kennedy. "If you're going to be stranded with anyone, be stranded with a movie crew. We had generators for lights and plenty of food and water. We were self-sustaining because we moved around on location all the time."

Camped out in rows of chaise longues on the ballroom floor, the cast and crew heard the winds pick up at about 4 p.m. and rumble by at almost

120 miles per hour. "It sounded like a freight train roaring past the building," recalled the producer.

When water seeped into one end of the ballroom, the crew huddled on the other side of the room. But at 7:30 p.m., Kennedy and Gary Hymes, the stunt coordinator, stepped outside into silence. "It was the eeriest thing I had ever seen," recalls Kennedy. "Here we were that morning on a beautiful tree-lined street adjacent to a golf course, and now virtually every single tree had been flattened."

Although the company had scheduled one more day of filming, the sheer force of Iniki had struck literally all of the sets. There was neither power nor working phones on the island, so at dawn the next morning, Kennedy jogged two miles to the airport to explore their options.

"The destruction in the airport was unbelievable," she recalled. "All the windows were blown out in the terminals, and the buildings were full of palms, trees, sand and water. Every single helicopter had been tipped on its side."

Thanks to her relentless efforts among airport and military personnel in Lihue, Kennedy was able to hitch a ride to Honolulu on a Salvation Army plane and began organizing there from a pay phone. Over the next 24 hours, she arranged for more than 20,000 pounds of relief supplies to be transported from Honolulu and Los Angeles to Kauai.

Upon the production's return to Los Angeles, *Jurassic Park* resumed filming at Universal Studios, returning only once more to Oahu to complete one day of location filming at Kualoa Ranch. Revenues totaling $4.5 million were spent in Hawai'i by the production of *Jurassic Park*.

EXIT TO EDEN
1994 Savoy

D: Garry Marshall

S: Deborah Amelon and Bob Brummer, based on Ann Rice's novel

P: Alexandra Rose and Gary Marshall

Cast: Dan Akroyd, Rosie O'Donnell, Dana Delaney, Paul Mercurio

A comedy about two cops from Los Angeles who go undercover to an island where sexual fantasy becomes reality under the watchful eyes of a beautiful dominatrix, Mistress Lisa.

Production on *Exit to Eden* began in September of 1993 on the Hawaiian island of Lanai at the exclusive Manele Bay Hotel resort, which was selected "because it's very beautiful and its exotic architecture has an eastern flavor that isn't typically Hawaiian," remarked producer Alexandra Rose in the press notes for the film. The Manele Bay resort has six different gardens on the premises with their own fountains, waterfalls and ponds, which provided a great deal of variety for filming purposes.

WATERWORLD
1995 U

D: Kevin Reynolds

S: Peter Rader and David Twohy

P: Charles Gordon, John Davis, Kevin Costner

Cast: Kevin Costner, Dennis Hopper, Jeanne Tripplehorn, Tina Majorino

An action-adventure set in the future, when the polar ice caps have melted and Earth is covered in water. Costner plays Mariner, a part-human, part-amphibian who rescues a woman and child from a man-made atoll being attacked by marauders and embarks on a search for fabled dry land.

To date, this was reportedly the most expensive film ever made, with a production budget of over $175 million and incorporating thrilling action sequences, revolutionary production design and dynamic visual effects.

Waterworld was filmed in Kawaihae, in the South Kohala district of the Big Island of Hawai'i, over a seven-month-long shooting schedule which began on June 27, 1994, extending to February 1995.

Universal built a huge floating platform set in Kawaihae Bay on the west coast of the Big Island to represent an incredible floating city in the film.

Almost 500 people worked in some form of production on the first and second units. *Waterworld* hired grips, electricians, medics, craft service and wardrobe out of Local 665, a mixed union that includes several trades and crafts.

Below
The massive floating set built for *Waterworld*.

Kirk Lee Aeder

▼ ▼

CHAPTER SIX

Films About Hawai'i and the South Seas Made Elsewhere

Many Hollywood films set on a Pacific island have been shot closer to the Sunset Strip than to the South Seas. Generally, authenticity is not a major goal; telling an entertaining story that sells well, is. Shooting in the Pacific Islands may provide the genuine islands and islanders, but it also presents obstacles and problems.

Travel to the islands is costly. Transportation, communication and accommodations for imported casts and crews to distant Pacific isles can be an extremely expensive proposition, and infrastructure in much of the South Pacific is not fully developed. On some islands there may be too much development if filmmakers want a primitive paradise background. A favorite trick of cameramen shooting on Waikiki Beach is to either strategically frame long shots of Diamond Head or place some extras or a beach umbrella in the beach foreground to block out buildings near the landmark crater.

Movie makers concerned with keeping costs down can solve the above problems in a number of ways. Sometimes second unit camera crews are dispatched to Oceania to shoot footage that is later incorporated into films primarily shot in Los Angeles studios. These scenes can be edited in with the L.A.-shot material or used in superimpositions, as in the blue-screen process. (Computer animation, etc., is creating a whole new high-tech possibility in this realm.) This gives the film the appearance of having been made on an island. Stock footage from previous cinematic island expeditions can also be used in this way. MGM's 1939 film *Honolulu*, starring Gracie Allen and George Burns, was cranked out on a Hollywood back lot, with a few Hawai'i exteriors added.

Another device is to use substitute islands that are more accessible or available. Metro's *Where the Pavement Ends*, directed by Rex Ingram and featuring Ramon

Opposite page
Adele Mara in *Wake of the Red Witch*.

Below

Sultry sarong gal Suzan Ball stars opposite genre veterans Jeff Chandler (*Bird of Paradise*) and Anthony Quinn (*Waikiki Wedding*, *Lust for Life*, etc.) in 1953's *East of Sumatra*, set near Indonesia. The natives are proverbially restless as Chandler plays a mining engineer and Quinn a heavy caught up in an indigenous rebellion. This film seems to reflect the realities of post-war Indonesia's anti-colonial struggle. The sarong comes from Southeast Asia, and is an Indonesian word. Some anthropologists theorize that Polynesians originally came from Southeast Asia, and Pacific sarongs are to some extent derived from tapa cloth wraparounds traditionally worn in Oceania.

Navarro, was filmed in Miami and Cuba in 1923. Paramount's *Aloma of the South Seas* was filmed in Puerto Rico and Long Island in 1926. United Artists' *Miss Sadie Thompson*, starring Gloria Swanson and Lionel Barrymore, was shot in 1928 not in Pago Pago, but on California's Catalina Island. As recently as 1979, the Pago Pago in Dino De Laurentiis' remake of *Hurricane* was filmed on Bora Bora, maybe because it was more scenic. Also, Bora Bora, unlike Pago Pago, includes a number of flat "motu" islets that resemble coral atolls, which were required by *Hurricane's* plot.

Why go "South of Tahiti" when you can recreate a reasonable filmic facsimile that will pass (on celluloid) for Oceania using elaborately designed studio sets and sound stages? Movies pretend all the time, and the feature film is not reality, but fantasy about imagined worlds.

SEVEN SINNERS

1940 U

D: Tay Garnett

S: John Meehan and Harry Tugend, based on a story by
     Ladislaus Fodor and Lazlo Vadnal

P: Joe Pasternak

Cast: Marlene Dietrich, John Wayne, Broderick Crawford,
        Mischa Auer, Albert Dekker

Bijou (Dietrich) a honky-tonk singer playing the South Sea Island circuit, visits the American naval base at Boni-Komba, where an American naval officer, Lt. Bruce Whitney (Wayne), falls for her.

Seven Sinners was filmed at the Universal Studios back lot in Hollywood.

Below
John Wayne at Universal's Hollywood backlot, tropical island set for a scene from *Seven Sinners*.

ALOMA OF THE SOUTH SEAS

1941 PAR

D:	**Alfred Santell**
S:	**Frank Butler, Seona Owen and Lillian Hayward**
P:	**B.G. De Sylva**
Cast:	**Dorothy Lamour, Jon Hall, Lynne Overman, Philip Reed, Katherine de Mille**

The original 1925 production starring Vivienne Osborne (who enjoyed a modest Hollywood career, mostly in the 1930s) was a huge Broadway stage hit. In 1926, Paramount released the first of two film versions starring famed "shimmy" dancer Gilda Gray. Exteriors were shot in Puerto Rico for this tale of a South Sea girl's love for a disillusioned white man.

In 1941, the studio decided to change the plot and remake the movie as a Technicolor showcase for young sarong queen Dorothy Lamour. *Aloma of the South Seas,* a lightweight, entertaining film, relied on romantic interludes and scenic backgrounds.

Born Dorothy Kaumeyer in New Orleans on December 10, 1914, Lamour started out as a band singer. Supper clubs, records and her own NBC radio show led to a Paramount Pictures contract, and Lamour made her screen debut in 1936 as *The Jungle Princess. The Hurricane,* released in 1937 and directed by John Ford, established Lamour as a Paramount star (even though it was made by independent producer Samuel Goldwyn and released by United Artists). Thanks to the film's costumer, Omar Kiam, Lamour made the sarong an international fashion statement. Though she made over fifty films and was a top star at Paramount, Lamour is most remembered for the eight "sarong movies" *(The Jungle Princess, The Hurricane, Her Jungle Love, Typhoon, Aloma of the South Seas, Beyond the Blue Horizon, Rainbow Island, Malaya)* and the famous "road" comedies with Bob Hope and Bing Crosby.

Of her 52 films, Lamour received first-star billing in 23. In fact, in the very first "road" movie *(Road to Singapore,* 1940), she was billed before Bob Hope. Lamour was the number one pin-up girl of the Armed Forces in 1941, 1942 and 1943.

In *Aloma of the South Seas,* two island children, Aloma (Lamour) and Tanoa (Hall), are promised to be married by a pact made by their island chief fathers. The boy is sent to the United States to school and the girl stays on

the island. When the young man returns as chief after his father's death, he at first does not want to marry the girl, but soon realizes that he loves her. Her jealous boyfriend (Reed) tries to take over the island, the volcano erupts, and the island is destroyed. Aloma, Tanoa and a few others survive to start their lives anew.

Director Alfred Santell, in a September 1, 1941 interview in *Technicolor News and Views*, remarked that "we decided to try something new in Technicolor work. We weren't going to make our mythical island a jungle . . . instead it would be an Eden, a sort of Paradise. Every object in the picture would have color of some kind. There would be no drab shades. We tinted our sand pink and our canyon walls lavender. Our trees had colorful flowers and our vines were stately and graceful."

Aloma of the South Seas received 1941 Academy Award nominations for Color Cinematography by Karl Struss, Wilfrid M. Cline and William Snyder, as well as for Special Effects and Sound Recording.

Lamour never really saw the South Seas until 1983, when she was a special guest on a Princess Cruise to such fabled ports of call as Pago Pago, Bora Bora, Tahiti and Tonga. Except for a trip to Hawai'i, all those sarong movies were filmed on the Paramount Studios back lot in Hollywood.

Opposite page
In ***Aloma of the South Seas***, **Tanoa (Jon Hall) and Aloma (Dorothy Lamour) are betrothed as children. But the childhood sweethearts grow apart when Tanoa travels overseas to pursue his education. When he returns, Tanoa is a changed grown-up man, and he has trouble relating to Aloma and the island society. Samoan novelist Albert Wendt—a self-confessed "movie addict" who left Samoa at a young age to pursue schooling in New Zealand—writes about a somewhat similar situation in his first book, *Sons For the Return Home*, which became a 1979 New Zealand film.**

SOUTH OF TAHITI   BRIAN

EVY with BROD CRAWFORD ANDY DEVINE MARIA and MONTEZ

GOOD PICTURES LIKE GOOD BOOKS NEVER GROW OLD

SOUTH OF TAHITI
1941 U

D:	George Waggner
S:	Gerald Geraghty, original story by Ainsworth Morge
P:	George Waggner
Cast:	Brian Donlevy, Broderick Crawford, Maria Montez, Andy Devine, Armida

Three adventurers on a small boat come upon an island in the Pacific ruled by a beautiful princess, whose cache of pearls they attempt to steal.

Left

South of Tahiti is most noteworthy for introducing the Hollywood Hispanic Maria Montez to the jungle genre. Next to Dorothy Lamour, she may be South Seas cinema's most celebrated Sarong Girl identified with the genre.

271

THE MOON AND SIXPENCE
1942 UA

D: **Albert Lewin**

S: **Albert Lewin**

P: **David L. Loew**

Cast: **George Sanders, Herbert Marshall, Elena Verdugo**

The story of the 1919 book and the 1942 film parallels the life story of Paul Gauguin, the great French painter (although W. Somerset Maugham's hero is named Charles Strickland). *The Moon and Sixpence* is the story of a middle-aged stockbroker, who, in his overpowering urge to paint, deserts his wife and children and later abandons others who love and befriend him. In Tahiti, free of all normal ties, he finally finds release for his great talent. He dies there of leprosy and in poverty.

Elena Verdugo, who played the Tahitian girl Ata, gave a poignant performance that established her in Hollywood. She later became famous to American television audiences for her starring roles in two series: *Meet Millie* in the 1950s and as Nurse Consuelo on *Marcus Welby, M.D.* in the late 1960s.

An entire Tahitian village was constructed on a sound stage for this South Sea setting.

The Gauguin family would not give the filmmakers the right to use the family name or the paintings in the film.

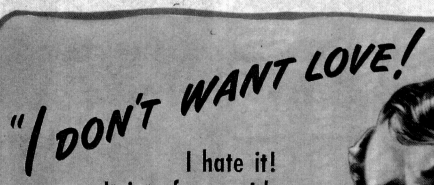

"**I DON'T WANT LOVE!**

I hate it!
It interferes with
my work...and yet
...I'm only human!"

W. Somerset Maugham's

THE
MOON AND SIXPENCE

STARRING

GEORGE
SANDERS · HERBERT **MARSHALL**

Doris Dudley · Elena Verdugo
Albert Basserman · Eric Blore

Adapted and Directed by
ALBERT LEWIN

Produced by **DAVID L. LOEW**

Released through
UNITED ARTISTS

*Maughams
Greatest
Story
becomes*

THE MOST TALKED-ABOUT PICTURE EVER MADE IN HOLLYWOOD!

PARDON MY SARONG

1942 U

D:	Erle C. Kenton
S:	True Boardman, Nat Perrin, John Grant
P:	Alex Gottlieb
Cast:	Bud Abbott and Lou Costello

This Abbott and Costello comedy takes the pair from Chicago to an exotic tropical island, where most of the comical action takes place.

In pre-war days, Hollywood producers would have thought nothing of sending a camera crew to Honolulu, Bali, Java or to the ends of the world to get proper backgrounds for a film. With World War II, studio technicians were put to the test to devise authentic backgrounds within the confines of the back lot. In creating a tropical background for *Pardon My Sarong,* Universal technicians created a set that at first glance resembled a Garden of Eden. More than 20,000 individual plants, many of them rare species, were arranged and placed to form a jungle.

THE TUTTLES OF TAHITI

1942 RKO

D: Charles Vidor

S: S. Lewis Meltzer and Robert Carson, based on the
        book by Charles Nordhoff and James Norman Hall

P: Sol Lesser

Cast: Charles Laughton, Jon Hall, Peggy Drake

Charles Laughton plays the wily head of an irresponsible clan of South Pacific beach bums in this gentle and completely charming film.

Above

Charles Laughton (who played Captain Bligh in Nordhoff and Hall's *Mutiny on the Bounty* and the title character in 1938's *The Beachcomber*) and Jon Hall in a cockfighting/gambling scene in the delightful, happy-go-lucky comedy *The Tuttles of Tahiti*, another movie based on a Nordhoff and Hall book titled *No More Gas*.

SON OF FURY

1942 TCF

D: John Cromwell

S: Phillip Dunne, based on the novel by Edison Marshall

P: Darryl F. Zanuck

Cast: Tyrone Power, Gene Tierney, George Sanders, Ray Mala

Benjamin Blake (Power) is heir to a dukedom that has been stolen by an unscrupulous uncle, who has taken Benjamin from his grandfather and

made him a bonded servant. Benjamin stows away on an India-bound ship, where he finds life even harsher. He jumps ship and makes his way to a South Sea island, where he and a friend make peace with hostile natives and become pearl divers. He meets an exotic native girl (Tierney), whom he calls Eve. Eventually, he returns to England with a fortune in pearls to clear his name and gain retribution against his cruel uncle. Afterward, he returns to the South Seas.

Son of Fury was filmed on the Twentieth Century Fox Studios backlot and on Southern California locations. A South Sea island village was built along the studio's "Lake Michigan," a lake that stood-in for half the world's rivers and oceans and cost $14,000 to build. Power wore a *pareu,* commonly known as a sarong, for the island sequences.

While swimming underwater with Tierney, Power kicked a sharp rock, cutting a three-inch gash on his left foot. Afterward, the studio refused to let the two stay underwater longer than two minutes.

California's first cold wave of the winter caught Tierney in a sarong, and she collapsed one morning with the flu.

She danced the *pao'a*, a native ceremonial dance, with 100 movie Polynesians for the picture. Hollywood could round up only one native Tahitian who could sing and dance, so the other 99 included Hawaiians, Hindus, Mexicans, one Indian and one Italian. The dance was staged by Augie Goupil, a French-Tahitian composer who recorded many native songs.

An Alaskan, Ray Mala, played a Tahitian chief. Ray Mala also starred in one of the few serials set in the South Seas, 1937's *Robinson Crusoe of Clipper Island.* John Reasin, an American who lived in Tahiti for ten years, served as technical advisor and taught Tierney the Polynesian she speaks in the film.

Opposite page

Gene Tierney and Tyrone Power garbed in sarongs on a Hollywood set with a rear projection of a tropical isle in *Son of Fury.*

Above

The island *wahine* of *Son of Fury* perform a Pacific-style dance. Several of this film's co-stars are veterans of the South Sea cinema genre: Frances Farmer stars in *Ebb Tide* (1937) (based on a Robert Louis Stevenson story) and *South of Pago Pago* (1940); Elsa Lanchester appears in *The Beachcomber* (1938) (based on a Somerset Maugham story. Her off-screen husband, Charles Laughton, plays Captain Bligh and is the patriarch of *The Tuttles of Tahiti*); George Sanders depicts Paul Gauguin in *The Moon and Sixpence* (1942), and John Carradine is in *The Hurricane* (1937).

WHITE SAVAGE

1943 U

D: Arthur Lubin

S: Richard Brooks

P: George Waggner

Cast: Maria Montez, Jon Hall,
        Sabu, Thomas Gomez,
        Sidney Toler, Turhan
        Bey, Al Kikume

Princess Tahia (Montez) rules Temple Island, which contains a sacred pool, the bottom of which is paved with gold. The white boss of a nearby town lusts for the princess and her gold. Sabu played the faithful palace boy. The film ends with a thrilling earthquake sequence set against the vivid South Sea island background.

White Savage was filmed on location at Dana Point, California. A jungle set was erected near Laguna Beach and at Universal Studios.

Right

Latino Maria Montez, Tahitian Jon Hall, and Indian Sabu were three of Hollywood's most popular stars in the 1940s. Here they star in *White Savage*. Hall plays a shark hunter in the first script written by avante garde director Richard Brooks.

WAKE OF THE RED WITCH

1948 REP

D:	Edward Ludwig
S:	Harry Brown and Kenneth Gamet
P:	Herbert J. Yates
Cast:	John Wayne, Gail Russell, Gig Young, Adele Mara, Luther Adler, Paul Fix, Duke Kahanamoku

Captain Ralls (Wayne) is a tempestuous scoundrel torn between love and vengeance, while Mayrant Ruysdaal Sidneye (Adler) is a shipping magnate whose vast empire reaches into every remote lagoon of the South Seas. He heads a giant enterprise called Batjak, LTD., which rose from a group of tramp schooners pirating their way through the Dutch East Indies to a gigantic network of vessels captained by men of dubious character and predatory tendencies. When Ralls loses the woman he loves, he sinks his ship, *The Red Witch,* with a fortune in gold bullion on board.

The ensuing tale is one of bloodthirsty revenge, with Ralls and Sidneye striking at each other in violent fury. Angelique (Russell), is innocently caught in the Batjak maelstrom, which ultimately destroys her.

Teleia (Mara) is a half-caste girl loved by Ralls' friend and partner, Sam Rosen (Young).

John Wayne's memorable octopus fight in *Wake of the Red Witch* was more than just another movie scene for him; it was a vindication. Several years previously, in *Reap the Wild Wind,* he had been felled by a huge, slimy, Technicolor red octopus that had emerged victorious in a battle to the death. In *Wake of the Red Witch,* the tables are turned, and Wayne kills the octopus.

A former football star at University of Southern California, Wayne once more found his athletic ability and experience paying off in difficult and hazardous underwater work, which he did himself without the use of a stunt double.

Olympic swimming champion, father of modern surfing and the man who best personified Hawai'i and its *aloha* spirit, Duke Kahanamoku played a Polynesian chieftain. This is the film in which Wayne, known to his friends as "Duke," meets the Duke of Hawai'i on screen.

Wake of the Red Witch was filmed on the Republic Studios back lot and at the Los Angeles County Arboretum.

S: **Stephanie Nardli**

P: **David E. Rose**

Cast: **Tab Hunter, Linda Darnell**

A young marine and a nurse, the only survivors of a torpedoed troop ship, are stranded on a deserted tropical island.
Island of Desire was filmed in Jamaica.

ALL THE BROTHERS WERE VALIANT

1953 MGM

D: Richard Thorpe
S: Harry Brown, based on the story by Ben Ames William
P: Pandro S. Berman
Cast: Robert Taylor, Stewart Granger, Ann Blyth, Betta St. John

The adventure-drama of 1850s New Bedford whaling brothers who find conflict in the sea and in romance. One brother, Mark (Granger) has an affair with a beautiful native girl among murderous pearl traders in the Gilbert Islands (now known as Kiribati).

South Sea Island scenes were filmed in Jamaica and at the MGM studios back lot.

Left
Betta St. John and Stewart Granger in *All the Brothers Were Valiant*.

DRUMS OF TAHITI
1953 COL

D: William Castle

S: Douglas Heyes and Robert E. Kent

P: Sam Katzman

Cast: Dennis O'Keefe, Patricia Medina, Francis C. Sullivan

An American buys a bride in San Francisco to conceal the fact that he is smuggling in a shipment of guns to be used to drive the French out of Tahiti in 1877. A tropical hurricane and an erupting volcano put an end to the insurrectionists at the film's finale.

Drums of Tahiti was filmed in 3D on the Columbia back lot and at the Los Angeles County Arboretum, though it was publicized as having been filmed in Tahiti.

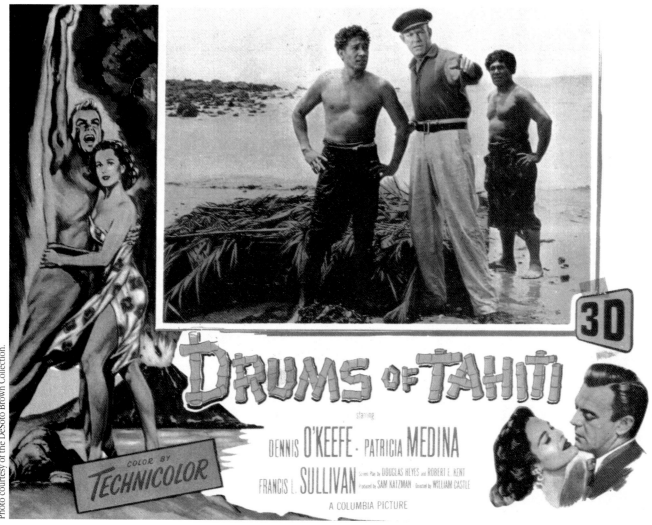

Photo courtesy of the DeSoto Brown Collection.

EAST OF SUMATRA
1953 U

D: **Budd Boeticcher**

S: **Frank Gill Jr., story by Jack Natteford and Louis L'Amour**

P: **Albert J. Cohen**

Cast: **Jeff Chandler, Anthony Quinn, Suzan Ball**

An American mining engineer promises supplies to a Pacific Island ruler. Double-crossed by the home office, he faces a native uprising.

East of Sumatra was filmed at the Universal Studios back lot in Hollywood.

Above

Jeff Chandler, who stars in *Bird of Paradise* (1951), is back in the Islands, along with genre alumnus Anthony Quinn, in *East of Sumatra*. Here, Chandler kisses an island woman. Geographical designations are common in South Seas cinema titles.

760-71

SOUTH SEA WOMAN

1953 WB

D:	**Arthur Lubin**
S:	**Edwin Blum, based on a stage play by William M. Rankin, adapted by Earl Baldwin and Stanley Shapiro.**
P:	**Sam Bischoff**
Cast:	**Burt Lancaster, Virginia Mayo, Chuck Connors**

A comedy adventure story in which two virile marines and a beautiful girl sit out the early days of World War II on a cozy South Sea island. The trio have escaped from Shanghai, where they got involved with waterfront scoundrels who prevented the marines from joining their regiment. They steal a boat, wind up on a Chinese junk, and are put off on a Vichy French-ruled island. Lancaster, as Sgt. O'Hearn, becomes a one-man liberation force as he busts up the marriage between PFC Davy White (Connors) and Ginger Martin (Mayo); commandeers a Nazi yacht, with the help of White, who loses his life; and sinks a Japanese invasion force.

South Sea Woman was filmed at the Warner Bros. studio back lot. Chuck Connors, former Los Angeles baseball player, made his film debut in this movie. He went on to play many film roles, but became best known as McCaine on the long-running television series *The Rifleman.*

288

THE HIGH AND THE MIGHTY
1954 WB

D: William Wellman

S: Ernest K. Gann, based on his novel of the same title

P: Wayne Fellows

Cast: John Wayne, Claire Trevor, Laraine Day, Robert Stack, Jan Sterling, Phil Harris

John Wayne stars as the co-pilot of a crippled airplane en route from Honolulu to San Francisco in which 22 lives hang in the balance. An engine erupts in flames and dangles crazily from a wing. Sullivan (Stack), the pilot, loses his composure, convinced that everyone's fate is sealed. But co-pilot

Dan Roman (Wayne) takes charge, ordering that cargo and baggage be thrown out in an attempt to successfully make the hazardous trip over the Pacific Ocean with their limited amount of fuel.

The passengers aboard the plane review and reevaluate their lives against the backdrop of impending disaster, and their true emotions and characters are revealed as the trip progresses.

Made in 1954 by William Wellman from the best-selling novel by Ernest K. Gann, *The High and the Mighty* established the basic formula for the modern disaster film, one that would be followed for the next forty years in such movies as *Airport* and its sequels. *The High and the Mighty* elevated the disaster itself to a preeminent position within the plot, whereas before, the people thrown together on a doomed journey were always the focus of the film.

The High and the Mighty was one of the most popular films of 1954. Wayne's whistling of the theme song at the film's end set off a national whistling craze, and the recorded song became number one on the record charts.

The Hawai'i sequences in the passenger office of TransOrient Pacific Airlines at Honolulu Airport were actually filmed at Samuel Goldwyn Studios in Los Angeles.

Opposite page

Co-stars Claire Trevor and John Wayne, as co-pilot Dan Roman, aboard the TransOrient Pacific Airline flight that flies from the West Coast to Hawai'i in *The High and the Mighty*, one of the first modern disaster movies.

Below

The High and the Mighty is one of many flight movies which have little to do with Hawai'i, except for the isles being the point of departure or ultimate destination. Here, the great director William Wellman discusses the filming with star John Wayne.

MA AND PA KETTLE AT WAIKIKI
1955 U

D: Lee Sholem

S: Harry Clark, Ellwood Ullman

P: Leonard Goldstein

Cast: Marjorie Main, Percy Kilbride, Lori Nelson, Hilo Hattie

The Kettles travel to Hawai'i, where Pa tries, with his unorthodox country ways, to manage a pineapple empire belonging to his overworked cousin. Ma and Pa meet their Hawaiian equivalents in the form of Hilo Hattie and Charly Lung as Mama and Papa Lotus and their dozen island children.

The comedy teaming of Main and Kilbride established the "hillbilly" characters of Ma and Pa Kettle in the 1947 film *The Egg and I*. Though first as supporting players, Ma and Pa Kettle became two of the most popular screen characters of the early fifties, and Main and Kilbride starred in a series of seven Kettle comedies for Universal.

Filmed on the sound stages and back lot at Universal Studios in Hollywood.

Below
The effervescent Hilo Hattie is on the left, appearing with Marjorie Main in the no-brainer comedy *Ma and Pa Kettle at Waikiki*. Hilo Hattie is the best part of this mildly amusing yarn about Pa as a pineapple king.

Opposite page
Marjorie Main and Percy Killbride as the hillbillies-go-Hawaiian Ma and Pa Kettle. At the end of *Ma and Pa Kettle at Waikiki*, the hicks attend an inevitable *luau*.

THE LITTLE HUT

1957 MGM

D:	Mark Robson
S:	F. Hugh Herbert, based on the play by Andre Roussin.
P:	F. Hugh Herbert and Mark Robson
Cast:	Ava Gardner, David Niven, Stewart Granger

Above

Stewart Granger and grass skirt-clad Ava Gardner in *The Little Hut*, a farce about infidelity amongst a marooned ménage-a-trois. As part of the promotion for *The Little Hut*, a contest was held to give away a Pacific isle.

A comedy about a wife, husband, and lover stranded together on a deserted island.

For the filming in Rome, Italy, a tropical island set was built at Cinecitta's huge stage 15. Background shots were filmed in Jamaica.

HEAVEN KNOWS, MR. ALLISON
1957 TCF

D: **John Huston**

S: **John Lee Mahin and John Huston, based on the novel by Charles Shaw**

P: **Buddy Adler and Eugene Frenke**

Cast: **Robert Mitchum, Deborah Kerr, Fusamoto Takasimi, Noboru Yoshida**

In *Heaven Knows, Mr. Allison,* Robert Mitchum played Allison, a World War II marine who is adrift at sea and washes up on a South Pacific island inhabited solely by a nun, Sister Angela (Deborah Kerr). Their struggle to survive the elements and the returning Japanese makes for a suspenseful and touching story. Although Mitchum and Kerr are practically the only characters in the film, the relationship they develop is of great interest because of the natural, witty dialogue and the dynamic chemistry between them.

Heaven Knows, Mr. Allison was shot on location on the island of Tobago, then a British colony eighteen miles off Trinidad at the southern end of the Caribbean.

"I picked Tobago for two reasons," said director John Huston in a November 18, 1956 New Yo*rk Times* interview by Nan Robertson. "I needed a place that was a dead ringer for a South Seas island, but I needed it nearer. And it had to be a spot where I could spend pounds sterling. This is what we call a 'British Quota' picture."

No Japanese were found in the Caribbean, so the casting search was extended to Sao Paulo, Brazil, where eight Japanese were finally hired and flown to Tobago. The rest of the "Japanese" soldiers in the film were Chinese. One hundred U.S. marines from nearby Trinidad were used in scenes depicting the Marine retaking of the island.

Deborah Kerr was nominated for an Academy Award as Best Actress for her performance in this film.

PEARL OF THE SOUTH PACIFIC
1957 RKO

D: Allan Dwan

S: Jesse Lasky Jr.

P: Benedict Bogeaus

Cast: Dennis Morgan, Virginia Mayo, David Farrar, Lance Fuller

The story of three adventurers seeking a fabulous treasure of pearls on an uncharted island.

Pearl of the South Pacific was filmed in Hollywood on RKO's Sound Stages 9 and 10, complete with a brightly sparkling lagoon, whose waters lapped a sandy beach; scores of natives in colorful costumes moving about beneath tall coconut palms; and a path leading to a temple containing a strange idol and actress Virginia Mayo as a lady missionary in a sarong.

Above
Saronged Virginia Mayo tries
to break a taboo in *Pearl of
the South Pacific*.

ENCHANTED ISLAND

1958 WB

D: Allan Dwan

S: James Leicester, Harold Jacob Smith

P: Benedict Bogeaus

Cast: Dana Andrews, Jane Powell, Don Dubbins, Arthur Shields, Ted de Corsia

Below

Dana Andrews plays Herman Melville's alter ego, and Jane Powell plays his Marquesan lover Fayaway in *Enchanted Island*, based on Melville's first novel, *Typee*, which is 150 years old in 1996 and the first great Western novel based on the South Seas.

Two American seamen in the 1840s jump ship in the Marquesas and take up with a friendly tribe of Polynesians who they later discover are cannibals. The film is loosely based on Herman Melville's novel *Typee*, which was reduced to a formula South Sea Island movie.

The film was made in Technicolor on the west coast of Mexico, which doubled for the South Seas.

"Jane Powell [was] the most unlikely blue-eyed Polynesian yet, with her maidenform bra always clearly visible beneath her Saks sarong..." wrote John Cutts in the May 1958 issue of *Films and Filming*.

Photo courtesy of the DeSoto Brown Collection.

ENCHANTED ISLAND
Technicolor
Starring
DANA ANDREWS
JANE POWELL
Co-starring
DON DUBBINS

Allan Dwan, who also directed *Pearl of the South Pacific*, lensed *Enchanted Island*, a weak adaptation of Herman Melville's first novel, *Typee*, although the movie uses the title from another Melville work. *Typee* is set at "the happy valley" of Taipivai (which Melville misspells) on Nuku Hiva in the Marquesas Islands, and recounts young Melville's real-life adventures after he jumps ship at Taiohae Bay to escape the tyrannical captain of his whaler. Melville (Dana Andrews) accidentally escapes to Taipivai,

reputedly the valley of the South Seas' fiercest inhabitants. Melville discovers, instead, that Taipivai is a paradise, and he falls in love with Fayaway (Jane Powell). Ultimately, he suspects that the Utopian villagers have one minor personality defect—a penchant for human flesh. Suspecting that they are merely fattening him up for the kill, Melville escapes again—returning to the rigors of life aboard a whaling ship. (Melville, of course, went on to write the masterpiece *Moby Dick*.) The story poses, once

again, the existential question of whether the white man can live in paradise after rediscovering it, or, must he be banished from Eden like Adam after the fall? Mexico doubles for the Marquesas in *Enchanted Island*, which has some good Melvillean philosophical dialogue about happiness, love, and freedom in an otherwise vapid version. Friedrich Ledebur, who plays Melville's indigenous attendant Kory-Kory, previously played the cannibal harpoonist Queequeeq in *Moby Dick* (1956).

OPERATION PETTICOAT

1960 U

D:	Blake Edwards
S:	Stanley Shapiro and Maurice Shiplin
P:	Robert Arthur
Cast:	Cary Grant, Tony Curtis, Joan O'Brien, Dina Merrill, Arthur O'Connell, Gene Evans

Grant is admiral Matt Sherman, commander of a battered submarine that can barely manage to crawl along the ocean floor. The only thing keeping the ship afloat is second-in-command Nick Holden (Curtis), who uses every felonious trick in the book to cadge parts and supplies for the vessel. Adding to the fun is an assignment to ferry a group of nurses led by Lt. Duran (Merrill), who are stranded in the Philippines at the start of World War II. The conflict between the crew's libido and the ladies' dramatic operation room rivals the war in intensity.

Together for the first and only time were Gary Grant, the accepted dean of sophisticated humor, and Tony Curtis, the newest star in the comedy field, who had parodied Grant in *Some Like It Hot*.

Operation Petticoat was the third-highest-grossing film of the year, with box-office returns of $6.8 million. The film helped advance the career of its young director, Blake Edwards, who would go on to success with such hits as *The Pink Panther, 10,* and *Victor, Victoria*.

Gavin MacLeod, who later became famous for his television portrayal of the captain on *The Love Boat* series, played one of his first roles in this film.

Photographed in color mostly on location in Key West, Florida, *Operation Petticoat* was filmed with the cooperation of the U.S. Navy.

Opposite page
Cary Grant and Tony Curtis on the set of the WWII comedy *Operation Petticoat*.

NO MAN IS AN ISLAND
1962 U

D: John Monks Jr., Richard Goldstone

S: John Monks Jr., Richard Goldstone

P: John Monks Jr., Richard Goldstone

Cast: Jeffrey Hunter, Marshall Thompson, Barbara Perez

The true story of U.S. Navy radioman George Tweed (Hunter), who was isolated for 31 months on Guam in the first years of World War II, evading capture, while the Japanese placed a price on his head. Tweed alerted the U.S. fleet to the positions of the Japanese defenses and task forces on the island.

No Man Is an Island was one of the first Hollywood-Filipino film co-productions. It was made on a budget of $650,000 and was based entirely on location in the Philippines, which doubled for Guam.

Richard Goldstone had produced 48 episodes of the popular television series *Adventures in Paradise* before turning to independent production with this film.

Jeffrey Hunter was a young actor who had been under contract to Twentieth Century Fox and featured in a number of important motion pictures. His most famous film credits include *Broken Lance, The Searchers* and *King of Kings.* His disappointing roles in bad films in the mid-1960s resulted in a mid-life career slump. He died after surgery following a bad fall in his home which severely injured his head on May 27, 1969.

PT 109

1963 WB

D: Leslie H. Martinson

S: Richard l. Breen

P: Jack L. Warner

Cast: Cliff Robertson, Ty Hardin, James Gregory, Robert Culp, Grant Williams, Robert Blake, Michael Pate

PT 109 was the first and only film so far produced about the life of a president of the United States while he was still in office. Cliff Robertson was cast as young John F. Kennedy.

The story focuses on Lt. John F. Kennedy's 1943 experiences as a torpedo boat skipper in World War II in the Solomon Islands. At approximately 0130 hours, on August 2, 1943, the Japanese destroyer *Amagiri* rammed JFK's

PT 109 in the Blackett Straits. The boat was sheared in half, and two of Kennedy's men were lost. Kennedy led what was left of his crew by swimming and wading to Plum Pudding Island.

All prints of the film were withdrawn by Warner Bros. in view of President Kennedy's assassination on November 22, 1963. The film was released six months earlier and was still playing in theaters.

PT 109 was filmed on the little island of Munson Key, near Key West, Florida.

ENSIGN PULVER
1964 WB

D:	Joshua Logan
S:	Joshua Logan and Peter S. Feibleman
P:	Joshua Logan
Cast:	Robert Walker, Burl Ives, Walter Matthau, Tommy Sands, Larry Hagman, Diana Sands

In this sequel to *Mister Roberts* by Joshua Logan, who directed the play on Broadway, Larry Hagman played a young lieutenant. (His mother, Mary Martin, created the role of Nellie Forbush in Logan's *South Pacific.*) Diana Sands played a Polynesian girl.

Acapulco, Mexico, was chosen as the location for the small fleet of cargo ships found operating there; these World War II-era ships were nearly extinct elsewhere. Filming could also be done there for a fraction of what it would have cost in the South Seas, and Acapulco offered a similar tropical beauty. In addition, it was only three hours away by air from Hollywood.

Actor Walter Matthau later teamed up with the original *Mr. Roberts* Ensign Pulver, Jack Lemmon, in a series of successful comedies (*The Fortune Cookie, The Odd Couple*).

Above
Walter Matthau and Robert Walker Jr. in Acapulco doubling for South Sea island locations in *Ensign Pulver*.

Below

A *McHale's Navy* feature film starring Ernest Borgnine and Tim Conway was released in 1964, based on the World War II TV comedy series of the same name set in the Pacific Theater.

Opposite page

The cast of *McHale's Navy* — on top in the straw hat and Aloha shirt is Ernest Borgnine (who also co-starred in 1953's WWII drama *From Here to Eternity*) as the PT boat commander McHale, and in uniform on the bottom is Tim Conway as Ensign Parker.

FATHER GOOSE
1964 U

D:	Ralph Nelson
S:	Peter Stone and Frank Tarloff, story by S.H. Barnett.
P:	Robert Arthur
Cast:	Gary Grant, Leslie Caron, Trevor Howard

A disheveled South Seas beachcomber (Grant) is pressed into service as a coast watcher to aid in the fight against the Japanese in the early days of World War II. Fun, romance and bits of poignancy and humor come about when Grant, on a rescue mission to another island, finds himself saving a schoolteacher and her seven students.

Outdoor sequences for *Father Goose* were photographed on location along the tropical north shore of Jamaica in the West Indies. Interiors were shot at Universal Studios, Hollywood. Charles Lang, Jr. *(Lives of a Bengal Lancer, One Eyed Jacks)* was the cinematographer.

McHALE'S NAVY
1964 U

D:	Edward J. Montagne
S:	Si Rose, Frank Gill Jr. and George Carleton Brown
P:	Edward J. Montagne
Cast:	Ernest Borgnine, Joe Flynn, Tim Conway

A feature-length color picture based on the zany escapades of the popular World War II television comedy series. The top-rated ABC network show starred Academy Award-winner Ernest Borgnine, who had co-starred in 1953's *From Here to Eternity.*

McHale's Navy centers around the hilarious adventures of a PT boat crew on a South Sea Island naval base. The group gets themselves deeply in debt by restaging week-old Australian horse race results and issuing fresh news sheets to excitement-hungry marines.

One of the most expensive outdoor sets in Universal history was constructed on the studio back lot for the filming of this full-color feature. An entire ten-acre South Pacific Naval base, including a $300,000, seventeen-building complex of Quonset huts and recreation halls, and a jungle were erected on the site.

Also constructed was a 1,500,000-gallon salt-water lagoon, the first of its kind anywhere. The lagoon, formerly of fresh water and approximately one-half the size, was used previously for the *Riverboat* television series. It was drained, deepened and widened by a fleet of bulldozers to accommodate two 85-foot World War II PT boats. Tons of sand were dumped and raked to create seven acres of beach, and studio technicians added green dye to the lagoon to match the ocean color tests, which were made off Catalina Island.

THE FINAL COUNTDOWN
1980 UA

D:	Don Taylor
S:	David Ambrose, Gerry Davis, Thomas Hunter, Peter Powell
P:	Peter Vincent Douglas
Cast:	Kirk Douglas, James Farentino, Katherine Ross, Martin Sheen

The largest nuclear-powered aircraft carrier in the world, the USS *Nimitz*, and its crew go back in time to the eve of December 7, 1941. They have the chance to stop the Japanese invasion and prevent the Pearl Harbor tragedy by blasting the attacking armada from the skies.

The Final Countdown was filmed in San Diego and at Norfolk Naval Base, Virginia. Some stock shots of Diamond Head and Pearl Harbor were interspersed in the beginning credits of an aerial helicopter transport.

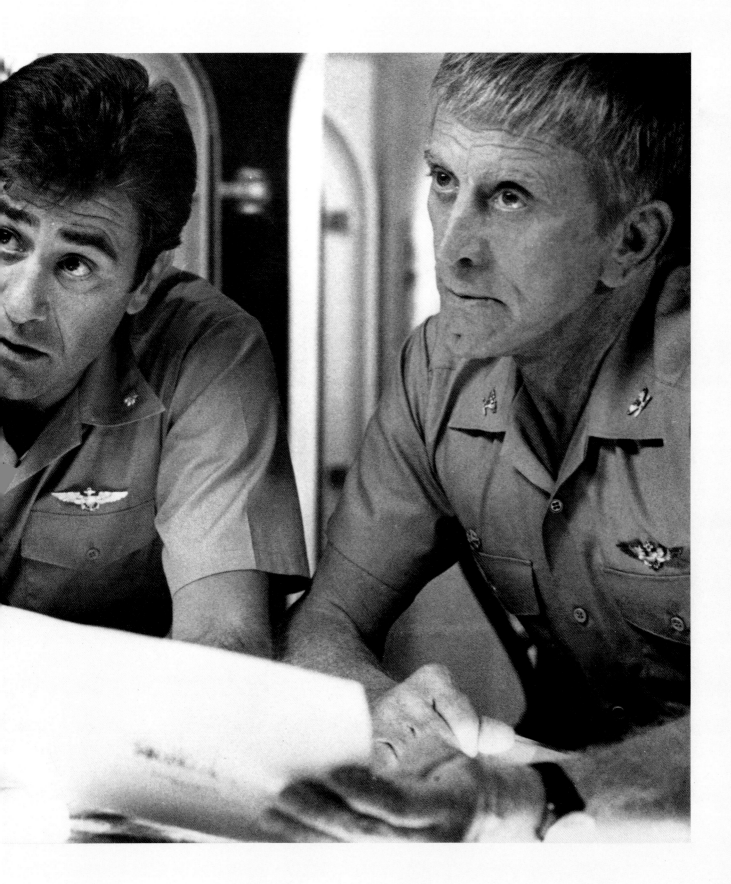

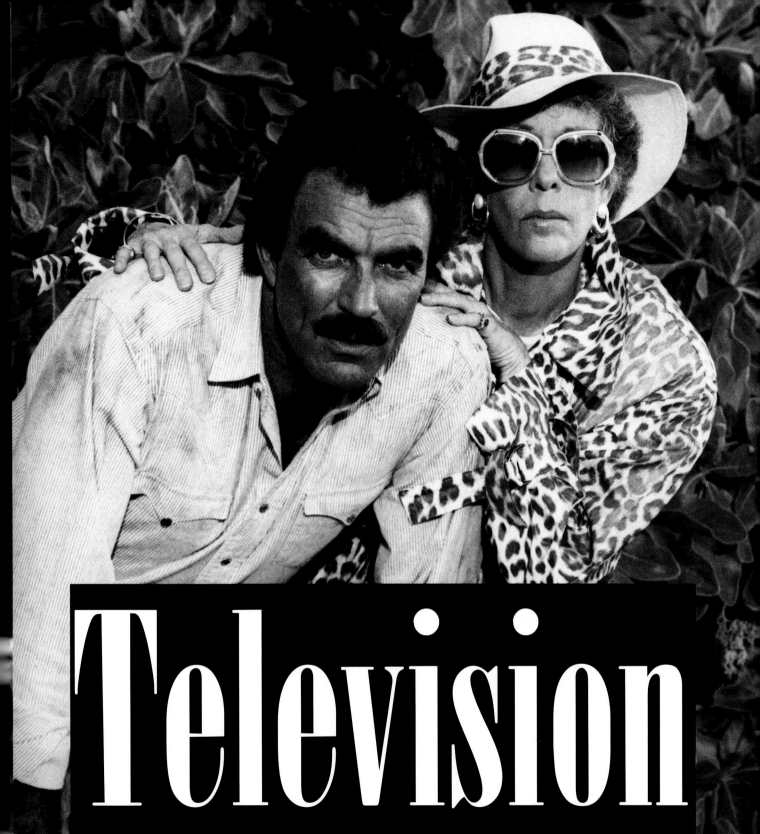

Television

Following are abbreviations for the American television networks used in the listings:

ABC—American Broadcasting Company
NBC—National Broadcasting Company
CBS—Columbia Broadcasting System

Hawai'i and South Sea Island-set Network Series, Movies-Of-The-Week and Specials

Previous pages
"Book 'em, Dano!"—Jack Lord in his signature role as special unit chief Steve McGarrett in *Hawaii Five-O*.

Tom Selleck as private investigator Thomas Sullivan Magnum in an episode of *Magnum, P.I.*, with guest star Carol Burnett, a former Hawai'i resident.

This page
Gardner McKay as the heartthrob Captain Adam Troy in the first Hollywood TV series set in the Pacific, the James Michener-created *Adventures in Paradise*.

South Seas TV goes back to the so-called "Golden Age" of television. *Adventures in Paradise*, based on an idea by James Michener, premiered in the 1950s and starred Gardner McKay, who still lives on Oahu. (*The Adventures of Captain David Grief*, a 1956 syndication, preceded *Adventures in Paradise*.) It was followed by *Hawaiian Eye*, starring Robert Contrad, in 1959, Hawai'i's Statehood year, and started the TV trend of detective shows in Hawai'i that has continued as recently as 1995's *Marker* series and the made-for-TV movie *Crowfoot*. The heroes of all these shows are mainland transplants—usually military veterans who, for mysterious personal reasons, end up in Hawai'i chasing criminals.

In terms of television productions and broadcasts, Hawai'i is one of the most successful states in the Union. From 1968 until 1989, with *Hawaii Five-O*, *Magnum P.I.*, and then *Island Son*, Hawai'i had an unbroken 21-year stretch of network series on the air. Only two other states, California and New York, equal and/or surpass this impressive record. Obviously, with beautiful locales and locals, trained casts and crews, and readily available film and TV facilities, Hawai'i is a popular place to shoot television series and productions (including commercials).

The Hawai'i of the 1990s is also a place for serious documentaries. Stephanie Castillo's poignant *Simple Courage*, which compares Father Damien's nineteenth-century struggle with Hansen's disease (formerly called leprosy) to the contemporary AIDS epidemic, won an Emmy and CINE Golden Eagle awards. Edgy Lee, another local documentarian, also had her work *Papakolea*, about the cause of Hawaiian homesteaders in Honolulu, broadcast nationwide on public television.

The TV mini-series *Pearl* (1978–79) was a *From Here to Eternity* knock-off combining torrid love triangles and warfare. The soap opera-ish *Pearl* co-starred Angie Dickinson, Dennis Weaver, Lesley Ann Warren, and Robert Wagner. Gregg Henry portrays a Navy pilot involved in a controversial affair with a Japanese woman played by Tiana Alexandra.

ADVENTURES IN PARADISE
1959-1962 ABC

Cast: Gardner McKay

Captain Adam Troy (McKay) in his freelance schooner, the *Tiki*, plies the South Pacific in search of passengers, cargo and adventure, which are found in abundance. Troy is a Korean War veteran who had found the Pacific to his liking.

James A. Michener created *Adventures in Paradise* and sold the original idea to television. The program was filmed primarily on the Twentieth Century Fox back lot, with some second unit location shooting in the South Pacific.

FLYING DOCTOR
SYNDICATED IN 1959

Cast: Richard Denning, Jill Addams

A half-hour adventure series about a doctor who brings medicinal care via airplane to the remote Australian outback and the Pacific Isles.

HAWAIIAN EYE
1959-1963 WB

Cast: Robert Conrad, Anthony Eisley, Connie
Stevens, Poncie Ponce, Troy Donahue

Hawaiian Eye is a Honolulu-based private detective agency owned and operated by Tom Lopaka (Conrad), born and raised in the Islands, and Tracy Steele (Eisley), who hails from Chicago. They are assisted by Crickett Blake (Stevens), a beautiful singer at what is now the Hilton Hawaiian Village. Together, through their investigative work, they strive to eliminate the sources of trouble that invade tropical paradise.

Kim, the taxi driver, a featured regular, was played by Native Hawaiian entertainer Poncie Ponce, who was

Above
Gardner McKay and Jo Morrow in *Adventures in Paradise*.

A scene from *Adventures in Paradise*, based on James Michener's Pacific-based story idea. Series star Gardner McKay is multi-talented; in addition to acting, he sculpts, writes plays and novels, and more.

Left
The cast of *Hawaiian Eye*.

The opening title sequence included such Hawaiian landmarks as Blow Hole, Diamond Head, Lanikai, Aloha Tower and the Royal Palace. A tag line for the series during its debut season was "If you haven't visited the newest state yet, 'Hawaiian Eye' television series is the next best thing to it."

This detective series with a Hawai'i background was originally based on the successful *77 Sunset Strip* TV series formula, which also included the Miami-set series *Surfisde 6* and the New Orleans locale of *Bourbon St. Beat*, where characters and story lines could be transferred from one Warner Bros. TV series to the other.

Hawaiian Eye made a concerned effort to offer viewers Hawaiian culture, music and history through its story lines and presentation of modern-day images of Hawai'i as America's newest state. The producers insisted that whenever possible stories be used that could happen nowhere else but in Hawai'i.

The popular series theme music, "Hawaiian Eye," was written by Mack David and Jerry Livingston.

discovered during a Los Angeles nightclub engagement by a Warner Bros. producer. Kim is the original small-time operator who buys and sells everything and, if he can't handle the problem, one of his many relatives can.

Douglas Kinilau Mossman, born in the Islands of Hawaiian-Scotch ancestry, played Moke, the night security guard at the agency. A graduate of Kamehameha School and the University of Hawai'i, Mossman also served as technical advisor on the series, making sure everything was island authentic. Actor Grant Williams, as Greg MacKenzie, joined the firm as a special investigator from the mainland after appearing in several previous episodes. In 1962, Troy Donahue joined the series as Don Barton, special events director at the hotel and became a love interest for Crickett Blake.

Warner Bros. produced 134 episodes of this one-hour filmed series for the ABC-TV network in black and white, which made its debut on October 7, 1959. The first four episodes' exteriors were shot in Hawai'i. The rest were shot largely in and around Los Angeles at the Warner Bros. studios in Burbank.

Hundreds of second-unit Hawaiian stock shots were used to create an island atmosphere. In 1962, the troupe filmed four episodes on location in Hawai'i.

THE ISLANDERS
1960-1961 ABC

Cast: William Reynolds, James Philbrook

The story of pilots flying their airline in the Spice Islands of the East Indies. Smugglers, escaped convicts, stolen goods, and mysterious beautiful women were always keeping them busy.

BEACHCOMBER
1961 SYNDICATED

Cast: Cameron Mitchell, Don Megowan, Sebastian Cabot

A wealthy San Francisco merchandising executive retreats to a South Pacific island paradise to seek the meaning of life. The half-hour adventure series pilot was filmed in Hawai'i.

GILLIGAN'S ISLAND
1964-1967 CBS

Cast: Bob Denver, Alan Hale Jr.

A half-hour comedy series about a diverse group of shipwrecked castaways on a deserted island.

September 26, 1964 marked the very first episode of *Gilligan's Island.* Creator Sherwood Schwartz had worked hard to convince CBS executives that his new comedy would be a success. With great reluctance, United Artists and CBS had finally shot the pilot at Moloaa Bay, off the island of Kauai, Hawai'i. The island shown behind the show's credits is Coconut Island, located in Kaneohe Bay on the northeast shore of Oahu. The actual series was filmed at CBS Studio Center in the San Fernando Valley on stage 2 and on the back lot, where a lagoon was built.

In the pilot, Bob Denver starred as Gilligan, Alan Hale Jr. as Skipper, Jim Backus as Thurston Howell III, and

Natalie Schafer as Lovey Howell. The other three castaways featured a high school teacher (John Gabriel) and two secretaries (Kit Smythe as Ginger and Nancy McCarthy as Bunny). After earning terrific scores in audience testing, the pilot was sold and *Gilligan's Island* had begun.

Schwartz then recast the other three roles with Russell Johnson as Professor, Tina Louise as sexy Hollywood actress Ginger Grant, and Dawn Welles as Mary Ann Summers. *Gilligan's Island* remained in the CBS lineup for three seasons. The series of 92 shows finished first in its time period all three seasons. The castaways were still stranded on that tiny deserted isle, never rescued when the show was canceled.

Gilligan's Island proved its staying power in a Saturday morning animated series and three made-for-television movies, including *Rescue From Gilligan's Island* (1978), *The Castaways on Gilligan's Island* (1979) and *The Harlem Globetrotters on Gilligan's Island* (1981).

SINGER PRESENTS HAWAII-HO
1968 NBC

Don Ho, Hawai'i's most popular export to the mainland since surfing, brought his casual and relaxed delivery of songs to television in his first network special.

Ho was joined by members of his traveling troupe, including the Aliis and Robin Wilson. Five hundred children from the choir of the Kamehameha School, which Ho attended as a boy, joined in singing aloha. Locations ranged from the lagoons and beaches of the five islands to the nightclubs and airport of Hawai'i.

HAWAII FIVE-O
1968-1980 CBS
Cast: **Jack Lord, James MacArthur, Kam Fong, Zulu, Herman Wedemeyer, Richard Denning as the Governor and Khigh Dhiegh as Wo Fat.**

Photo courtesy of Rita Ractliffe photo archives.

Hawaii Five-O was a crime series set in the lush surroundings of Hawai'i. The plot centers on a four-man Hawai'i state police unit headed by Steve McGarrett (Lord), who, according to the script, reported only to the Governor. The unit tackled such high felony crimes as espionage and drug traffic. The other members of the unit were Dan "Dano" Williams, played by James MacArthur; Chin Ho Kelly, played by Kam Fong; and Kono, played by Zulu. Kam Fong is a former Honolulu policeman and Zulu is a Native Hawaiian.

Supposedly, writer Leonard Freeman originated the popular show after his mother-in-law, who lived in Honolulu, suggested he develop "something about Hawai'i so that he and his wife would visit more often."

During a meeting with Governor John Burns, Freeman learned that Burns was planning to start a special police task force to deal with unusual crimes in the islands and was going to call the force "Five-O." According to Oseransky, "Lenny went back and wrote a television series called 'Hawaii Five-O' based on that unit."

The long-running series was filmed on location in the Hawaiian Islands primarily on Oahu and in and around Honolulu. Each time a move was made, the cameras, cables, mikes, sound equipment, etc., were piled into trucks and lugged to the next spot. It was a good deal more cumbersome than using a sound stage or the back lot of a Hollywood studio, but the effect was far more realistic and interesting.

Filming was comprised of almost 70 percent exterior shots to take advantage of the exotic beauty of the islands. Leonard Freeman and Jack Lord were partners, Freeman watching the shop in Hollywood, developing scripts, hiring guest stars and directors, and Lord running the show in Hawai'i. The film was flown daily to Hollywood for processing and editing.

Also contributing to the authentic atmosphere of the show were the bit and walk-on parts filled by island residents, the majority of them nonprofessionals. Everyone,

Opposite page
Hawaii Five-O star Jack Lord came to represent Hawai'i in the minds of millions of viewers around the world. Lord is a native New Yorker.

Above
Chinese-French beauty France Nuyen specialized in so-called "exotic" roles, and appeared in several Pacific-related productions, such as *South Pacific* and *Diamond Head.* Nuyen was a guest star on *Hawaii Five-O;* here, she's on location near Waikiki with series star Jack Lord.

Photo courtesy of Rita Ractliffe photo archives.

from the doorman of a well-known hotel (cast as a legislator) to real legislators, lawyers and housewives, auditioned.

At the time, it was technically difficult to film a series in Hawai'i because no permanent production facilities were available. Filmmakers who shot in the islands virtually moved in, bringing cameras and building sound stages and sets, and then moved out, taking everything with them.

An on-the-job production training program was carefully planned by local producer and production manager, Bernie Oseransky, which resulted in today's small army of trained film professionals, many of whom after twelve years of *Hawaii Five-O* went on to work on *Magnum P.I.* and other shows and films.

Hawaii Five-O conveyed a representative image of Hawai'i, its beauty, its racial mixtures and way of life.

Lord worked seventy to eighty-hour weeks on *Hawaii Five-O*. The role of McGarrett made him an internationally known television star and gave him financial security.

Lord directed a number of *Five-O* episodes over the years and was nominated for a Directors Guild of America award for the critically acclaimed episode "Why Won't Linda Die?" The show traveled on location to Hong Kong for the opening presentation of the 1977-78 season and to Singapore for a two-hour episode in February of 1979.

Every great detective has his arch-adversary, and Steve McGarrett, head of Hawai'i's elite Five-O unit, was haunted for twelve exciting seasons by that malevolent master criminal, Wo Fat. This sinister thorn in McGarrett's side first appeared in the two-hour motion picture for television that preceded the show.

This CBS television series, which ended its twelve-year run in 1980, provided benefits of over $100,000,000 to Hawai'i via the tourism it attracted. The spending effect the series had on Hawai'i's economy was almost $180,000,000—it paid an estimated $16,000,000 in state taxes, created 7,992 jobs a year, and developed Hawai'i as a film center in the Pacific.

HAWAII FIVE-O BROADCAST HISTORY

After 12 seasons on the air and 290 hours, virtually every big-name actor or actress guest-starred on the series, as well as lesser-known talents who have gone on to fame.

The list includes: Victoria Principal, Barry Bostwick, George Lazenby, Manu Tupou, James Darren, Ed Asner, Charles Cioffi, Cameron Mitchell, Robert Loggia, John Saxon, Erik Estrada, Richard Yniguez, Edward James Olmos, Henry Darrow, Robert Vaughn, Diana Scarwid, Mildred Natwick, Ross Martin, Nehemiah Persoff, Cyd Charisse, Rory Calhoun, Tim Thomerson, Janis Paige, Martin Sheen, Samantha Eggar, Tab Hunter, Barbara Luna, Harry Guardino, Jackie Coogan, Moses Gunn, Ricardo Montalban, Pernell Roberts, Jack Soo, France Nuyen and Hawai'i's own Hilo Hattie.

Some of the Oahu, Hawai'i, locations used on the series include: Honolulu Stadium, Hilton Hawaiian Village, Kahala Park, Dillingham Fountain, Diamond Head Crater, Honolulu International Airport, Hawaii State Library (main location), Iolani Palace and Grounds, Hawai'i Kai, North Shore of Oahu, Ilikai Hotel, Diamond Head Tunnel, Leahi Hospital, Hawai'i State Capitol, Cannon Club-Fort Ruger, Kaimana Beach Hotel, Ewa Sugar Plantation, Crosley Ranch-Mililani, Ala Moana Park, Makapuu Beach and Cliff, Bellows Air Force Base, Chinese Cultural Center.

Below

(left-right) Kam Fong, James MacArthur and Jack Lord are surprised to see the corpse get up after a scene is shot on location in Hawai'i for *Hawaii Five-O.*

HAWAII FIVE-O 1968-1969 Season

Pilot: Cocoon

1. FULL FATHOM FIVE
2. STRANGERS IN OUR OWN LAND
3. TIGER BY THE TAIL
4. SAMURAI
5. ...AND THEY PAINTED DAISIES ON HIS COFFIN
6. TWENTY-FOUR KARAT KILL
7. THE WAYS OF LOVE
8. NO BLUES SKIES
9. BY THE NUMBERS
10. DEATHWATCH
11. PRAY, LOVE, REMEMBER—PRAY, LOVE, REMEMBER
12. KING OF THE HILL
13. UPTIGHT
14. FACE OF THE DRAGON
15. THE BOX
16. ONE FOR THE MONEY
17. ALONG CAME JOEY
18. ONCE UPON A TIME, PART 1
19. ONCE UPON A TIME, PART 2
20. NOT THAT MUCH DIFFERENT
21. SIX KILOS
22. THE BIG KAHUNA
23. YESTERDAY DIED AND TOMORROW WON'T BE BORN

1969-1970 Season

1. A THOUSAND PARDONS—YOU'RE DEAD!
2. TO HELL WITH BABE RUTH
3. FORTY FEET HIGH AND IT KILLS!
4. JUST LUCKY, I GUESS
5. SAVAGE SUNDAY
6. A BULLET FOR MCGARRETT
7. SWEET TERROR
8. THE KING KAMEHAMEHA BLUES
9. THE SINGAPORE FILE
10. ALL THE KING'S HORSES
11. LEOPARD ON THE ROCK
12. THE DEVIL AND MR. FROG
13. THE JOKER'S WILD, MAN, WILD!
14. WHICH WAY DID THEY GO?
15. BLIND TIGER
16. BORED, SHE HUNG HERSELF
17. RUN, JOHNNY, RUN
18. KILLER BEE
19. THE ONE WITH THE GUN
20. CRY, LIE
21. MOST LIKELY TO MURDER
22. NIGHTMARE ROAD
23. THREE DEAD COWS AT MAKAPUU, Part 1
24. THREE DEAD COWS AT MAKAPUU, Part 2
25. KISS THE QUEEN GOODBYE

1970-1971 Season

1. ...AND A TIME TO DIE
2. TROUBLE IN MIND
3. THE SECOND SHOT
4. TIME AND MEMORIES
4. THE GUARNERIUS CAPER
6. THE RANSOM
7. FORCE OF WAVES
8. THE REUNION
9. THE LATE JOHN LOUISIANA
10. THE LAST EDEN
11. OVER 50?—STEAL
12. BEAUTIFUL SCREAMER
13. THE PAYOFF
14. THE DOUBLE WALL
15. PANIOLO
16. TEN THOUSAND DIAMONDS AND A HEART
17. F.O.B. HONOLULU, PART 1
18. F.O.B. HONOLULU, PART 2
19. THE GUNRUNNER
20. DEAR ENEMY
21. THE BOMBER AND MRS. MORONEY
22. THE GRANDSTAND PLAY, PART 1
23. THE GRANDSTAND PLAY, PART 2
24. TO KILL OR BE KILLED

1971-1972 Season

1. HIGHEST CASTLE, DEEPEST GRAVE
2. NO BOTTLES...NO CANS...NO PEOPLE
3. 3000 CROOKED MILES TO HONOLULU
4. TWO DOVES AND MR. HERON
5. ....AND I WANT SOME CANDY AND A GUN THAT SHOOTS....
6. AIR CARGO-DIAL FOR MURDER
7. FOR A MILLION, WHY NOT?
8. THE BURNING ICE
9. REST IN PEACE, SOMEBODY
10. A MATTER OF MUTUAL CONCERN
11. NINE, TEN, YOU'RE DEAD
12. IS THIS ANY WAY TO RUN A PARADISE?
13. ODD MAN IN....
14. BAIT ONCE, BAIT TWICE
15. THE 90 SECOND WAR, PART 1
16. THE 90 SECOND WAR, PART 2
17. SKINHEAD
18. WHILE YOU'RE AT IT, BRING IN THE MOON
19. CLOTH OF GOLD
20. GOOD NIGHT, BABY—TIME TO DIE!
21. DIDN'T WE MEET AT A MURDER?
22. FOLLOW THE WHITE BRICK ROAD
23. R&R&R
24. WEDNESDAY, LADIES FREE

1972-1973 Season

1. DEATH IS A COMPANY POLICY
2. DEATH WISH ON TANTALUS MOUNTAIN
3. YOU DON'T HAVE TO KILL TO GET RICH, BUT IT HELPS
4. PIG IN A BLANKET
5. THE JINN WHO CLEARS THE WAY
6. FOOLS DIE TWICE
7. CHAIN OF EVENTS
8. JOURNEY OUT OF LIMBO
9. "V" FOR VASHON: THE SON
10. "V" FOR VASHON: THE FATHER
11. "V" FOR VASHON: THE PATRIARCH
12. THE CLOCK STRUCK TWELVE
13. I'M A FAMILY CROOK-DON'T SHOOT!
14. THE CHILD STEALERS
15. THANKS FOR THE HONEYMOON
16. THE LISTENER
17. HERE TODAY-GONE TONIGHT
18. THE ODD LOT CAPER
19. WILL THE REAL MR. WINKLER PLEASE DIE?
20. LITTLE GIRL BLUE
21. PERCENTAGE
22. ENGAGED TO BE BURIED
23. THE DIAMOND THAT NOBODY STOLE
24. JURY OF ONE

1973-1974 Season

1. HOOKMAN
2. DRAW ME A KILLER
3. CHARTER FOR DEATH
4. ONE BIG HAPPY FAMILY
5. THE SUNDAY TORCH
6. MURDER IS A TAXING AFFAIR
7. TRICKS ARE NOT TREATS
8. WHY WAIT TILL UNCLE KEVIN DIES?
9. FLASH OF COLOR, FLASH OF DEATH
10. A BULLET FOR EL DIABLO
11. THE FINISHING TOUCH
12. ANYBODY CAN BUILD A BOMB
13. TRY TO DIE ON TIME
14. THE $100,000 NICKEL
15. THE FLIP SIDE IS DEATH
16. THE BANZAI PIPELINE
17. ONE BORN EVERY MINUTE
18. SECRET WITNESS
19. DEATH WITH FATHER
20. MURDER WITH A GOLDEN TOUCH
21. NIGHTMARE IN BLUE
22. MOTHER'S DEADLY HELPER
23. KILLER AT SEA
24. 30,000 ROOMS AND I HAVE THE KEY
25. THE MINDS OF DR. IMMACULARI (2 hrs)

1974-1975 Season

1. THE YOUNG ASSASSINS
2. A HAWAIIAN NIGHTMARE
3. I'll KILL 'EM AGAIN
4. STEAL NOW, PAY LATER
5. BOMB, BOMB, WHO'S GOT THE BOMB?
6. RIGHT GRAVE, WRONG BODY
7. WE HANG OUR OWN
8. THE TWO FACED CORPSE
9. HOW TO STEAL A MASTERPIECE
10. A GUN FOR MCGARRETT
11. WELCOME TO OUR BRANCH OFFICE
12. PRESENTING IN THE CENTER RING—MURDER
13. HARA-KIRI: MURDER
14. BONES OF CONTENTION
15. COMPUTER KILLER
16. A WOMAN'S WORK IS WITH A GUN
17. SMALL WITNESS LARGE CRIME
18. RING OF LIFE
19. STUDY IN RAGE
20. AND THE HORSE JUMPED OVER THE MOON.
21. HIT GUN FOR SALE
22. THE HOSTAGE
23. DIARY OF A GUN
24. 6,000 DEADLY TICKETS

1975-1976 Season

1. MURDER—EYES ONLY
2. McGARRETT IS MISSING
3. TERMINATION WITH EXTREME PREJUDICE
4. TARGET? THE LADY
5. DEATHS NAME IS SAM
6. THE CASE AGAINST MCGARRETT
7. THE DEFECTOR
8. SING A SONG OF SUSPENSE
9. RETIRE IN SUNNY HAWAII—FOREVER
10. HOW TO STEAL A SUBMARINE
11. THE WATERFRONT STEAL
12. HONOR IS AN UNMARKED GRAVE
13. A TOUCH OF GUILT
14. WOODEN HULL OF A RAT
15. DEADLY PERSUASION
16. LEGACY OF HONOR
17. LOOSE ENDS GET HIT
18. ANATOMY OF A BRIBE
19. TURKEY SHOOT AT MAKAPUU
20. A KILLER GROWS WINGS
21. CAPSULE KIDNAPPING
22. LOVE THY NEIGHBOR, TAKE HIS WIFE
23. A SENTENCE TO STEAL
24. VENDETTA FOR A MIXED TRIO

1976-1977 Season

1. NINE DRAGONS
2. ASSAULT ON A PALACE
3. OLDEST PROFESSION, LATEST PRICE
4. MAN ON FIRE
5. TOUR DE FORCE—KILLER ABOARD
6. THE LAST OF THE GREAT PAPER HANGERS
7. HEADS, YOU'RE DEAD
8. LET DEATH DO US PART
9. DOUBLE EXPOSURE
10. YES, MY DEADLY DAUGHTER
11. TARGET—A COP
12. THE BELLS TOLL AT NOON
13. MAN IN A STEEL FRAME
14. READY, AIM
15. ELEGY IN A RAIN FOREST
16. DEALERS CHOICE—BLACKMAIL
17. A CAPITOL CRIME
18. TO DIE IN PARADISE
19. BLOOD MONEY IS HARD TO WASH
20. TO KILL A MIND
21. REQUIEM FOR A SADDLE BRONC RIDER
22. SEE HOW SHE RUNS
23. PRACTICAL JOKES CAN KILL YOU

1977-1978 Season

1. UP THE REBELS
2. YOU DON'T SEE MANY PIRATES THESE DAYS
3. THE COP ON THE COVER
4. THE FRIENDS OF JOEY KALIMA
5. THE DESCENT OF THE TORCHES
6. THE NINTH STEP
7. SHAKE HANDS WITH THE MAN ON THE MOON
8. DEADLY DOUBLES
9. DEEP COVER
10. TSUNAMI
11. EAST WIND, ILL WIND
12. TREAD THE KING'S SHADOW
13. THE BIG ALOHA
14. A SHORT WALK ON THE LONG SHORE
15. THE SILK TRAP
16. HEAD TO HEAD
17. TALL ON THE WAVE
18. ANGEL IN BLUE
19. WHEN DOES A WAR END?
20. INVITATION TO A MURDER
21. FROZEN ASSETS
22. MY FRIEND, THE ENEMY
23. A STRANGER IN HIS GRAVE
24. A DEATH IN THE FAMILY
25. DIE-HARD ON DIAMOND HEAD

1978-1979 Season

1. THE SLEEPER
2. HOROSCOPE FOR MURDER
3. DEADLY COURIER
4. THE CASE AGAINST PHILIP CHRISTIE
5. SMALL POTATOES
6. A DISTANT THUNDER
7. DEATH MASK
8. THE MIRACLE MAN
9. A LONG TIME AGO
10. WHY WON'T LINDA DIE?
11. NUMBER ONE WITH A BULLET, PART 1
12. NUMBER ONE WITH A BULLET, PART II
13. THE MEIGHAN CONSPIRACY
14. THE SPIRIT IS WILLIE
15. THE BARK AND THE BITE
16. STRINGER
17. THE EXECUTION FILE
18. A VERY PERSONAL MATTER
19. THE SKYLINE KILLER
20. THE YEAR OF THE HORSE
21. THE PAGODA FACTOR
22. THE STALKING HORSE

1979-1980 Season

1. A LION IN THE STREETS
2. WHO SAYS COPS DON'T CRY?
3. THOUGH THE HEAVENS FALL
4. SIGN OF THE RAM
5. GOOD HELP IS HARD TO FIND
6. IMAGE OF FEAR
7. USE A GUN, GO TO HELL
8. VOICE OF TERROR
9. A SHALLOW GRAVE
10. THE KAHUNA
11. LABYRINTH
12. SCHOOL FOR ASSASSINS
13. FOR OLD TIMES SAKE
14. THE GOLDEN NOOSE
15. THE FLIGHT OF THE JEWELS
16. CLASH OF SHADOWS
17. A BIRD IN HAND
18. THE MOROVILLE COVENANT
19. WOE TO WO FAT

THE LITTLE PEOPLE A/K/A THE BRIAN KEITH SHOW
1972-1974 CBS
Cast: Brian Keith, Shelley Fabares

Two pediatricians, a widowed father and his daughter, run a free clinic, as well as a private practice, on Oahu. The office was run by a Hawaiian nurse played by Hawai'i-born Victoria Leialoha Young (who became the third Mrs. Brian Keith in real life). Concern for kids formed the crux of the stories. In the second season the show underwent a title and character changes. It was filmed on location in Hawai'i.

Above
Brian Keith in *The Little People.*

Below
Perry Como's 1976 Hawaiian special.

ELVIS PRESLEY, ALOHA FROM HAWAII VIA SATELLITE
1973 NBC
Cast: Elvis Presley

This historic, highly rated Elvis Presley concert special was broadcast worldwide via satellite on January 14, 1973, from the Honolulu International Center Arena in Honolulu, Hawai'i, as a benefit concert for the Kui Lee Cancer Fund.

THE DON HO SHOW
1976 ABC
Cast: Don Ho, Patti Swallie, Angel Pablo, Sam Kapu and Tokyo Joe

A daily comedy variety program starring Don Ho as host and originating at Waikiki Beach, the show premiered on ABC on October 25 and ran for thirteen weeks. It was taped at the Cinerama Reef Hotel in Honolulu in a new studio designed to provide an exterior-interior feeling.

PERRY COMO'S HAWAIIAN HOLIDAY
1976 NBC

Cast: Perry Como

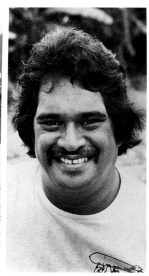

A musical travelogue special set in Hawai'i starred Perry Como as he visited many of the Hawaiian Islands' scenic wonders, intergrating local music, song and dance with old standards.

BIG HAWAII
1977 NBC

Cast: John Dehner, Cliff Potts, Elizabeth Smith, Moe Keale

A sprawling paradise ranch on the island of Hawai'i is the private domain of autocratic Barrett Fears (Dehner). Mitch Fears (Potts) is a son who has returned to help run the ranch. Bill Lucking is Oscar Kalahani, ranch foreman, and Elizabeth Smith is Lulu Kalahani.

M STATION HAWAII
1979 CBS

Cast: Jack Lord

A feature-length pilot film created, starring and directed by Jack Lord, from a script written by Bob James. The pilot, filmed in Hawai'i, was not picked up as a series.

BAA BAA BLACK SHEEP A/K/A THE BLACK SHEEP SQUADRON
1976-1978 NBC

Cast: Robert Conrad

One-hour series based on the real-life exploits of Marine Corps Major Gregory "Pappy" Boyington, a World War II flying ace, and his squadron of misfits in the Solomon Islands.

Above

Elizabeth Smith, Moe Keale and Remi Abellira in *Big Hawaii*. Moe Keale is a gifted Hawaiian musician, who has also acted in a number of Hawai'i-based productions. He had a recurring role as Leon, the chauffeur, in the 1995 action series *Marker*, and appeared in 1995's *Picture Bride*.

Below

Hawaiian Eye's Robert Conrad in another Pacific-related role, as "Pappy" Eddie Boyington in *Baa Baa Black Sheep*, a World War II series set in the Solomon Islands.

Though set in the South Pacific, it was filmed just outside of Los Angeles in an area near Newhall called Indian Dunes and at Universal Studios, utilizing actual World War II aerial combat color footage.

MAGNUM P.I.
1980-1988 CBS

Cast: Tom Selleck, John Hillerman, Roger E. Mosley, Larry Manetti

Thomas Sullivan Magnum (Selleck), retired from the Navy after serving in Vietnam, turns private eye and lives an idyllic life keeping tabs on security at a lush beachfront mansion on Oahu's North Shore. His companion is the estate's knowledgeable but stuffy major domo, Jonathan Q. Higgins (John Hillerman), who disapproves intensely of Magnum's freewheeling ways.

In the first two-hour special episode, on December 11, 1980, the fun-loving private detective boldly takes on Navy higher-ups to track down the cold-blooded murderers of his best friend. Magnum becomes a target in the process and calls for help from resourceful fellow members of his special combat team in Vietnam, helicopter charter pilot T.C. Calvin (Roger E. Mosley) and Rick Wright (Larry Manetti).

Thus began the eight-year, 162-episode run of *Magnum P.I.*, the one-hour detective series filmed entirely in Hawai'i.

A veteran of television movies, Tom Selleck in 1978 had guest-starred in *The Rockford Files* as detective Lance White. The oil-and-water combination of the noble, pristine and slightly pompous Lance White and Rockford worked so well that CBS wanted to make a series with Selleck as a private eye.

The charming, tall, dark and handsome Selleck had already played a cop in the 1977 NBC pilot *Bunco*, with Robert Urich, and portrayed an Army captain in CBS's *The Gypsy Warriors*, with James Whitmore Jr. In 1979,

CBS reteamed him with Whitmore as private eye Tom Boston in *Boston and Kilbride*, which was not successful.

The network asked Glen Larson, producer of *McCloud* and *Switch*, two popular series, for a script. He gave them *Magnum*, the story of a James Bond-style private eye, ex-CIA agent who lived on the private estate of an author named Robin Masters. Magnum lived in the guest house all by himself except for his killer Doberman and a roomful of fantastic gadgets.

Larson didn't want to proceed with the project and turned the script over to Don Bellisario, who had his own private eye pilot script, *H.H. Flynn.* He combined his script with Larson's to create *Magnum P.I.*

Hawaii Five-O was going off the air after twelve seasons, and CBS persuaded Bellisario to set *Magnum* in Hawai'i to make use of the production facilities built there. The pilot, made in the spring of 1980, got an order to go to series before it was even aired. The initial episode, shown on December 11, 1980, ranked number 14 for the year and had an overall rating of 21.0.

Magnum aired all over the world, well before the end of its primetime life, and continues to be popular.

The supervising producer in Hawai'i was Charles Floyd Johnson, and the music was by Mike Post and Pete Carpenter. *Magnum P.I.* contributed $100 million directly into Hawai'i's economy during its initial series run.

Opposite page

Murder, She Wrote's Angela Lansbury as Jessica Fletcher and Tom Selleck as Magnum, P.I. guest–starred on each other's show. Here, they are near Waimanalo Beach, Oahu; twin-peaked Olomana is in the background.

Above

Tom Selleck with Frank Sinatra, who won an Academy Award when he first donned an aloha shirt in From Here to Eternity (1953). "Old Blue Eyes" put a Hawaiian shirt back on for a guest star role in an episode of Magnum, P.I.

Magnum P.I. Broadcast History

1980-81 Season

1. DON'T EAT THE SNOW IN HAWAII (2-HOUR PILOT)
2. NEVER PLAY WITH A CHINA DOLL
3. THANK HEAVEN FOR LITTLE GIRLS AND BIG ONES, TOO
4. NO NEED TO KNOW
5. SKIN DEEP
6. NEVER AGAIN...NEVER AGAIN
7. THE UGLIEST DOG IN HAWAII
8. MISSING IN ACTION
9. LEST WE FORGET
10. THE CURSE OF THE KING KAMEHAMEHA CLUB
11. THICKER THAN BLOOD
12. ALL ROADS LEAD TO FLOYD
13. ADELAIDE
14. DON'T SAY GOOD-BYE
15. THE BLACK ORCHID
16. J. DIGGER DOYLE
17. BEAUTY KNOWS NO PAIN

1981-82 Season

1. BILLY JOE BOB
2. DEAD MAN'S CHANNEL
3. WOMAN ON THE BEACH
4. FROM MOSCOW TO MAUI
5. MEMORIES ARE FOREVER (2-HOUR)
6. TROPICAL MADNESS
7. WAVE GOODBYE
8. MAD BUCK GIBSON
9. THE TAKING OF DICK MCWILLIAMS
10. THE SIXTH POSITION
11. GHOST WRITER
12. JORORO KILL
13. COMPUTER DATE
14. TRY TO REMEMBER
15. ITALIAN ICE
16. ONE MORE SUMMER
17. TEXAS LIGHTNING
18. DOUBLE JEOPARDY
19. THE LAST PAGE
20. THE ELMO ZILLER STORY
21. THREE MINUS TWO

1982-83 Season

1. DID YOU SEE THE SUNRISE?
2. KI'IS DON'T LIE
3. THE EIGHT PART OF THE VILLAGE...
4. PAST TENSE
5. BLACK ON WHITE
6. FLASHBACK
7. FOILED AGAIN
8. MISTER WHITE DEATH
9. MIXED DOUBLES
10. ALMOST HOME
11. HEAL THYSELF
12. ...OF SOUND MIND
13. THE ARROW THAT IS NOT AIMED
14. BASKET CASE

15. BIRDMAN OF BUDAPEST
16. I DO?
17. FORTY YEARS FROM SAND ISLAND
18. LEGACY FROM A FRIEND
19. TWO BIRDS OF A FEATHER
20. ...BY ITS COVER
21. THE BIG BLOW
22. FAITH AND BEGORRAH

1983-84 Season

1. HOME FROM THE SEA
2. LUTHER GILLIS: FILE #521
3. SMALLER THAN LIFE
4. DISTANT RELATIVE
5. LIMITED ENGAGEMENT
6. LETTER TO A DUCHESS
7. SQUEEZE PLAY
8. A SENSE OF DEBT
9. THE LOOK
10. OPERATION: SILENT NIGHT
11. JORORO FAREWELL
12. THE CASE OF THE RED FACED THESPIAN
13. NO MORE MR. NICE GUY
14. REMBRANDT'S GIRL
15. PARADISE BLUES
16. THE RETURN OF LUTHER GILLIS
17. LET THE PUNISHMENT FIT THE CRIME
18. HOLMES IS WHERE THE HEART IS
19. ON FACE VALUE
20. DREAM A LITTLE DREAM
21. I WITNESS

1984-85 Season

1. ECHOES OF THE MIND - PART I
2. ECHOES OF THE MIND - PART II
3. MAC'S BACK
4. THE LEGACY OF GARWOOD HUDDLE
5. UNDER WORLD
6. FRAGMENTS
7. BLIND JUSTICE
8. MURDER 101
9. TRAN QUOC JONES
10. LUTHER GILLIS: FILE #001
11. KISS OF THE SABER
12. LITTLE GAMES
13. PROFESSOR JONATHAN HIGGINS
14. COMPULSION
15. ALL FOR ONE - PART I
16. ALL FOR ONE - PART II
17. THE LOVE-FOR-SALE BOAT
18. LET ME HEAR THE MUSIC
19. MS. JONES
20. THE MAN FROM MARSEILLES
21. TORAH, TORAH, TORAH
22. A PRETTY GOOD DANCING CHICKEN

1985-86 Season

1. DEJA VU (2-HOUR)
2. OLD ACQUAINTANCE

3. THE KONA WINDS
4. THE HOTEL DICK
5. ROUND AND AROUND
6. GOING HOME
7. PANIOLO
8. THE TREASURE OF KALANIOPU'U
9. BLOOD AND HONOR
10. RAPTURE
11. I NEVER WANTED TO GO TO FRANCE, ANYWAY
12. SUMMER SCHOOL
13. MAD DOGS AND ENGLISHMEN
14. ALL THIEVES ON DECK
15. THIS ISLAND ISN'T BIG ENOUGH
16. THE WAY OF THE STALKING HORSE
17. FIND ME A RAINBOW
18. WHO IS DON LUIS AND WHY IS HE DOING THESE TERRIBLE THINGS TO ME?
19. A LITTLE BIT OF LUCK...A LITTLE BIT OF GRIEF
20. PHOTO PLAY

1986-87 Season

1. L.A. (2-HOUR)
2. ONE PICTURE IS WORTH...
3. STRAIGHT AND NARROW
4. A.A.P.I.
5. DEATH AND TAXES
6. LITTLE GIRL WHO
7. PAPER WAR
8. NOVEL CONNECTION
9. KAPU
10. MISSING MELODY
11. DEATH OF THE FLOWERS
12. AUTUMN WARRIOR
13. MURDER BY NIGHT
14. ON THE FLY
15. SOLO FLIGHT
16. FORTY
17. LAURA
18. THE AUNT WHO CAME TO DINNER
19. OUT OF SYNC
20. THE PEOPLE VS. ORVILLE WRIGHT
21. LIMBO

1987-88 Season

1. INFINITY AND JELLY DOUGHNUTS
2. PLEASURE PRINCIPLE
3. INNOCENCE...A BROAD
4. TIGERS FAN
5. FOREVER IN TIME
6. THE LOVE THAT LIES
7. A GIRL NAMED SUE
8. UNFINISHED BUSINESS
9. THE GREAT HAWAIIAN ADVENTURE COMPANY
10. LEGEND OF THE LOST ART
11. TRANSITIONS
12. RESOLUTIONS (2-HOUR)

FANTASY ISLAND
1978-1984 ABC
Cast: Ricardo Montalban, Herve Villechaize

During the first and second seasons of this popular series, four episodes were filmed in Hawai'i. The pilot exterior shots and two episodes were filmed on Kauai. Numerous stock shots, backgrounds and inserts were used in most episodes through the life of the series, including Kauai's Wailua Falls, which was featured in the establishing island shots where Tatoo and Mr. Roarke welcome guests to the island.

THE ISLANDER
1978 ABC
D: Paul Krasny

Cast: Dennis Weaver, Bernadette Peters, Sharon Gless, Robert Vaughn

Above
"The plane, boss! The plane!"—Ricardo Montalban and Herve Villechaize in *Fantasy Island*, with dancers dressed Tahitian-style.

Below
Dennis Weaver stars as flamboyant attorney Gable McQueen in *The Islander*.

A famous trial lawyer retires to Honolulu to buy a small hotel and escape the tension of criminal law, but island mobsters and a U.S. senator friend wanted by the police for allegedly beating a woman keep pressures at the boiling point. This two-hour movie pilot for a series that never sold was filmed on location in Hawai'i.

PEARL
1978-79 ABC
D: Hy Averback and Alex Singer

S: Stirling Silliphant

P: Sam Manners

Cast: Angie Dickinson, Dennis Weaver, Robert Wagner, Lesley Ann Warren, Tiana Alexandra, Gregg Henry, Katherine Helmond, Adam Arkin, Brian Dennehy, Max Gail, Char Fontane, Marian Ross, Christian Vance

One of the most popular multipart (five hours) dramas in television history, *Pearl* is the explosive story of men and women living in the peacetime paradise of Hawai'i in 1941. Their lives are suddenly shattered on a quiet December morning, when a Japanese attack from the skies ends the innocence of a nation.

Written by Oscar-winning Stirling Silliphant (*In the Heat of the Night*), *Pearl* interwove the lives of a diverse group of people who, despite personal upheavals, live in the peaceful community of Honolulu in early December 1941.

Pearl was filmed entirely on location on Oahu, Hawai'i.

Above

Angie Dickinson, Dennis Weaver, Lesley Ann Warren and Robert Wagner in *Pearl.*

Below

Starting with the Oscar-winning 1953 film, James Jones' brilliant novel *From Here to Eternity* has inspired many adaptations, spinoffs, and imitators. *Pearl* is a soap opera-ish knock-off of *Eternity.* In 1979, NBC adapted *Eternity* into the mini-series format. William Devane plays the Burt Lancaster role (Sgt. Milton Warden) and Natalie Wood plays the Deborah Kerr part (Karen Holmes), the adulterous lovers.

THE MACKENZIES OF PARADISE COVE
1979 ABC

Cast: Clu Gulagher

A one-hour series filmed in Hawai'i starring Clu Gulagher as Cuda Weber, a crusty, free-spirited operator of a fishing boat who becomes unofficial guardian to five lovable, orphaned children. Moe Keale is featured as Big Ben Kalikini, and Scott Kingston, as Richie Kalikini. The series was created by William Blinn and Jerry Thorpe, and was also directed by Thorpe.

FROM HERE TO ETERNITY
1979 NBC

D:	**Buzz Kulik**
S:	**Don McGuire**
P:	**Buzz Kulik**
Cast:	**Natalie Wood, William Devane, Peter Boyle, Roy Thinnes, Andy Griffith, Joe Pantoliano, Kim Basinger**

Three-time Oscar nominee Natalie Wood, Wiliam Devane, Peter Boyle, Roy Thinnes and Andy Griffith head the all-star cast of *From Here to Eternity,* the unabridged television version of James Jones' powerful best seller.

The six-hour miniseries about the lives of soldiers on and off duty in Hawai'i just prior to Pearl Harbor traces the love affair between a company commander's wife and a sergeant, and the near brutal treatment of a young, stubborn career soldier who pays a heavy price for his principles.

From Here to Eternity was filmed on location in Hawai'i. It was not a remake of the 1953 movie, for which only a portion of the 858-page novel was used. The contemporary miniseries format allowed for the full and frank dramatization of the story for the first time.

The original movie won eight Academy Awards, including one for Best Picture. The novel sold more than seven million copies and topped the nation's best-seller list for a year, winning the National Book Award in 1952. Because of its frank language and love scenes, it was considered a daring novel when it was first published in 1951.

FROM HERE TO ETERNITY
1979 NBC

Cast: **William Devane, Barbara Hershey, Roy Thinnes, Don Johnson, Rocky Echevarria**

This weekly one-hour drama series was drawn from the monumental best-selling novel by James Jones about Army life in Hawai'i. It was a continuance of the story originally presented in the highly successful six-hour miniseries. The locale is Honolulu, Hawai'i, six months following the Japanese attack on December 7, 1941.

Devane and Thinnes return to their miniseries roles as the crusty Sgt. Milt Warden and the social-climbing Major Holmes. Kim Bassinger also returns as prostitute Lorene Rogers. New to the cast are Barbara Hershey as Karen, Holmes' wife; Don Johnson, as Jefferson Davis Prewitt; Rocky Echevarria, as Pfc. Ignacio Carmona; and David Spielberg, as Lt. Ross.

Above
Kim Basinger as Prewitt's girlfriend, the prostitute Lorene (originally played by Donna Reed in the 1953 film) in the miniseries version of *From Here to Eternity*.

Left
Sgt. Milton Warden (William Devane) makes love to his commanding officer's wife, Karen Holmes (Natalie Wood).

Below
William Devane reprises his role as Sgt. Milton Warden, and Barbara Hershey plays his lover, Mrs. Karen Holmes, in the short-lived episodic series which grew out of the *From Here to Eternity* mini-series of the same name in 1979. Another James Jones novel, *The Thin Red Line*, about the battle of Guadalcanal, became a film in 1964. Director Terrence Malick has optioned the rights to the book in order to shoot a remake. And Kaylie Jones' novel *A Soldier's Daughter Never Cries*, about the death of her father, James Jones, has been optioned by the prestigious Merchant-Ivory film team.

Above
David Carradine stars as
Paul Gauguin and Edwige
Taie portrays Teha'amana,
the Tahitian who was the
model for many of the
French artist's paintings
1891—1903 in *Gauguin
the Savage*.

Below
Stephen Shortridge, Debbie
Reynolds, Pat Klous and Bill
Daily in *Aloha Paradise*.

GAUGUIN THE SAVAGE
1980 CBS

D: **Fielder Cook**

S: **J.P. Miller**

P: **Douglas Benton**

Cast: **David Carradine, Lynn Redgrave, Barrie
Houghton**

A two-and-a-half-hour dramatic film of the turbulent artistic career of French painter Paul Gauguin from 1885, the year in which he left his successful job as a Parisian stockbroker to devote his life to painting, until the time of his death as a virtually unkown artist in 1903.

In abandoning his family and sailing to Tahiti to protest what he called the "disease" of civilization, Gauguin was forced to leave behind the most important person in his life, his young daughter Aline. It was for Aline, his favorite child, that Gauguin aspired to greatness.

In Tahiti, although living in poverty, Gauguin was initially at one with the world. The island's beauty and its primitive people served as a continual source of inspiration, and it was there that the artist created many of his finest works. But the poverty he endured, together with failing health and the realization that artistic fame had eluded him, eventually took their toll, and in 1903, several years after an unsuccessful suicide attempt, Gauguin died forlornly on the Marguesas island of Hiva Oa. It remained for history to fulfill Gauguin's promise to his daughter Aline that he one day would achieve artistic stature. Today, he is recognized as one of the founding fathers of modern art.

David Carradine attained worldwide recognition for his role as Caine in the television series *Kung Fu*.

Gaugain the Savage was filmed in Southern France, Paris, Tahiti and Los Angeles.

ALOHA PARADISE
1981 ABC

Cast: Debbie Reynolds, Stephen Shortridge, Bill Daily

Reynolds stars as the manager of a lush hotel resort on the Kona Coast in Hawai'i in this two-hour pilot film for a series.

TALES OF THE GOLD MONKEY
1982 ABC

Cast: Stephen Collins, Caitlin O'Heaney, Jeff MacKay

In this high-style series set in 1938, Stephen Collins stars as Jake Cutter, an expatriate American flyer who is drawn into adventure and intrigue as he transports passengers and cargo throughout a remote South Seas Island chain in a well-worn Grumman Goose. The pulse-pounding adventure set in the South Pacific pits Jake and his friends against sinister Nazi spies, a Eurasian princess and a host of other colorful characters.

Tales of the Gold Monkey was created by executive producer Don Bellisario and filmed in Hawai'i and in Los Angeles at Universal Studios.

Above

Executive producer Donald Bellisario, who produced *Magnum, P.I.*, returns to paradise with the high flying series *Tales of the Gold Monkey*, a South Sea saga in the 1930s adventure-movie mode. The ABC series, set before America entered World War II, stars Jeff MacKay, Stephen Collins, Caitlin O'Heaney and Leo the dog.

Below

Ali MacGraw and Robert Mitchum in the World War II-era mini-series *The Winds of War*, based on Herman Wouk's novel.

THE WINDS OF WAR
1983 ABC

D: Dan Curtis

S: Herman Wouk

P: Dan Curtis

Cast: Robert Mitchum, Ali MacGraw, Jan-Michael Vincent, John Houseman, Peter Graves, David Dukes, Polly Bergen

This eighteen-hour miniseries was focused on U.S. naval commander "Pug" Henry (Mitchum) between 1939

and the Japanese bombing of Pearl Harbor. A military attache on a series of personal missions for President Franklin Delano Roosevelt, Pug meets all the historic titans of the period—Churchill, Hitler, Mussolini, Stalin. He watches as the lives of his family and everyone in Europe are increasingly threatened by the gathering storm of World War II.

That global conflict forms the turbulent backdrop for the personal stories of Pug and his errant wife Rhoda; their children, Byron, Warren and Madeline; Byron's wife-to-be, Natalie Jastrow, an American Jew in Italy; Natalie's expatriate American uncle, philosopher Aaron Jastrow; and Pamela Tudsbury, the English woman who extends her love to Pug.

The bombing of Pearl Harbor was recreated at a Navy base in Port Hueneme, California, where the Navy allowed only four days of filming. Rented Navy destoyers were wired with simulated explosives.

THE THORN BIRDS
1983 ABC

D: **Daryl Duke**
S: **Carmen Culver**
P: **David L. Wolper, Stan Margulies**
Cast: **Richard Chamberlain, Rachel Ward, Philip Anglim, Bryan Brown, Earl Holliman, Ken Howard, Richard Kiley, Piper Laurie, Sydney Penny, Christopher Plummer, Jean Simmons, Barbara Stanwyck and Mare Winningham**

Above
Rachel Ward and Richard Chamberlain in *The Thorn Birds*.

Bryan Brown and Richard Chamberlain in *The Thorn Birds*.

Right
Rachel Ward and Richard Chamberlain in *The Thorn Birds*.

A ten-hour dramatization of Colleen McCullough's romantic best-selling novel about one Australian family's epic tragedy and triumph. Richard Chamberlain stars as the handsome priest, Father Ralph, and Rachel Ward stars as the strong-willed beauty, Meggie Cleary.

The Thorn Birds begins in 1920, as the Clearys, a New Zealand farming family, migrate to a great sheep ranch in Australia. Within this vast canvas of characters and settings emerges Meggie Cleary, a woman as beautiful and indomitable as the surrealistic landscape, and the man she loves but can never marry—Father Ralph, a magnetic, outspoken parish priest whose own ambitions lead him into the inner circles of the Vatican.

The production was filmed during a five-month shooting schedule on locations that included the Simi Valley near Los Angeles, as well as other locations in Southern California, and on the Garden Island of Kauai, Hawai'i, for scenes set in subtropical Queensland, Australia, and the Great Barrier Reef.

HART TO HART
1984 ABC, "HARTS AND PALMS" EPISODE
Cast: **Robert Wagner, Stephanie Powers**

While on vacation in Hawai'i, the Harts become involved in a murder plot when Jennifer fears that Jonathan's business acquaintance is being poisoned. This episode was filmed entirely on location on Maui, Hawai'i.

The Harts returned to Hawai'i ten years later for a two-hour movie filmed on Oahu.

HAWAIIAN HEAT
1984 ABC
Cast: **Robert Ginty, Jeff McCracken, Tracy Scoggins, Mako and Branscombe Richmond**

Robert Ginty and Jeff McCracken star as two Chicago policemen who trade in street traffic duty, the cold of Chicago, and no chance for promotions for the lush paradise of Hawai'i and positions on the Honolulu police force. As detectives fighting crime in this action drama, the two *haoles* (outsiders, Caucasians) do things their way, using Chicago street smarts, but they also learn to interface with the Hawaiian Islands' culture and customs.

Above
Stephanie Powers and Robert Wagner shot several *Hart to Hart* episodes and a TV movie in Hawai'i.

Left amd below
Jeff McCracken and Robert Ginty as Chicago cops who go Hawaiian on Waikiki Beach as detectives in *Hawaiian Heat*.

Art director John Leimanis, who designed the interior set for the ABC television network's *Hawaiian Heat* series, considered the success of his work to be a miracle. In just two short months, a 120-by-60-foot warehouse in an industrial complex near Honolulu was converted into a studio for the island-based show. From design to the first day of filming interiors for the series, a scant eight weeks had passed.

PERRY COMO'S CHRISTMAS IN HAWAII
1985 ABC

Cast: **Perry Como, Marie Osmond, Burt Reynolds**

Marie Osmond and Burt Reynolds are Perry Como's guest stars in a tropical paradise holiday musical special. Highlights are visits to the glorious natural wonders of the islands, where at each stop the singers raise their voices in Christmas tunes, backed by local talents such as the Tihati Dancers, the Kamehameha Choir, the Hawai'i Young Singers and Hualani's Pipers. Perry runs into Burt on the beach, and they blend their voices in something not so traditional.

BLOOD AND ORCHIDS
1985 CBS

D: **Jerry Thorpe**
S: **Norman Katkov**
P: **Andrew Adelson**
Cast: **Kris Kristofferson, Jane Alexander, Sean Young, Jose Ferrer, Susan Blakely, Haunani Minn, James Saito, Mat Salinger, Madeline Stowe, Robert Andre, Warren Fabro, Shaun Shimoda, Russell Omori**

A four-hour miniseries set in Hawai'i in 1937, the drama deals with the improprieties of justice and the resultant civil unrest when four local Hawaiian youths

Above
Perry Como and Burt Reynolds in *Perry Como's Christmas in Hawaii* episode, 1985.

Below
Sean Young plays the wife of the prosecuting attorney, and Kris Kristofferson portrays the investigator, in the mini-series *Blood and Orchids*, a dramatization of the real-life 1931 Massie case in Hawai'i.

are wrongly accused of the assault and rape of a Navy lieutenant's wife. In the process of unraveling the facts in the case, a local captain of detectives falls in love with the young wife of a celebrated mainland attorney who is summoned to the islands at the behest of the rape victim's powerful socialite mother. To complicate matters, the Navy lieutenant commits the ultimate insurrection when he takes civilian police matters into his own hands.

Another vital element in the production of *Blood and Orchids* was the use of as many Hawai'i actors as possible. Of the 63 roles in *Blood and Orchids,* 43 were cast in Hawai'i. Of the twenty actors who traveled over from the mainland, three—Haunani Minn, Elizabeth Lindsey and Henry Kaimu Bal—are Hawai'i-born. Three of the four boys who play the alleged assailants charged with assaulting and raping the wife of a Navy lieutenant were discovered in community theaters or acting schools. Russell Amori was a member of a local repertory company, the Honolulu Theatre for Youth. His only television credit prior to the miniseries was a local show called *Pidgin to da Max,* which aired on KGMB, the Honolulu CBS affiliate.

T.J. HOOKER
1986 CBS
Cast: William Shatner, Heather Locklear, James Darren

A special two-hour Movie-of-the-Week episode of the police series *T.J. Hooker* entitled "Blood Sport" was filmed on Oahu, Hawai'i. Hooker and his team are sent to Hawai'i as personal bodyguards to a U.S. senator stalked by political terrorists.

Below

The cast of *Tour of Duty*, a drama series about the Vietnam war and the young Americans who fought it.

ISLAND SONS
1986 ABC

Cast: Timothy Bottoms, Joe Bottoms, Sam Bottoms, Ben Bottoms

This pilot for a proposed series filmed in Hawai'i revolved around four individualistic brothers from an oldtime *kamaaina* Caucasian family in Hawai'i who are reunited by the death of their father. The brothers have vastly different careers: one runs a ranch, one is a businessman, one operates a schooner and another is a district attorney. *Island Sons* was written and created by Jim Parriot.

TOUR OF DUTY
1987-1988 CBS

Cast: Terence Knox, Ramon Franco, Steve Akahoshi, Kevin Conroy, Steven Caffrey, Eric Bruskotter, Miguel Nunez

The story of a group of young American infantrymen fighting in the Southeast Asian jungles of Vietnam in 1967.

All twenty episodes of *Tour of Duty*'s first season were filmed in Hawai'i, primarily at the Army's Schofield Barracks, 45 minutes from Honolulu on the island of Oahu. Other key locations were a warehouse in an industrial section of Pearl City; the old *Five-O* sound stage near Diamond Head; and Omega Station, a Coast Guard facility at the base of the Koolau Mountains. The series moved to Southern California locations during its second season.

WAR AND REMEMBRANCE
1988 ABC

D: **Dan Curtis**

S: **Herman Wouk, Dan Curtis and Earl Wallace**

P: **Barbara Steele**

Cast: **Robert Mitchum, Polly Bergen, Jane Seymour, Sir John Gielgud, Hart Bochner**

This thirty-hour miniseries sequel to *The Winds of War* miniseries follows Victor "Pug" Henry (Mitchum), an American career naval officer whose family becomes caught up in the horrors and triumphs of World War II. In the first chapters Pug and his son Byron (Bochner) are off fighting the war in the Pacific.

The war in the Pacific scenes were actually filmed during the summer of 1987 at Pearl Harbor, Hawai'i, and near the coast off Oahu in Waianae Bay on vintage Naval ships. The World War II-era vessels, the reserve tanker *Nodaway*, and the destroyer *Edwards*, were taken out of mothballs and refitted for the Pacific Theater recreation. One hundred fifty extras, many of them certified Hawai'i lifeguards, were hired for scenes involving sailors being rescued at sea after a Naval engagement. Most of the submarine scenes were shot using the USS *Bowfin*, a submarine, which, as part of the Pearl Harbor Memorial, hadn't been to sea in eighteen years and was restored to seaworthiness. The sub was fitted with an underwater tow bridle and towed by a tugboat for scenes on the surface.

EMMA, QUEEN OF THE SOUTH SEAS
1988 SYNDICATED

Cast: Barbara Carrera , Hal Holbrook

A four hour mini-series based on the true story of Emma Eliza Coe, the beautiful daughter of a princess of

the Samoan Royal Family and of the first American consul in Apia, Samoa during the latter half of the nineteenth century. Emma acquired a vast fortune and was known by many eminent figures in Europe and the U.S. Filmed in Fiji and Australia.

JAKE AND THE FATMAN
1988-92 CBS
Cast: William Conrad, Joe Penny

Starring William Conrad as the voluminous district attorney J.L. McCabe and Joe Penny as Jake Styles, his high-living partner in crime-busting, *Jake and the Fatman* began production in Hawai'i on November 15, 1988. The two-hour debut saw the shift of locale from the show's previous Southern California setting to Hawai'i, where the production took full advantage of the beauty of the tropical islands. The series was filmed in Hawai'i during the 1989-90-91 seasons.

Above
Scene from *Emma, Queen of the South Seas*.

Right
Joe Penny and William Conrad in *Jake and the Fat Man*.

Below
The cast of *Life Goes On* (left—right), Kellie Martin, Chris Burke, Bill Smitrovich and Patti LuPone.

LIFE GOES ON
1989-1992 ABC, "THATCHERS GO HAWAIIAN" EPISODE
Cast: Patti Lupone, Kellie Martin, Bill Smitrovich, Chris Burke

It's a dream come true for the Thatcher family when Corky wins a vacation to Hawai'i, a trip that holds sudden surprises for everyone. A guest appearance was made by Don Ho, and the episode was filmed on location in Hawai'i.

ISLAND SON
1989 CBS
Cast: Richard Chamberlain, Brynn Thayer, Clyde Kusatsu, Timothy Carhart, Betty Carvalho, Ray Bumatai, Kwan Hi Lim

A one-hour drama series about Dr. Daniel Kulani (Chamberlain), a man at a turning point in his life at a large hospital in Honolulu.

After many years on the U.S. mainland, pursuing first his medical education and then the highly successful private practice that brought him notoriety and considerable finanacial reward, Dr. Kulani has recently returned to the island home of his childhood to reassess his life and reorder his priorities.

Island Son was unique as a medical series in that much of Kulani's medical practice took him outside the confines of the hospital setting, putting him among the island people he had come to know and understand. The series was filmed entirely on location in Hawai'i.

TRENCHCOAT IN PARADISE
1989 CBS

Cast: **Dirk Benedict, Sydney Walsh, Bruce Dern**

A motion picture for television in which a small-time New Jersey private detective crosses a big-time crime boss and ends up with a one-way ticket to Hawai'i.

MIRACLE LANDING
1990 CBS

D: **Dick Lowry**

S: **Garner Simmons**

P: **Dick Lowry**

Cast: **Connie Sellecca, Wayne Rogers, Ana-Alicia, Nancy Kwan, James Cromwell, Jay Thomas, Ray Bumatai**

A motion picture for television depicting the remarkable true story of the extraordinary courage of ordinary people that turned a tragedy into a modern miracle, based on the true story of a Hawai'i commercial airliner that was severely damaged when the top skin of its fuselage ripped off during flight. The instinctive actions of

the crew, heroic and unprecedented, made aviation history. *Miracle Landing* was filmed on location in Hawai'i and in Hollywood.

MURDER IN PARADISE
1990 NBC
Cast: **Maggie Han, Kevin Kilner, Barbara Carrera**

World premiere movie about a burned-out, big-city cop seeking refuge in Hawai'i, only to become embroiled in a serial murder case that appears to be identical to his last case in New York City.

RAVEN
1992 CBS
Cast: **Jeffrey Meek, Lee Majors**

In the tropical setting of the Hawaiian Islands, the mysterious Jonathon Raven (Meek), a martial arts master, seeks to escape the murderous world of international assasins. *Raven* was an hour-long action-adventure series produced by Columbia Pictures Television and aired on CBS.

Raven is joined by his buddy, Herman "Ski" Jablonski (Majors), a grizzled, ex-alcoholic private eye who once served in the special forces with him in Vietnam. The series was filmed entirely in Hawai'i.

BYRDS OF PARADISE
1994 ABC
Cast: **Timothy Busfield, Elizabeth Lindsey, Seth Green, Jennifer Love Hewitt, Ryan O'Donohue, Arlo Guthrie**

Set against the backdrop of rural Hawai'i was a family drama from Steven Bochco Productions starring Busfield as Sam Byrd, a widower who, with his three children, moves from New England to Hawai'i searching

Above

Maggie Han, Kevin Kilner and Barbara Carrera in *Murder in Paradise*.

Below

Jeffrey Meek and Lee Majors in front of Diamond Head in the martial arts series *Raven*.

for a new life. A former Yale professor, Sam has been hired as the headmaster of the Palmer School, a private plantation school.

Once in Hawai'i, the family tries to adjust to their new home, which isn't easy, given some islanders' attitudes toward mainlanders. Sam encounters just such an attitude when he meets Healani Douglas (Lindsey), the school's Dean of Students, a beautiful Native Hawaiian.

As time goes by, the Byrds and their neighbors, colleagues and classmates accept one another and settle into a relatively normal life in "Paradise."

The cast featured Robert Kekaula and Lani Opunui Ancheta, two Native Hawaiians who portrayed the Byrds' housekeepers, Manu and Sonny Kaulukukui.

The series began production on December 6, 1993, and was shot entirely on location in Hawai'i, primarily on the island of Oahu. Thirteen episodes were filmed and twelve aired before the series was cancelled in May of 1994. The Byrd home facade was located in the Kualoa Valley, and the Palmer School was on the site of the Mokuleia Land Company in Waialua on the North Shore.

ONE WEST WAIKIKI
1994 CBS
Cast: Cheryl Ladd, Richard Burgi

Introduced as part of the summer CBS lineup on August 4, 1994, the series stars Cheryl Ladd as a feisty forensics expert, Dr. Dawn Holiday, and Richard Burgi as a good cop with some rough edges. They work together to solve complex and mysterious homicide cases in Honolulu.

One West Waikiki was one of the first shows to use the new Diamond Head studio facilities as its headquarters and for most of the permanent interiors. Glen Larson is the executive producer of the series.

Above

The cast of *Byrds of Paradise* (left—right), Seth Green, Lani Opunui-Ancheta, Timothy Busfield, Jennifer Love Hewitt, Robert Kekaula, Arlo Guthrie, Elizabeth Lindsey and Ryan O'Donohue on location at Kualoa Ranch, Oahu, where *Blue Hawaii*, *Jurassic Park*, and other films have been shot. It is believed that *Byrds* had too many multicultural Hawai'i references to attract a large Continental–U.S. viewership.

Below

Cheryl Ladd and Richard Burgi in another Hawai'i crime series, *One West Waikiki*, which is still in international syndication.

MARKER

1995 United Paramount Network

Cast: Richard Grieco, Gates McFadden, Keone
Young, Andy Bumatai

Combining the bright, paradise setting of Hawai'i with fast-paced action, personal stories and humor, *Marker* was a one-hour series created by Emmy award-winning writer/producer Stephen J. Cannell, which made its debut on the new United Paramount Network on January 17, 1995.

Richard Grieco stars as Richard DeMorra, a carpenter from New Jersey who returns to Hawai'i for his estranged father's funeral to find that he has inherited a mysterious legacy of personal debts, or "markers," which his wealthy industrialist father had bestowed on islanders to reward good deeds. In the process of redeeming the markers, Richard learns more about his father and himself.

Gates McFadden is Kimba Hills Rose, Richard's young stepmother whose antagonistic relationship with Richard is tempered with a grudging respect. Young plays Taki "Moch" Mochadomi, Richard's late father's lawyer, who brings wise counsel and a calming influence.

Stand-up comic and Hawai'i resident Andy Bumatai portrays Andy "Pipeline" Kahala, a local who shares the beachfront property that Richard has inherited from his father.

Each episode of *Marker* was filmed entirely on location in Hawai'i, using Honolulu as a base and tapping into the various locales of Oahu. The former Henry Kaiser estate, a sprawling pink stucco home near Koko Head, doubled as Joe Rose's home, the Hale o Loke Estate.

"I always feel that audiences long for the tropical environs of a place like Hawai'i. It gives us a bird's-eye view of a paradise that's both diverting and entertaining. Marker will present a weekly escape to a lush, sun-drenched fantasy that viewers will relish," remarked Stephen J. Cannell in press notes for the series.

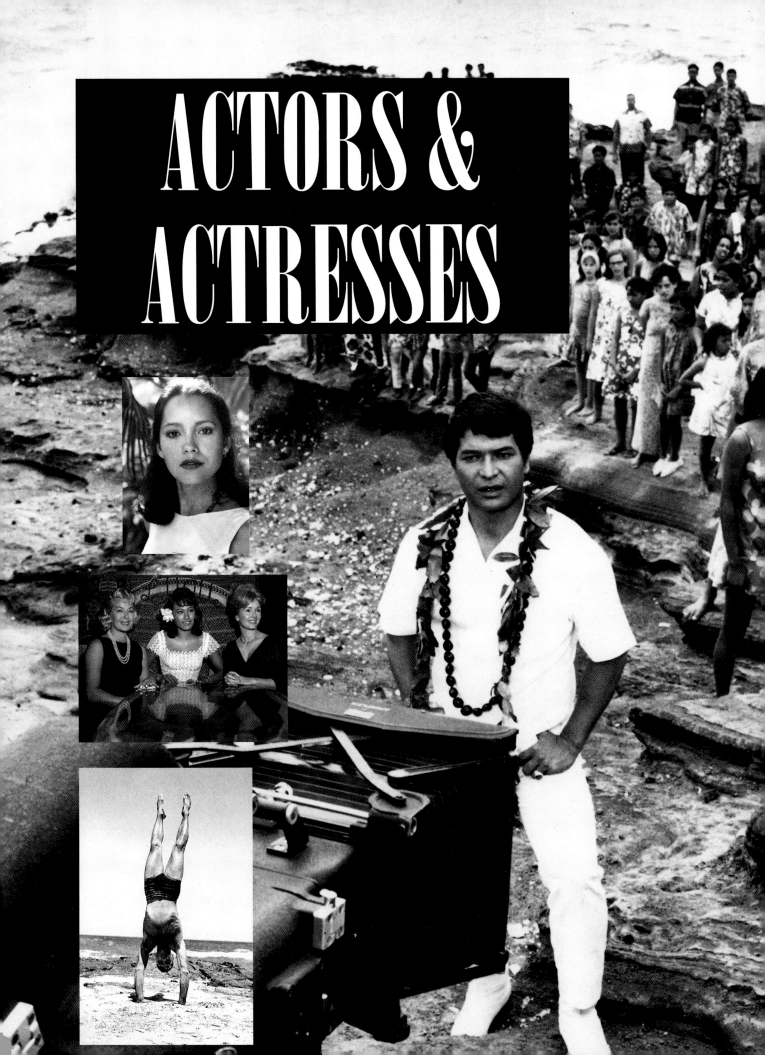

ACTORS & ACTRESSES

Right
Jon Hall co-stars with sarong girl Susan Cabot in one of his later pictures, 1950's *On the Isle of Samoa.*

Previous page
Don Ho on location in Hawai'i for his 1968 TV special.

Inset (top) Barbara Carrera as she appeared in the Warner Bros. release *When Time Ran Out.*

Inset (center) Tahitian starlet Tarita goes Hollywood, sitting between Lana Turner (herself a South Seas cinema veteran) and Debbie Reynolds. Note the rattan furniture and Maori carving on what appears to be a bamboo wall.

Inset (bottom) Former circus acrobat Burt Lancaster between takes while filming 1953's *From Here to Eternity* on location on Oahu.

Hawai'i and South Sea Film and Television Personalities

More often than not, the major actors and actresses in South Seas cinema have not been indigenous Pacific talent. Non-Islanders have flooded the screen playing "natives" (Hollywood's ethnographic term for Oceania's aboriginal peoples) or half-castes. Often these thespians were of Latino origin, such as Dolores Del Rio (*Bird of Paradise*, 1932), Raquel Torres (*White Shadows in the South Seas*, 1928, and *The Sea Bat*, 1930), Conchita Montenegro (*Never the Twain Shall Meet*, 1931), Movita Castenada (this co-star of the 1935 *Mutiny on the Bounty* married Marlon Brando, the lead in the 1962 *Bounty* epic), Maria Montez (*South of Tahiti* and *Moonlight in Hawaii* in 1941 and *White Savage* in 1943), and Lupe Velez (*Honolulu*, 1941).

The strange career of Dorothy Lamour is an excellent example of a Caucasian actor or actress passing as a non white in the movies. Wearing her ubiquitous sarong, Lamour starred in movies like *The Jungle Princess* (1936), *The Hurricane* (1937), *Her Jungle Love* (1938), *Tropic Holiday* (1938), *Typhoon* (1940), *Moon Over Burma* (1940), *Road to Singapore* (1940), *Aloma of the South Seas* (1941), *Beyond the Blue Horizon* (1942), *Rainbow Island* (1944), *Road to Bali* (1952), and *Donovan's Reef* (1963). Lamour portrayed Polynesian types with names such as Ulah, Marama, Tura, Manuela, Dea, Mima, Aloma, Tama, Princess Shalmar, Lonah, Lalah, and Fleur, although she did not have a drop of islander blood. The Hollywood studios had to apply dark body makeup to the French-Irish-Spanish-American actress to "native" her up.

There have been some exceptions over the years where Pacific Islanders have appeared on screen, sometimes playing themselves. These professional Polynesians were usually of Hawaiian heritage, such as Olympic champion Duke Kahanamoku, renowned for his swimming and surfing prowess. Duke strutted his stuff in a string of flicks, including Paramount's 1925 *Adventure*, based on a Jack London saga set in the Solomon Islands, and RKO's 1930 *Girl of the Port*, which took place in Fiji. Hilo Hattie, master of *hula*, danced in 1942's *Song of the Islands*, which included scenes of her native Big Island. Mamo Clark appeared in a number of Pacific films, including Gable's *Mutiny on the Bounty*, *Wallaby Jim of the Islands* (1937), *Hawaii Calls* (1938), and *Mutiny on the Blackhawk* (1939). Dayton Ka'Ne starred in the De Laurentiis productions of *Hurricane* and *Beyond the Reef* (1981). Credits sometimes reveal *Kanaka* sounding names like Libby Keanini, Winona Love, Mona Maris, Kealoha Holt, etc.

Other Polynesians have appeared in Hollywood movies from time to time. Hollywood's Tahitians include Reri and Matahi, who graced the screen in Flaherty and Murnau's *Tabu*, which was shot on location on Bora Bora and won an Oscar for cinematography. William Bambridge appeared in 1935's Best Picture, *Mutiny on the Bounty*. Tarita showed talent and was quite becoming opposite future husband Marlon Brando as Fletcher Christian in 1962's version of the *Bounty* epic. Tevaite Vernette, who studied philosophy at a French university, played opposite Mel Gibson in 1984's *The Bounty*. Perhaps the most famous Tahitian actor is Jon Hall, who starred as a sarong boy in countless South Sea flicks opposite Dorothy Lamour and other South Sea starlets.

The silver screen's Samoans include Moira Walker, who co-starred with Gary Cooper in 1953's *Return to Paradise*. When he was a lad, Felise Va'a, future editor of *The Samoa Times*, portrayed Rori opposite Cooper in the production shot at Lefaga village, on Western Samoa.

The best-known nonnative actor who was born and raised in the Oceanic region was Errol Flynn, who originally hailed from Tasmania. Flynn's first starring role was in the second screen version of *Mutiny on the Bounty*. Flynn portrayed Fletcher Christian in the 1932 Australian movie *In the Wake of the Bounty*, which incorporated dramatic scenes with documentary footage of Pitcairn Island. It is fascinating to note that Flynn was, in real life, descended from one of the *Bounty* mutineers.

Hopefully, filmmakers and audiences are now more conscious of, and sensitive to, ethnic issues, and there will be more Pacific Islanders playing themselves and having greater input into Hollywood's South Seas cinema and TV. Greater authenticity and realism enhances the imagery of both the big and little screens.

DUKE KAHANAMOKU

B: 1890

D: 1968

The one man who best personified the Hawaiian during the first half of this century was Duke Kahanamoku, who helped to shape the public image of Hawai'i and the Native Hawaiian people. A Native Hawaiian, Duke overcame severe racial discrimination on the mainland United States to become an internationally recognized gold medal-winning Olympic swimmer, a motion picture actor, a Hawaiian goodwill ambassador, the father of modern surfing and a Hawaiian folk hero. Born in Honolulu in 1890, the six-foot-one, bronze, panther-lean Kahanamoku in 1911 broke the AAU American swim record in Honolulu Bay. He won gold medals in the Olympics of 1912 and 1920. He participated and won medals in the 1924 and 1932 Olympics.

Kahanamoku's swim record was broken in the 1924 Paris Olympics by Johnny Weissmuller, who later became the "Tarzan" of movie fame.

Kahanamoku, offered a motion picture contract in the 1920s, found himself in Hollywood portraying a number of Native American, Arab, and assorted tribal roles that allowed him to display his athletic, if not thespian, abilities in such silent films as *Pony Express, Lord Jim, Old Ironsides, Hula* and the 1927 Pathe serial, *Isle of Sunken Gold.* He was sought out by such Hollywood personalities as Charlie Chaplin, Ronald Coleman and Douglas Fairbanks, who featured Kahanamoku in his 1931 travelogue *Around the World in Eighty Minutes.*

After World War II, Kahanamoku returned to Hollywood for a role as a native chieftain in *Wake of the Red Witch,* a Republic film with John "Duke" Wayne. In 1953 he made a cameo appearance as a native chief who boards the cargo ship in the film *Mister Roberts,* with Henry Fonda.

Duke died at the age of 77, after a lifetime of service to sports, Hawai'i and humanity.

Below
Aloha oe, **Duke—Olympic champion swimmer, surfer, beachboy, official greeter, and actor Duke Kahanamoku in front of his nightclub at the International Market Place in Waikiki. In the lifetime of this full-blooded Hawaiian, Hawai'i went from an independent kingdom to a provisional government to a republic to a territory to a state.**

AL KIKUME

Hawaiian character actor active in Hollywood for more than 40 years, Kikume is best known for his role as Dorothy Lamour's father in *The Hurricane*. Other credits include *Operation Pacific* and *Hurricane Smith*.

HILO HATTIE

B: 1901

D: 1979

With her bright muumuu, funny hat and bandanna tied around her *opu*, Hilo Hattie clowned, danced and sang the song "When Hilo Hattie Does the Hilo Hop," which delighted live audiences of soldiers, sailors, locals, tourists and moviegoers and television viewers for almost forty years.

She was as famous to most Americans as Diamond Head. Hattie, a full-blooded Hawaiian, had entered show business as a lark in 1936, when, as a Honolulu grammar school teacher, she joined a group of housewives, secretaries and other teachers in serenading guests at the Royal Hawaiian Hotel.

"We called ourselves the 'Serenaders' and we used to perform at the Royal Hawaiian for a dollar a night," Hattie recalled in an August 23, 1968 interview in the *Los Angeles Times*. "I always liked to clown and mimic the hula folks, so that was my part of the show. One night we were performing at a luau and a man invited me to do my act the next day at the Eastman Kodak show. I accepted, but a strange thing happened. The people were so interested in watching my performance, they forgot to take pictures. I had to do the number again so they could take pictures a second time."

After continuing her dual teaching-entertainment career for sixteen years, Hattie decided to give up the classroom and become a full-time entertainer. Her first big break came in 1942 with a motion picture called *Song of the Islands*, starring Betty Grable and Victor Mature. The producers of the picture made her adopt the name "Hilo Hattie" because of her association with the song (her real name was Clara Haili, which she had legally changed in 1948).

After her motion picture debut, Hattie cut records for Columbia and Decca and was featured with Harry

In movies like *Song of the Islands*, Hilo Hattie proved herself to be an adept comedienne on a performance par with many of Hollywood's comic talents. She was a genuinely charming and mirthful performer.

Owens and His Royal Hawaiians on a weekly television series from 1949-1955.

Her later movies included *Miss Tatlock's Millions*, *Ma and Pa Kettle at Waikiki*, *City Beneath the Sea* and *Blue Hawaii*, with Elvis Presley.

Hilo Hattie made a rare dramatic appearance in 1968 on an episode of the television series *Hawai'i Five-0*, in which she portrayed the mother of a boy accused of murder.

JON HALL

B: 1913

D: 1979

Hall won movie stardom playing a South Sea native opposite Dorothy Lamour in the original *The Hurricane* in 1937. He quickly made a career of exotic and barechested roles in future films, such as *South of Pago Pago* and *Aloma of the South Seas.*

Born in Fresno, California, as Charles Loeher, the son of a former ice skating champion and a Tahitian woman, he grew up in Tahiti and was educated in Europe.

Hall made his movie debut in 1935 in *Charlie Chan in Shanghai.* He later starred with Maria Montez in a number of Technicolor escapist extravaganzas at Universal, including *Arabian Nights, White Savage, Ali Baba and the Forty Thieves, Gypsy Wildcat* and *Lady in the Dark,* with Ginger Rogers.

In his later years, he starred in his own television series called *Ramar of the Jungle* from 1952-1955. Hall also headed a film library of stock footage, which he licensed out to producers. In addition, he developed an underwater camera for the Navy, a shark-killing weapon, a distortion-free camera and a projector called Optivision.

BUSTER CRABBE

B: 1908

D: 1983

A top gold medal Olympic swimmer of his day who went on to become a popular movie actor, Crabbe was best known as the star of the old *Flash Gordon* and *Buck Rogers* serials.

Born in Oakland, California, in 1908, Crabbe was 18 months old when his family moved from California to Hawai'i so that his father could take a new job as overseer at a pineapple plantation.

He learned to swim by age five and attended Punahou School in Honolulu, where he developed into a magnificent swimmer, surfer and all-around athlete. As he recalled

Jon Hall out of uniform—sans saraong.

years later, simply carrying a surfboard to the water's edge was a feat of strength. Crabbe's April 24, 1983 *Los Angeles Times* obituary quoted him as having said, "That was back when we had 150-pound redwood slabs for surfboards. They didn't have fiberglass in those days."

Buster Crabbe, who is best known for his outer space serials, grew up on Oahu.

He won a place on the U.S. Olympic team during his first year on the mainland studying law at the University of Southern California. He participated in the 1928 Olympics in Amsterdam, but did not win until the 1932 Olympics in Los Angeles, where he won the gold medal for the 400-meter freestyle event.

MAMO CLARK

B: 1914

D: 1986

Clark was practically snatched from a classroom at the University of Southern California, where she was pursuing the study of law, to portray Clark Gable's native sweetheart in *Mutiny on the Bounty*. Her performance won her a contract, but also established her in the public's eye as a "native girl." Typed as such, she was billed simply as "Mamo" in about twenty film appearances through 1941. Her film credits include *The Hurricane, Hawaii Calls, Air Devils, Wallaby Jim of the Islands,*

long-time actor, Richard Denning, better known as the governor on *Hawaii Five-O.*

Mutiny on the Blackhawk, One Million B.C., Girl From God's Country, and *Robinson Crusoe of Clipper Island.*

A native of Honolulu, she was adopted as a small child by the Clarks, Mrs. Clark being her mother's cousin. She attended both the American and Chinese schools in Honolulu and the Sacred Heart Academy in Hawai'i. She is also the authoress of *Except Their Sun*.

RICHARD DENNING

Though perhaps best known now for his role as the Governor on the long-running television series *Hawaii Five-O,* Denning's career includes more than 150 movies and 300 television shows, a radio series and four television series. The actor's association with tropical islands began with his costarring role opposite Dorothy Lamour in *Beyond the Blue Horizon.* He later starred for Roger Corman in *Naked Paradise* filmed entirely on Kauai, and on television, he starred in the series *Flying Doctor* about a physician in the Pacific. In the mid-1960s, Denning made his home on Maui with his wife, former actress Evelyn Ankers.

Known primarily as an actress, Mamo Clark also was an author, writing the book *Except Their Sun.*

Actress Jocelyn LaGarde
is probably the only
Tahitian to have been
nominated for an
Academy Award.

JOCELYN LAGARDE

This Tahitian star made her film debut as Queen Malama in the film *Hawaii,* for which she won an Academy Award nomination in 1966 as Best Supporting Actress and a Golden Globe award.

Six feet tall and weighing 400 pounds, the regal LaGarde was found in her native Tahiti by the film's director, George Roy Hill, and casting director Marion Dougherty. She was signed for the film even though she had never acted before and could not speak English.

LaGarde was a direct descendant of Tahiti's last reigning monarch, Queen Pomare IV.

Prior to LaGarde, only two other Tahitian actresses had found fame in Hollywood—Anna Chevalier, who starred in *Tabu* (1931), and Tarita of *Mutiny on the Bounty* (1962).

MANU TUPOU

The Fiji actor Manu Tupou starred on Broadway opposite Stacy Keach in *Indians* and Ingrid Bergman in *Captain Brassbound's Conversation,* and on the screen as Prince Keoki in *Hawaii* and as the Indian chief in *A Man Called Horse.* On television, he played roles in episodes of *Hawaii Five-O* and *Magnum P.I.* In 1994, Tupou played opposite Katharine Hepburn and Warren Beatty in *Love Affair* (its French Polynesia exteriors included shots of Moorea, and the cargo-cruise ship *Aranui,* which sails from Tahiti to the Marquesas). Tupou is the founder of, and acting teacher for, Los Angeles' American Repertory Company.

ZULU

Zulu, who played Kono on the popular television series *Hawaii Five-O,* was born Gilbert Kauaihi on the Big Island of Hawai'i. When he was eleven, the family moved to Honolulu, where he attended Kamehameha School.

Zulu, three-quarters Hawaiian, one-quarter English, grew up loving water sports. At age twelve he became a beachboy in his free time, giving surfing lessons and outrigger rides to tourists at Waikiki Beach.

At seventeen he joined the U.S. Coast Guard and served for four years in Atlantic and Pacific ports. He toured with a Polynesian revue in Japan. He has appeared in many movies made in Hawai'i, including *Rampage, Hawaii, Gidget Goes Hawaiian,* and *Diamond Head,* as well as Japanese and Italian movies filmed in Hawai'i. Later, Zulu became one of Hawai'i's most popular disc jockeys and performed in nightclubs throughout the islands.

DON STROUD

This Honolulu-born character and supporting actor has more than forty feature film and hundreds of televi-

From *Hawaiian Eye* to *Baywatch*, Don Stroud's acting career has stretched across four decades.

sion credits, including *Madigan, Coogan's Bluff, The Buddy Holly Story* and *The Choir Boys*.

Stroud's first break into show business occurred in 1961, when he doubled for Troy Donahue, surfing in the series *Hawaiian Eye*, which was partly filmed in the islands. In the opening scene, Stroud was pictured riding a big wave, then a close-up of Troy Donahue was shown with water being thrown in his face.

Son of a famous island blues singer and owner of a Honolulu nightclub, Stroud attended Kaimuki High School. "I was the only *haole* [Caucasian] kid in school and it was tough," he remarked to Larry Ketchum in the August 23-29, 1984 edition of *Drama Logue Interview*. He played football, dropped out of school, and at 15 he broke through an ultra-select circle of Polynesians at Waikiki to become a professional beachboy. "The way I came to be accepted at the beach [was] I used to clean the canoes of all the greats … Steamboat, Blackout, Rabbitt, all the beachboy immortals."

Stroud traveled to Los Angeles and wound up with a contract at Universal Studios. He often played the heavy in a succession of film and television roles. His most recent credits include the series *Mike Hammer*, with Stacey Keach; the television movie *Gidget's Summer Reunion*; and a guest-starring role on an episode of *Baywatch*.

BETTE MIDLER

Midler first appeared on the big screen as an extra in the film *Hawaii*. She hit the Hollywood big time with the 1979 release *The Rose*; but her second movie, *Jinxed*, in 1982, was a flop. For a long while after that she wasn't seen on the Hollywood circuit.

Then came an association with Walt Disney Studio's Touchstone Pictures and a string of hits, including *Down and Out in Beverly Hills, Ruthless People, Outrageous Fortune, Big Business, Stella* and *Scenes From a Mall*. Most recently, she starred in the television film of the Broadway musical *Gypsy*. Midler is best known as a singer.

GERRY LOPEZ

Born and raised in Honolulu, the two-time Pipeline Classic surf champion is considered to be the unofficial godfather of Hawaiian surfing. Lopez has appeared in the films *Big Wednesday, Conan the Barbarian* and *Farewell to the King*, all directed by John Milius. He also appeared in *North Shore* and has guest-starred on television's *Hawaii Five-O* and *Magnum P.I.*

Gert Frobe as Goldfinger, Sean Connery as agent 007, James Bond, and Harold Sakata as Oddjob in *Goldfinger*.

HAROLD SAKATA

Sakata is best remembered for his silent but deadly method of eliminating enemies as the sinister bodyguard Oddjob in the James Bond thriller *Goldfinger.*

A former Olympic silver medal-winning wrestler, Sakata also appeared in such television shows as *Quincy, Batman, The Rockford Files* and *Hawaii Five-0.*

Born in Kona on the island of Hawai'i, the eldest of ten children, Sakata worked in the plantation fields and as a stevedore in his youth and never finished high school. In the 1948 Olympic Games in London, he was awarded the silver medal in weightlifting. In 1949, known as one of the strongest men in the world, he became a professional wrestler, playing the villain Tosh Togo before wrestling fans around the world. It was while wrestling on London television in the early 1960s that he was discovered by producer Harry Saltzman and director Guy Hamilton for the *Goldfinger* role. After retiring from acting and wrestling, Sakata became a popular figure around Oahu, where he lived. He died of cancer at age 62.

JACK LORD

Lord achieved worldwide television stardom with his role as Steve McGarrett, the stern, no-nonsense head of the elite police investigations unit, Hawaii Five-O. After twelve seasons, the series finally ended, and Lord dropped out of the business. The actor was born in New York City, the son of a steamship company executive. Spending his teenage summers working as a seaman, he developed his love of art, painting and sketching, which was inspired by his views from the decks of freighters in the Mediterranean and off the coasts of China, Persia and Africa.

After serving as a merchant marine

officer, Lord attended New York University on a football scholarship, majoring in fine arts.

While making Maritime Service training films during the Korean War, Lord became fascinated with motion picture techniques. Later, he studied acting under Sanford Meisner at New York's Neighborhood Playhouse. His first acting break came in the Ralph Bellamy television series, *Man Against Crime,* and was followed by dozens of live television appearances.

On Broadway, he played the lead in *Traveling Lady,* opposite Kim Stanley, and Brick in *Cat on a Hot Tin Roof,* directed by Elia Kazan.

His motion picture credits include *Man of the West, The Court Martial of Billy Mitchell, God's Little Acre* and *Dr. No,* among others. Before his starring role as Steve McGarrett, Lord had become known to television audiences as rodeo rider Stoney Burke in the short-lived series of the same name.

Lord has received many tributes for his civic activities in Hawai'i. He and his wife, Marie, a former fashion designer, reside in Kahala.

Jack Lord also has a 007 tie-in: he played CIA agent Felix Leiter in the first James Bond feature, *Dr. No.* Whether jogging, riding a bicycle or a horse, or out busting bad guys, Jack Lord has been an action star.

JAMES MACARTHUR

James MacArthur is perhaps best known for his role as Danny "Dano" Williams, McGarrett's trusted young lieutenant on the long-running *Hawaii Five-O* television series.

The son of famous creative parents—actress Helen Hayes and newspaperman-playwright Charles MacArthur—James was raised in an environment of creative people and made his acting debut at the age of eight in *The Corn is Green*, in summer stock. By the time he was sixteen, he decided on acting as a career. During school vacations and whenever time permitted, he performed on television, his most notable early role being the juvenile lead in *Strike Me a Blow* on the CBS television network under the direction of John Frankeheimer. He repeated this role in the movie version of the play *The Young Stranger* in 1956.

In 1960 MacArthur appeared in the Broadway production of *Invitation to a March*, with Celeste Holm and Jane Fonda. His film credits include *Kidnapped, Spencer's Mountain, Swiss Family Robinson, The Light in the Forest, The Interns, To Be a Man, The Battle of the Bulge,* and *The Love-Ins.*

RICHARD BOONE

This craggy-faced, crusty, charismatic actor is best remembered for his role as the professional black-clad gunfighter for hire, Paladin, on *Have Gun, Will Travel,* the 1960s Western television series.

Boone moved from Hollywood to Honolulu, where he lived from 1964 to 1971. He helped induce the late television producer Leonard Freeman to film the series *Hawaii Five-0* in Honolulu and turned down the part of McGarrett, which made actor Jack Lord a worldwide television star.

Boone tried unsuccessfully for many years to found a major movie studio in Hawai'i and was able to make only one low-budget film, *Kona Coast.* He served as ex-

Actor Richard Boone was a Hawai'i resident; he produced and starred in *Kona Coast* (1968).

ecutive producer and star for this Pioneer production released by Warner Bros.

"I love Hawaii. I live there and I want to work there, too," he said in a June 3, 1968 UPI interview. "Most people don't realize the wealth of backgrounds we have over there for shooting movies and television series. There are sections of the Big Island that look exactly like Arizona. You couldn't tell the difference; sand, cactus, the whole bit. Then there are snow-capped mountains with skiing seven months a year. Or if you like, we have volcanoes. The Parker Ranch has 240,000 acres and 42,000 head of cattle. You could make a western without leaving the Islands."

Among Boone's many motion picture credits are *The Alamo, The Shootist, The Kremlin Letter* and *Hombre.*

TOM SELLECK

The handsome, six-foot-four-inch Tom Selleck progressed from a comparatively unknown actor to an internationally famous star of television and motion pictures with his role as the Hawai'i-based detective Thomas Magnum.

Magnum P.I. ran on the CBS television network from 1980 through 1988 and was syndicated worldwide. In addition to starring in the series, Selleck also served as executive producer for the final two seasons.

During the eight years of *Magnum P.I.* production, Selleck earned one Emmy award and four nominations, one Golden Globe award and seven nominations.

Selleck was Steven Spielberg's first choice to star as Indiana Jones in the film *Raiders of the Lost Ark.* He asked CBS to let Selleck out of his series commitment on *Magnum P.I.*, but CBS refused. The rest is history: Harrison Ford became Indiana Jones.

Originally from Detroit, Michigan, Selleck spent his early youth in the Los Angeles suburb of Sherman Oaks.

After attending the University of Southern California, he was signed by Twentieth Century Fox and played small roles in numerous features and television series. Following two appearances as a detective in James Garner's hit television series *The Rockford Files* and a starring role in the NBC series *The Sacketts,* he landed the role of Magnum. His starring feature film credits include *High Road to China, Lassiter, Runaway* and the 1988 release *Three Men and a Baby.* This film marked his comedic debut and became a worldwide box-office smash. His other films include *An Innocent Man, Her Alibi, Quigley Down Under, Folks, Mr. Baseball* and 1970's *Myra Breckinridge* (for which he was discovered by Mae West).

DANNY KAMEKONA

Kamekona's television credits include *Burke's Law, L.A. Law, 21 Jump Street, Miami Vice, Sanford and Son, The Rockford Files, Barnaby Jones, Magnum P.I., Hawaii Five-O* and *Tour of Duty.* His feature film credits include *Karate Kid II, Problem Child, Black Widow* and *Goodbye Paradise.*

Magnum, P.I.—and Hawai'i—started Tom Selleck on his way to film fame.

KWAN HI LIM

Born on the island of Oahu, Lim is the son of a Methodist minister. He grew up on Oahu, and, after completing his undergraduate work at the University of Hawai'i, attended law school at Duke University in Durham, North Carolina. Following graduation, he became a practicing attorney in Hawai'i, but has always maintained an active hand in film and television acting, as well.

Beginning with a role in the feature film *The Hawaiians,* Lim also appeared in the film *Uncommon Valor,* starring Gene Hackman. He is probably most recognizable to television audiences from his recurring role as Lieutenant Tanaka of the Honolulu Police Department

Tahitian actress Tarita appears in a publicity still after making *Mutiny on the Bounty* (1962) opposite real-life love Marlon Brando.

Born and raised on the small Tahitian island of Bora Bora, she was discovered by producer Aaron Rosenberg while he was shooting some island dance sequences. Rosenberg picked her out of a bevy of Polynesian beauties. At the time, Tarita could speak only French and Tahitian.

Tarita entered into a torrid real-life romance with Marlon Brando and bore him two children. After the filming company returned to MGM studios for filming, she came to the U.S., but her limited English and acting abilities made it impossible for her to pursue an acting career. It is rumored that Brando discouraged her acting career. On and off, Tarita and Brando lived together for many years in Tahiti and on Tetiaroa, the actor's privately owned atoll. Their daughter, Cheyenne Brando, took her own life in April 1995 in Tahiti.

TIA CARRERE

Born Althea Janairo in Kalihi, Oahu, of Hawaiian-Filipino parents, Carrere has carved out quite a career for

on *Magnum P.I.* and in 31 episodes of *Hawaii Five-O*, in which he portrayed a number of different characters.

He also played John Kulani in the *Island Son* series starring Richard Chamberlain.

DAYTON KA'NE

Dayton was born on the windward side of Oahu, in the village of Waimanalo, and educated at the University of Hawai'i in Honolulu, where he prepared himself for an agricultural career.

A surfing and water enthusiast, Dayton was picked for the important role of Matangi in Dino De Laurentiis' *Hurricane* and *Beyond the Reef.*

TARITA

Tarita Teriipaia was catapulted into international stardom at nineteen, when she landed the lead role of the island beauty opposite Marlon Brando in the 1962 remake of MGM's *Mutiny on the Bounty.*

Pouting beauty Tia Carrere was discovered while *Aloha Summer* was made in Oahu, and she has gone on to star with some of moviedom's top leading men, including Sean Connery and Arnold Schwarzenegger.

herself as a model, actress and singer. In 1988, immediately after high school graduation, she was cast in her first film, *Aloha Summer*. After that, she moved to Los Angeles, where she became a much sought-after print and commercial model. She spent two years on daytime's popular series *General Hospital*, where she played the role of Jade Soong. She has co-starred in such films as *Harley Davidson and the Marlboro Man* and *Showdown in Little Tokyo*. She attained stardom when she landed the female lead in *Wayne's World* and its sequel *Wayne's World 2*. Her most recent film credits are *Rising Sun* and *True Lies*.

JULIA NICKSON

Former top Hawai'i model turned actress, born to a Chinese mother and British father in Singapore, Nickson moved to the islands in 1976. She made her film debut

Julia Nickson in *Rambo*.

opposite Sylvester Stallone in the worldwide box-office hit film *Rambo*. The actress was featured in the television miniseries *Around the World in Eighty Days*, opposite Pierce Brosnan.

ELIZABETH LINDSEY

Lindsey's career has seen her play a number of exotic schoolteacher roles in a number of television films, including her role as Healani Douglas, a Hawaiian-English teacher in Steven Bochco's ABC series *The Byrds of Paradise*.

Lindsey's recurring role in the acclaimed ABC series *China Beach* attracted a loyal following and won her great industry attention for her portrayal of Mai, a widowed French-Vietnamese schoolteacher. She played a Hawaiian schoolteacher in the CBS TV miniseries *Blood and Orchids*.

Lindsey has amassed a number of guest-starring roles in such series as *Simon and Simon*, *Dynasty*, *Magnum P.I.*, and *Knight Rider*, and in the NBC Movie-of-the-Week, *The Last Flight Out*, with James Earl Jones.

The actress grew up on the North Shore of the island of Oahu in the little town of Laie. Her father, Henry Lindsey, of Chinese, Hawaiian, French and English ancestry, was a

Actress Elizabeth Lindsey is a local girl who has made good in several network TV series.

genealogist specializing in the history of the peoples of the South Pacific. She attended Kamehameha School and Brigham Young University on Oahu.

In Hawai'i she created, co-produced and directed a series of documentaries for television called *Legacy of Light,* which pays tribute to outstanding Hawaiians of the 20th century. The series won the prestigious Kahili award for its contribution to the perpetuation of Hawaiian culture.

DON HO

This famous Hawaiian singer and entertainer emerged from the obscurity of his mother's bar to headline in Waikiki's biggest nightclubs. He then rose to even greater mainland and international fame in the late 1960s. One of six children, Don grew up on Oahu and served in the U.S. Air Force during the Korean War.

Soon after leaving the service, Don went to work singing at the family bar. His easy-going style and natural singing ability made him an island favorite. He came to the attention of Kimo McVay, owner of Duke Kahanamoku's, where he became the star attraction.

Don's rendition of the song "Tiny Bubbles" became his signature tune and continues to be a favorite among tourists from the mainland. His television appearances on the popular variety shows of the time include *The Dean Martin Show, The Andy Williams Show, Laugh In* and *The Glen Campbell Show.* He starred in his own NBC network special, *Hawai'i-Ho!* in 1968 and in his own short-lived daily variety program originating from Hawai'i: *The Don Ho Show,* in 1976.

KAM FONG

Kam Fong Chun was born in Honolulu and attended the Fern School, Kalakaua Intermediate School and McKinley High School. Although he appeared in school plays in both intermediate and high school, it was only after working for seventeen years as a Honolulu policeman that Kam Fong decided on a full-time acting career.

World famous Don Ho sings on location in his native Hawai'i.

When not in front of the *Hawai'i Five-0* cameras as Chin Ho Kelly, he spent much of his time working as an actor and master of ceremonies for the Honolulu Community Theatre, the Honolulu Theatre for Youth and other charitable organizations.

His film credits include such movies filmed in Hawai'i as *Gidget Goes Hawaiian, Ghost of the China Sea, Seven Women From Hell* and *Diamond Head.*

Kam Fong appeared regularly on Hawai'i radio and television stations and once was billed as "Hawai'i's Only Chinese Disc Jockey."

On television he conducted a series of children's programs called *Kam Fong's Comedies.* Always interested in children's welfare, he is a board member of W.A.I.F., founded by actress Jane Russell.

ANDY BUMATAI

Bumatai became known as "Hawaii's First Stand-Up Comic," receiving raves, attention and film and television roles. He co-starred as Andy "Pipeline" Kahala on the UPN TV series, *Marker*.

Born and raised in Hawaii, Bumatai toured the islands as well as the mainland with his unique brand of ethnic humor in a celebrated stand-up routine which pokes fun at a kaleidoscope of stereotypes.

In addition to headlining comedy clubs including the Punchline and Caesar's Tahoe, and opening for such performers as Tom Jones and the Beach Boys, Bumatai began to guest star on such series as *Riptide* and *The Jeffersons*. In films, the young comedian has appeared in *A Man Called Sarge, Aloha Summer* and *The Whoopie Boys*. Bumatai has also recorded a number of comedy albums.

RAY BUMATAI

Ray is an actor and comedian, who performed with Hawai'i's famous Booga Booga comic trio. Ray has appeared in the 1991 independent Hawai'i feature *Goodbye Paradise*, co-starring KHON news anchor Joe Moore, Pat Morita, James Hong, Danny Kamekona, and Varoa Tiki. In 1992's made-for-TV *Miss America: Behind the Crown*, Ray depicted Samoan pro-football player Nuu Faaola, who allegedly abused Carolyn Sapp before she became Miss America. Ray's real-life brother Andy portrayed his on-screen brother, too, in this production supposedly based on a true story. The Waianae native also played a Polynesian villager in the made-for-television *Danger Island*, co-starring June Lockhart and Richard Beymer. Ray also was in the short-lived ABC-TV series *Big Wave Dave's* about transplanted mainlanders who try to "go Hawaiian" and surf at Oahu's North Shore; and Ray played King Kamehameha in the 1995 comedy *Under the Hula Moon*.

JASON SCOTT LEE

Jason Scott Lee is to many in Hawai'i a local hero. Like many island sons, he is "chop suey," or of mixed ancestry—seven-eighths Chinese and one-eighth Native Hawaiian. He thus has his feet planted in both the Asian and Polynesian communities. Born in Los Angeles to parents from Hawai'i, Jason moved to Honolulu when he was two. He has one sister and three brothers. Lee graduated from Pearl City High School, located in the urban sprawl north of Honolulu along Oahu's western coast, near Pearl Harbor.

Jason briefly attended Leeward Community College. He has said that he quit a drama class, wondering "Who's Shakespeare and what's a sonnet?" Jason dropped out and moved to California in 1987 to pursue acting. Lee cites his parents' supportiveness as being a major factor in the success of his career.

Jason had small parts on TV and in Cheech Marin's 1987 pre-Prop 187 comedy *Born in East L.A.*, and as a bully who picks on Michael J. Fox in *Back to the Future II*. His first starring role came in 1993's *Map of the Human Heart*, a highly artistic World War II drama about an interracial love affair in Canada between an Eskimo (Lee) and a French-Indian woman (Anne Parillaud), who remeet in war-torn London during the blitz. Later that year, Lee burst onto the screen in *Dragon, The Bruce Lee Story*, which became an international hit (Jason is no relation to Bruce). The producers decided to go for an actor first and a martial artist second, although Jason underwent extensive jeet kune do training for the role. *Dragon* is arguably better than any of Bruce Lee's own kung fu films, because the biopic went beyond "chop socky" stunts and into the life and mind of an Asian male battling society's and Hollywood's stereotyping of men of Asian ancestry.

In *Rapa Nui*, Jason got to indulge his Polynesian side, playing a Pacific islander in a love triangle set against the carving of the monumental *moai* stone statues on Easter Island.

In late 1994, Jason donned a loin cloth to play Mowgli, the jungle boy raised by wolves in India, in *Rudyard Kipling's The Jungle Book*, reprising the role that Sabu originally played in the 1942 version of the Kipling classic.

Left
Dorothy Lamour as Marama ("the light") gets "lei'd," Pacific-style, in this still from 1937's *The Hurricane*, based on the Nordhoff and Hall novel. The Tahiti-based co-authors' fifth bestseller in a row, *The Hurricane* was their second book which Hollywood turned into a major motion picture (1935's Best Picture *Mutiny on the Bounty* was the first). Nordhoff and Hall's story is set in French Polynesia on the atolls of the Tuamotus, the world's largest archipelago. *The Hurricane* is one of the genre's best and is an anti-colonial fable loosely based on a true tale of injustice. Raymond Massey co-stars as the iron-fisted French governor who persecutes Lamour's love interest, played, but of course, by Jon Hall as a victim of racism and colonialism. Ironically, France has been conducting nuclear tests since the 1960s at Moruroa atoll in the Tuamotus, unleashing an atomic force even greater than that of cyclonic winds. Tahiti's popular anti-nuclear independence movement is led by Oscar Temaru, who worked at Moruroa and saw firsthand the effects of nuclearism in the Tuamotus.

CHARLIE CHAN

Chang Apana, a real-life detective with the Honolulu Police Department, was the Charlie Chan inspiration for Earl Derr Biggers, who created the fictional Honolulu detective.

Biggers had visited Hawai'i in the early 1920s and for several years had contemplated writing a mystery tale set there. In 1924, while doing research at the New York Public Library, he came across an article in the *Honolulu Star-Bulletin* describing how Apana had risked his life to smash an island drug ring. A year later, in 1925, Biggers published the first Charlie Chan mystery, *The House Without a Key*. The others were *The Chinese Parrot* (1926); *Behind That Curtain* (1928); *The Black Camel* (1929); *Charlie Chan Carries On* (1930); and *Keeper of the Key* (1932).

The celebrated Charlie Chan film series followed. A total of 48 Chan films were made, featuring such actors as Warner Oland, Sidney Toler, Roland Winters and Peter Ustinov. Charlie Chan radio and television shows, and even comic books featuring the great detective, were also created. The Chan plots are constructed so similarly that their conventions become a kind of ritual for the reader or the moviegoer. Always there is the obvious suspect whom everyone is willing to accept. Then Chan meanders, spotting clues, spouting aphorisms, and keeping everyone in the dark until, at the last moment, gathering all the possibilities together, he exposes the true culprit, usually the last person anyone would expect.

In 1926, Chan (played by George Kuawa) made his first appearance in a ten-chapter serial, *House Without a Key,* produced by Pathe Studios. Though this was an adaptation of the first Chan novel, the Asian detective was reduced to a minor character. Two years later, Universal obtained the rights to the second Chan book, *The Chinese Parrot*, which was filmed by German director Paul Leni and featured Kamiyama Sojin as Chan. In 1929, Fox (which produced all the subsequent Chan films until 1942), filmed the third book in the series, *Behind That Curtain*, as a vehicle for Warner Baxter and Lois Moran. Chan, played by E.L. Park, was again relegated to a part of very little importance.

Not until 1931 and *Charlie Chan Carries On* did the role of Chan find its first really effective interpreter, Warner Oland, a Swedish-born actor who was well known for his many screen roles as an oriental villain. From then

Sidney Toler as Chan in *Charlie Chan's Murder Cruise*. Along with *King Kong*, *Moby Dick*, and *Jurassic Park's* dinosaurs, Honolulu detective Charlie Chan is one of the most popular characters associated with South Seas cinema.

on, on the right side of the law, Oland won even greater fame and continued in the role until his death in 1938. He was then replaced by Sidney Toler.

Only five films were based directly on the six Chan books created by Biggers, including *The Black Camel* (filmed partly in Hawai'i) and *Charlie Chan's Murder Cruise,* a remake of *Charlie Chan Carries On.* With the exception of *Charlie Chan in Reno*, an adaptation of Philip Wylie's *Death Makes a Decree,* the other films are original screenplays featuring Bigger's detective.

After the Chan books became best-sellers, author Biggers journeyed to Hawai'i to meet the man who had inspired the novel. The two men became friends, and Biggers frequently used details from Apana's life to add to Charlie's image. For example, Apana had nine children, including a daughter named Rose, as did Charlie. Both crime fighters lived on Punchbowl crater, and both were promoted to Detective First Grade following a police department scandal.

Apana was only five feet tall, but he was fearless. He once crawled under a porch and did battle with an escaped murderer twice his weight. When the dust cleared, the escapee was in handcuffs.

Born on December 26, 1864 in Waipio, Oahu, to a Chinese immigrant couple, Chang returned with his family to China, where he lived until he was ten, when he returned to live with an uncle in Waipio. In his youth, he became an expert horseman and worked for the Humane Society.

Apana became a master at using the horse whip, and, when he joined the Honolulu Police Department in 1898, he was allowed to carry a whip instead of a revolver. Though he did not have a formal education, the detective could speak three languages: English, Chinese and Hawaiian.

Apana's investigative brilliance was not limited to drug cases. His work on what the press billed in 1929 as "The Frances Ashe Disappearance" was considered outstanding. The police had searched without success for Ashe, daughter of a socially prominent family from the mainland, and for her abductor. Meanwhile, Apana was painstakingly piecing together bits and pieces of clues, retracing his steps several times until he could prove that she had in fact drowned.

Apana received several medals and citations for his detective work, and he retired from the Honolulu Police Department on May 22, 1932, at the age of 68. Just as the books and films were becoming wildly popular, Earl Derr Biggers passed away on April 13, 1933, less than a year after completing his last Charlie Chan novel. Chang Apana died eight months later on December 8 at Queens Hospital in Honolulu. He was buried in the Moana Chinese Cemetery.

Asian-American groups have been sensitive to the portrayal of Charlie Chan for many years. Chan had been played mainly by Caucasian actors (with Asians in minor supporting roles) and was based on stereotypical Caucasian conceptions of Asians.

World War II, the Korean conflict and the Vietnam War, in which American GIs called the enemy Charlie, extended the popular myth of the inscrutable, not-to-be-trusted (especially after Pearl Harbor) Asian. With his shuffling walk, goatee and oriental Confucius philosophy, Chan is considered an offensive Asian stereotype.

During the 1920s, 1930s, and 1940s, Chan was America's best-known Asian. Together with his Americanized number one son, Lee, played by Chinese-American actor Keye Luke, he portrayed Chinese assimilation into a rigid segregated American society of the time in a somewhat idealized and simplistic Hollywood manner.

During World War II, the Chinese were still considered to be the good guys because they were fighting the Japanese. Unlike the mainland Japanese-Americans, they were not interned in detention camps by Executive Order 366 (nor were most of Hawai'i's residents of Japanese ancestry).

Most Americans could not tell the difference between Japanese and Chinese Americans, so both groups for the most part were seen as an Asian menace. Charlie Chan, born in Honolulu of Chinese heritage, was indeed American, though Hawai'i was still a territory at that time.

The last Charlie Chan film was made in 1981, when Peter Ustinov portrayed Chan in an awful stereotypical interpretation in *Charlie Chan and the Curse of the Dragon Queen.* The film provoked the ire of Asian-American groups, who openly picketed U.S. theaters showing the film.

Obviously, the time has come for a new adaptation and reinterpretation of Charlie Chan that features an Asian-American actor in the lead role.

Though there have been changes in detective fiction, the form is still quite alive on television. Angela Lansbury in *Murder, She Wrote* and Peter Falk as *Columbo* have continued to carry on the tradition.

Opposite page
Bela Lugosi, second from left, with Warner Oland as the inscrutable number one detective Charlie Chan, in *The Black Camel*.

Above

Charlton Heston stars as the Big Five-type land baron Whip Hoxworth opposite Tina Chen as Nyuk Tsin, the Chinese girl who rises from poverty to become matriarch of a business dynasty in haole-dominated Hawai'i, in 1970's *The Hawaiians*. This is probably the only Hollywood feature that shows (although briefly) the overthrow of Queen Liliuokalani and the independent Kingdom of Hawai'i.

Center

Cyd Charisse portrays a character derived from *Miss Sadie Thompson*, while Rock Hudson is the archetypal sea captain in *Twilight for the Gods*.

Below

By the 1940s, South Seas cinema was such an established film genre that it was even the subject of a spoof, starring Dorothy Lamour, no less. Here, Lamour appears with, from left to right, Gil Lamb, Noel Neil, Eddie Bracken, Barry Sullivan and Yvonne DeCarlo in 1944's risque send-up *Rainbow Island*. Perhaps this musical was tongue in cheek because wartime audiences would not buy the Pacific paradise cliche while thousands were dying in WWII's island hopping campaign in the Pacific Theater.

Video Film Source Guide

Video and laser disc are two of the most popular formats available in which old films can be seen today. Hawai'i film titles available on video cassette or laser disc are noted here along with distribution source. N/A means that the film is not available.

A

Aloha Summer	Lorimar Home Video
Aloma of the South Seas	N/A
American Guerrilla in the Philippines	N/A

B

The Black Camel	N/A
Big Jim McLain	WB Home Video
Big Wednesday	WB Home Video
Bird of Paradise (1932)	Nostalgia Family Video
Beachhead	N/A
Behold Hawaii	N/A
Black Widow	Fox Home Video
Between Heaven and Hell	Fox Home Video
Beyond the Reef	N/A
Bird of Paradise (1951)	N/A
Blue Hawaii	Fox Home Video
The Blue Lagoon (1949)	N/A
The Blue Lagoon	Col Home Video
Body Heat	Warner Bros. Home Video
The Bounty	Orion Home Video

C

The Caine Mutiny	Col Home Video
The Castaway Cowboy	Buena Vista Home Video
Cinerama South Sea Adventure	N/A

D

Death Wish	Paramount Home Video
The Devil at Four O'Clock	Good Times/ Kids Klassics Dist

Donovan's Reef	Paramount Home Video
Diamond Head	Col Home Video

E

East of Sumatra	N/A
Enchanted Island	Video Communications Inc.
The Enemy Below	Fox Home Video
Ensign Pulver	Warner Home Video
Exit to Eden	HBO/Savoy Home Video

F

Father Goose	Republic Pictures Home Video
Feet First	Time-Life Video
The Final Countdown	Vestron Home Video
Forbidden Island	N/A
From Here to Eternity	Columbia Home Video
Flight of the Intruder	Paramount Home Video
Flight to Hong Kong	N/A
Four Frightened People	N/A

G

Ghost of the China Sea	N/A
Gidget Goes Hawaiian	Columbia Home Video
Girls! Girls! Girls!	Fox Home Video
Goodbye Paradise	York Home Video

H

Hawaii	MGM/UA Home Video
Hawaiian Nights	N/A
Hawaiian Buckaroo	Nostalgia Family Video
The Hawaiians	N/A
Hawaii Calls	Discount Video Tapes
Heaven Knows, Mr. Allison	N/A
The High and the Mighty	N/A
His Majesty O'Keefe	Warner Home Video
Hell Below	N/A
Hell in the Pacific	Fox Home Video
Hell's Half Acre	N/A
Honeymoon in Vegas	New Line Home Video
Honolulu	MGM Home Video
Honolulu Lu	N/A
Hook	Tri Star Col Home Video
Hula	Grapevine Home Video
The Hurricane (1931)	Sultan Entertainment
Hurricane	Paramount Home Video

I

In Harm's Way	Paramount Home Video
Island of Desire	Mike Lebell's Video
Island of the Alive	Warner Home Video
Island in the Stream	Paramount Home Video

J

Joe Versus the Volcano	Warner Home Video
Jurassic Park	MCA/Universal Home Video

K

Kona Coast	N/A
Karate Kid Part II	Columbia Home Video
King Kong	Paramount Home Video

Above

The jalopy is stuck near a Kauai beach shortly after Rita Hayworth, as *Miss Sadie Thompson*, arrives on a tropical island with a U.S. military base.

Center

American skipper Morgan (Cliff Robertson) and members of his crew, Will (Matthew Modine) and Charley (Ned Vaughn), must defend the America's Cup against the Australians in *Wind*.

Below

Dorothy Lamour first donned her famous sarong in 1936's *The Jungle Princess*, opposite Ray Milland as a downed pilot who crashes in paradise. This film poses the existential dilemma found in much of South Seas cinema: once the Westerner discovers utopia, he/she must choose between staying or going.

Opposite page
Left

Jose Ferrer between scenes of *Miss Sadie Thompson*.

Center

Connie Steven appearing as Cricket Blake in the television series *Hawaiian Eye*.

Right

"Papillon" is the French word for "butterfly," the apropos nickname for Steve McQueen's freedom-loving character, Henri Charriere, who strives to escape from the dreaded penal colony, Devil's Island. Charriere's jump from the cliffs was filmed at the Hana cliffs on Maui as executed by stunt man Dar Robinson for actor McQueen. His fellow inmates include Dustin Hoffman, who returned to Hawai'i for location shooting for 1995's *Outbreak*. Director Franklin J. Schaffner's 1973 two-and-a-half-hour epic is a powerful plea for prison reform. Dalton Trumbo, of Hollywood 10 and blacklisting fame, co-wrote the screenplay with Lorenzo Semple, Jr., based on Charriere's book.

L

The Last Flight of Noah's Ark   Buena Vista Home Video

The Little Hut   N/A
Lord of the Flies (1990)   Orion Home Video
Love Affair   Warner Home Video

M

Ma and Pa Kettle at Waikiki   MCA/Universal Home Video
Making of Jurassic Park   MCA/Universal Home Video
McHale's Navy   MCA/Universal Home Video
Merry Christmas, Mr. Lawrence   MCA/Universal Home Video
Million Dollar Weekend   N/A
Miss Sadie Thompson   Columbia Home Video
Mister Roberts   Warner Home Video
Moana   Grapevine Home Video
The Moon and the Sixpence   MGM Home Video
Mutiny on the Bounty (1933)   MGM Home Video
Mutiny on the Bounty (1962)   MGM Home Video

N

Naked Paradise/Thunder Over Hawaii   N/A
No Man Is an Island   N/A
None But the Brave   Warner Bros. Home Video
North   Columbia/TriStar Home Video
North Shore   MCA/Universal Home Video

O

Old Man and the Sea   Warner Home video
Operation Pacific   Warner Home Video

Operation Petticoat   Republic Pictures Home Video
Outbreak   Warner Home Video

P

The Pagan   N/A
Pagan Love Song   MGM Home Video
Papillon   CBS/Fox Home Video
Paradise, Hawaiian Style   Fox Home Video
Pardon My Sarong   MCA/Universal Home Video
Pearl of the South Pacific   N/A
Picture Bride   N/A
Point Break   Fox Home Video
PT 109   Warner Home Video

R

Rampage   N/A
Rapa Nui   Warner Home Video
Raiders of the Lost Ark   Paramount Home Video
Return to Paradise   MGM/UA Home Video
Return to the Blue Lagoon   Col Home Video
The Revolt of Mamie Stover   N/A
Ride the Wild Surf   Col Home Video
Rough Cut   Paramount Home Video

S

The Sea Chase   Warner Home Video
Seven Sinners   MCA Universal Home Video
Seven Women From Hell   N/A
She Gods of Shark Reef   N/A
Son of Fury   Fox Home Video
Song of the Islands   Key Home Video
South of Pago Pago   The Nostalgia Merchant
South of Tahiti   N/A
South Pacific   Fox Home Video

South Sea Woman   N/A

T

Tabu   Milestone Film & Video
Ten   Warner Bros. Home Video
Throw Momma From the Train   Orion Home Video
Tiko and The Shark   N/A
Too Late, The Hero   Fox Home Video
Tora! Tora! Tora!   Fox Home Video
The Tuttles of Tahiti   Hollywood Home Theatre
Twilight for the Gods   N/A

U

Uncommon Valor   Paramount Home Video
Under Seige   Warner Home Video
Underwater   Turner Home Video

V

Voodoo Island   N/A

W

The Wackiest Ship in the Army   Col Home Video
Waikiki Wedding   N/A
Wake of the Red Witch   Republic Home Video
Waterworld   MCA/Universal Home Video
When Time Ran Out   Warner Home Video
The White Flower   N/A
White Heat/Cane Fire   N/A
White Savage   N/A
White Shadows of the South Seas   Facets MultiMedia

Above

It's 1959 in Hawai'i, the surf is crashing and the juke box is rocking for Mike (Chris Makepeace), Kilarney (Warren Fabro), Scott (Scott Nakagawa), Chuck (Don Michael Paul), Kenzo (Yuji Okumoto) and Jerry (Blaine Kia) in *Aloha Summer.*

Center

Shortly after statehood, teen idol James Darren starred in two made-in-Hawai'i movies with plots set in the Fiftieth State— *Gidget Goes Hawaiian* (1961) and *Diamond Head* (1963). Here, the star arrives on Oahu to a warm, *aloha* spirit welcome in a publicity still.

Below

A young Robert Conrad in the first detective-in-paradise TV series set in Hawai'i, *Hawaiian Eye*, which ran from 1959-1963. The private investigator's offices were supposedly at the Hawaiian Village Hotel (now the Hilton Hawaiian Village), which is seen here. Connie Stevens as singer Crickett Blake performed in the hotel, too.

Bibliography

Baltake, Joe. *Jack Lemmon: His Films and Career.* N.J.: Citadel Press, 1986.

Belafonte, Dennis, and Alvin H. Marill. *The Films of Tyrone Power.* N.J.: Citadel Press, 1979.

Blum, Daniel. *A New Pictorial History of the Talkies.* N.Y.: G.P. Putnam Sons, 1973.

Brooks, Tim, and Earle Marsh. *The Complete Dictionary to Prime Time Network TV Shows 1946-Present.* N.Y.: Ballantine, 1981.

D'Agostino, Annette M. *Harold Lloyd: A Bio-Bibliography.* Westport, CT: Greenwood Press, 1994.

diFranco, Philip J. *The Movie World of Roger Corman.* N.Y.: Chelsea House, 1979

Doll, Susan. *Films of Elvis Presley.* Lincolnwood, Illinois: Publications Int., 1991

Eames, John Douglas. *The MGM Story.* N.Y.: Crown Pub, 1979.

Eyles, Allen. *John Wayne and the Movies.* N.J.: A S Barnes and Co., 1976.

Fitzgerald, Michael E. *Universal Pictures.* N.Y.: Arlington House, New Rochelle, 1977

Hanson, Patricia King. *American Film Institute Catalogue of Motion Pictures Produced in the United States: Feature Films 1911-1920.* Vol F-1, 1931-1940, Vol F-3, Berkeley: University of California Press, 1988.

Hirschhorn, Clive. *The Universal Story.* N.Y.: Crown Publishers, 1983.

Hunter, Allan. *Gene Hackman.* London: W.H. Allan, 1987.

Lamour, Dorothy. *My Side of the Road—As Told to Dick McInnes.* N.Y.: Prentice Hall, 1980.

Logan, Josh. *Movie Stars, Real People and Me.* N.Y.: Delacorte, 1978.

Marill, Alvin H. *The Films of Anthony Quinn.* N.J.: Citadel Press, 1975.

McCarty, John. *The Complete Films of John Huston.* N.J.: Citadel Press, 1987.

Munden, Kenneth W. *American Film Institute Catalogue of Motion Pictures Produced in the United States: Feature Films 1921- 1930.* Vol F-2, New York, R.R. Bowker & Co., 1971

Munn, Michael. *Trevor Howard: The Man and His Films.* Chelsea, MI: Scarborough House, 1990.

Osterholm J. Roger. *Bing Crosby A Bio–Bibliography.* Westport, CT: Greenwood Press, 1994.

Parrish, James Robert. *The Swashbucklers.* N.Y.: Arlington House, 1976.

Ricci, Mark, Boris Zmijewsky, and Steve Zmijewsky. *The Films of John Wayne.* N.J.: Citadel Press, 1978.

Rovin, Jeff. *The Films of Charlton Heston.* N.J. Citadel Press, 1987.

Schmitt, Robert C. *Hawaii in the Movies 1898-1959.* Honolulu, Hawaii: Hawaiian Historical Society, 1988.

Schultz, Margie. *Eleanor Powell: A Bio-Bibliography.* Westport, Conn: Greenwood Press, 1994.

Taves, Brian. *The Romance of Adventure.* Mississippi: University Press, 1973.

Taylor, Deems. *Some Enchanted Evenings: The Story of Rogers and Hammerstein.* N.Y.: Harper and Row, 1953.

Thomas, Tony. *The Cinema of the Sea.* N.C.: McFarland, 1988.

Thomas, Tony, and Aubrey Slomon. *The Films of 20th Century Fox.* N.J.: Citadel Press, 1978, 1985.

Vidor, King. *A Tree is a Tree.* N.Y.: Harcourt, Brace & Company, 1952.

Whisler, John A. *Elvis Presley: Reference Guide and Discography.* N.J.: Scarecrow Press, 1981.

Zinnemann, Fred. *An Autobiography: A Life in the Movies.* N.Y.: Charles Scribner Sons, 1992.

Index

H

Hackman, Gene, 139, 248
Haena Beach, Kauai, 109
Hagman, Larry, 305
Hale, Alan Jr., 317
Halekulani Hotel, 171
Hall Street, 18
Hall, Jack, 70, 346, 351
Hall, Jon, xxvii, 55, 103, 202, 266, 275, 278, 350
Hall, Juanita, 27, 107
Halliday, John, 44
Halona Cove (Oahu), xii, 72
Hamel, Veronica, 160
Hamilton, Bernie, 119
Han, Maggie, 342
Hanalei (Bay), Kauai, 27, 84, 108
Hanalei, Ralph, 122, 158
Hanamaulu Beach, 125
Hanauma Bay (Oahu), 170
Hanks, Tom, 175
Hanna, Mark, 100
Hannemann, Nephi, 158
"Happy Talk," xxvii
Hardin, Ty, 304
Harris, Phil, 290
Harris, Richard, 139, 212
Harrison, Gregory, 167
Hart to Hart, 335
Hartman, Don, 49
Harvey, Raymond, 157
Haskin, Byron, 209
Hatta, Kayo, 184
Hatta, Mari, 184
Hattie, Hilo, 7, 57, 58, 122, 292, 348, 350
"Hawai'i 7," 70
Hawai'i Film Office, 26, 30, 236
Hawai'i Film Studio, 30, 236
Hawai'i International Film Festival, 30, 194
Hawaii, 6, 29, 139
"Hawaii Calls," 51
Hawaii Five-O, xviii, xix-xxi, 318-323
Hawaii in the Movies, xv, xxvii
Hawaiian Buckaroo, 52
Hawaiian culture, 5-8
Hawaiian Eye, 315-316, 368, 370
Hawaiian Heat, 335
Hawaiian Love, xxiii
Hawaiian Memories, ii
"Hawaiian Memories," 52
Hawaiian Nights, 53
The Hawaiians, 15, 151, 366
Hawaiian Village Hotel (Hilton Hawaiian Village), 315, 370
Hawkins, Jack, 242
Haworth, Jill, 135
Hayakawa, Sessue, 15
Hayes, Flora K., 122
Haynes, Roberta, 207
Hayward, Leland, 89

Hayward, Lillian, 266
Hayworth, Rita, 10, 22, 78, 368
"Heaven is in Blue Hawaii," 59
Heaven Knows, Mr. Allison, 295
Hecht, Harold, 209
Hedemann, Hans, 168
Heggen, Thomas, 89
Heisler, Stuart, 84, 282
Hell Below, 237
Hell in the Pacific, 216
Hell's Half Acre, xx, 82
Heller, Lukas, 218
Helmond, Katherine, 329
Hemingway, Ernest, 244
Hemmings, David, 244
Henry, Gregg, 329
Henry Kaiser Estate, 344
Hepburn, Katharine, ii
Her Jungle Love, 2
Herbert, F. Hugh, 294
Hershey, Barbara, 331
Heston, Charlton, 128, 151, 366
Hewitt, Jennifer Love, 342
Heyes, Douglas, 286
Hibler, Winston, 158
The Hidden Pearls, 15
The High and the Mighty, 290
Hill, George Roy, 139
Hill, James, 209
Hill, Robert, 114
Hillerman, John, 326
Hilo, 165
Hilton Hawaiian Village (Hawaiian Village Hotel), 315, 370
His Majesty O'Keefe, 209
Hispanics, xxviii, 4, 39, 49, 63, 67, 199, 271
Hitu, 200
Ho, Derek, 168
Ho, Don, 318, 324, 345, 359, 360
Hoffman, Dustin, 368
Hogan, Michael, 205
Holbrook, Hal, 339
Holden, William, 160
Holliman, Earl, 334
Hollywood Images of the Pacific, xxxi
Holmes, Burton, 15
Holt, Kealoha, 348
Holt, Robert I., 242
Holt, Sandrine, 231
Homeier, Skip, 84
Honda, Ralph, 70
Honeymoon in Vegas, 176
Hong, James, 179
Honolulu, 16, 54, 263
Honolulu Harbor (Oahu), 104, 187
Honolulu Lu, 56
Hopkins, Anthony, 225
Hopper, Dennis, 164, 260
Hornblow, Arthur Jr., 49
Hough, Richard, 225
Houghton, Barrie, 332
Houseman, John, 333

Houston, Donald, 205
Howard, Ken, 334
Howard, Leslie, 39
Howard, Trevor, 212, 218, 306
Hubler, Richard G., 84
Hudson, John, 207
Hudson, Rock, 104, 366
Huie, William Bradford, 92
bukilau, 213
Hula, 40-41, 214
hula, xx, 9, 40, 45, 60, 64
human sacrifice, 5, 175
Hunter, Jeffrey, 303
Hunter, Tab, 132, 282
Hunter, Thomas, 308
Hurricane, 218
The Hurricane, 30, 202
Hurricane Iniki, 258
Hurricane Smith, 5
Huston, John, 295
Huston, Walter, 237
"Hymn to the Sun," 54
Hyun, Peter, 48

I

"I Left Her on the Beach at Waikiki," 52
I've Got Mine, 84
Ihat, Steve, 145
Ikuma, Bishop Kinai, 70
Ilikai Hotel, 136, 144
IMAX, 162
In Harm's Way, 18, 135
In the Wake of the Bounty
interracial love, xxiii, xxviii-xxxii, 39, 55, 62, 64, 128, 167, 170, 213
Iona, Andy, 54
Island of Desire, 282
Island of the Alive, 252
Island Son, 340
Island Sons, 338
The Islander, 329
The Islanders, 317
Islands in the Stream, 244
Ito, Jiroomi, 251
Ito, Robert, 144, 169
Ivers, Julia Crawford, 40
Ives, Burl, 305

J

Jackson, Sammy, 133
Jacobs, Alexander, 216
Jake and the Fatman, 340
Janis, Dorothy, 196
Japanese immigrants, 184
Jarrett, Dan, 52
Jarrott, Charles, 160

Jean, 200
Jennings, Talbot, 47
Jensen, Maren, 223
The Jetty in Nawiliwili, 129
Joe Versus the Volcano, 175
Joe, Tokyo, 324
Johnson, Brad, 254
Johnson, Don, 331
Johnson, Lamont, 145
Johnson, Russell, 317
Johnson, Van, 81
Johnston, Mary, 94
Jones, Barry, 207
Jones, James, 19, 73
Jones, Kaylie, 19
Jones, Tommy Lee, xxxi, xxxii, 177
Jourdan, Louis, 64
Jovovich, Milla, 232
Jungle Heat, 96
The Jungle Princess, xxvi, 2, 368
Jurassic Park, xxv, 256
Jurgens, Curt, 239

K

Ka'Ne, Dayton, 218, 219, 223, 348, 357, 358, 372
Kahala Beach (Oahu), 45
Kahaluu (Oahu), 250
Kahanamoku, Duke, iv, 40, 41, 90, 280, 347, 349
Kahoano, Kimo, 162
kahuna, 61, 158, 255
Kai, Lani, 122
Kailua-Kona, 145
Kaina, Rev. William, 29
Kalapana, ii, 16, 55, 165
Kalaupapa Settlement, 71
Kalua, Peter, 162
Kaluana, George, 49
The Kamaaina, 16
Kamae, Eddie, 194
Kamai, Kolimau, 46
Kamehameha Schools choir, 318, 336
Kamekona, Danny, 179, 250, 357
Kamen, Robert Mark, 250
Kanakas Diving for Money, 189
Kanarek, Jules, 252
Kaneohe Bay (Oahu), 90, 135
Kanraku Tea House (Oahu), 187
Kanter, Hal, 121
Kapingamarangi, 192
Kaoluolani, 16
Kapu, Sam, 324
Kapu, Sam Jr., 145
Karate Kid part II, 250
Karloff, Boris, 99
Karlson, Phil, 242
Kasdan, Lawrence, 247
Katkov, Norman, 336
Kato, Takeshi, 133

1. JOHN WAYNE	12. DOROTHY LAMOUR	23. BURT LANCASTER
2. JULIE ANDREWS	13. DEANNA DURBIM	24. DEBORAH KERR
3. CHARLTON HESTON	14. BING CROSBY	25. MARY PICKFORD
4. BETTE MIDLER	15. JACK LORD	26. DUKE KAHANAMOKU
5. TOM SELLECK	16. CHARLEY CHAPLIN	27. JAMES CAGNEY
6. WARNER OLAND	17. FRANCES FARMER	28. HARRY OWENS
7. TOSHIRO MIFUNE	18. GEORGE BURNS	29. CLARE BOW
8. HILO HATTIE	19. GRACY ALLEN	30. FRANK SINATRA
9. SHIRLEY TEMPLE	20. HENRY FONDA	31. KIRK DOUGLAS
10. SESSUE HAYAKAWA	21. ELEANOR POWELL	32. MITZI GAYNOR
11. ELVIS PRESLEY	22. HAROLD LLOYD	33. BUSTER CRABBE